THE LAST HOLIDAY

In a musical career spanning five decades, from *Small Talk at 125th and Lennox* to *I'm New Here*, Gil Scott-Heron (1949–2011) released twenty albums and many seminal singles including 'The Revolution Will Not Be Televised', 'Home Is Where the Hatred Is', 'Winter in America', 'B Movie', 'Johannesburg' and 'Lady Day and John Coltrane'. He is also the author of three previous books: two novels, *The Vulture* and *The Nigger Factory*, and *Now and Then: The Poems of Gil Scott-Heron*.

'The mesmerizing posthumous memoir of "a poet and polemicist whose lyrics have inspired and galvanized generations"' *GQ*

'Gil Scott-Heron is timeless'
New York Times

'One of the great pioneers of late-twentieth-century music'
Independent

'For more than two decades, [Gil Scott-Heron] has been committed to examining those facts of the human condition that most of us would rather forget ... he is an artist who has crafted witty but crucial insights for Black America'
Washington Post

'Scott-Heron's memoir comes beautifully to life when talking about other musicians'
Telegraph Review

'Scott-Heron is undeniably a trickster wordsmith, reaching into his bag of goodies for turns of phrase and figures of speech that effortlessly hold attention. He veers from a slangy, conversational, wisecracking style to the tone of a perceptive philosopher . . . or suddenly dropping on us the sort of rhythmic street poetry . . . equally able to evoke a mood of urgency or tenderness' *Observer*

'What is most remarkable about Scott-Heron's account of his progress . . . is his delight in telling the story. Almost by way of explanation for his dazzling command of language, the first chapter opens thus "Words have been important to me for as long as I can remember" . . . His scope as a writer, evident even in the most casual passages of this memoir, is a testament to his reach'
New Statesman

'*The Last Holiday* is humble, charming and intelligent throughout, and the author clearly has no time for the trappings of modern celebrity, preferring to focus on the craft of what he does, and the social and political context of his work'
Scotsman

Also by Gil Scott-Heron:

The Vulture
The Nigger Factory
Now and Then: The Poems of Gil Scott-Heron

GIL SCOTT-HERON
THE LAST HOLIDAY
A MEMOIR

CANONGATE

LIST OF ILLUSTRATIONS

Dr. King

I admit that I never had given much thought
As to how much of a battle would have to be fought
To get most Americans to agree and then say
That there actually should be a Black holiday.
But what a hell of a challenge. How far would Stevie go
To make them pass legislation tabled ten years in a row?

I didn't doubt for a second that the brother was sincere
But how many minds had come together in the last twelve years?
How many folks recognized that America had to grow?
And who else could convince them that yesterday had to go?
I had liked the idea of a minister being around
When racing for high stakes, to have his foot near the brakes
Because of what truly could have gone down.
I thought America could have blown up
Before it could ever be said that we had grown up.
And for whatever reason were there Americans who never knew
That Dr. King prevented chaos and would give him his due.
I admired Stevie's enthusiasm and that he spoke his mind
But right does not triumph over wrong every time.
Ghandi took nonviolence with him when he died.
Over here there was nonviolence, but only on one side.
When white folks beat up and killed people that you knew

You might direct your anger at a building or two.
Instead of making the Old Testament a civil rights guide
And saying that "an eye for an eye" would now be justified
We were told to accept that some white folks had no class
And instead of condemning white people "en masse"
We were told remaining peaceful would be the best thing
And directing that philosophy were men like Dr. King.

Through a storm of provocation to fight we saw
That in order to change America you must change the law.
They called us "militants" and "radicals" and were made to look bad
For trying to secure rights all Americans had.
But behind what's often written is where you find the real thing
So America might not have made it without Dr. King.

PROLOGUE

I always doubt detailed recollections authors write about their childhoods. Maybe I am jealous that they retain such clarity of their long agos while my own past seems only long gone.

What helped me to retain some order was that by the age of ten I was interested in writing. I wrote short stories. The problem was that I didn't know much about anything. And I didn't take photos or collect mementos. There were things I valued, but I thought they would always be there. And that I would.

There was Jackson, Tennessee. No matter where I went—to Chicago, New York, Alabama, Memphis, or even Puerto Rico in the summer of 1960—I always knew I'd be coming back home to Jackson. It was where my grandmother and her husband had settled. It was where my mother and her brother and sisters were all born and grew up. It was where I was raised, in a house on South Cumberland Street that all of them called home, regardless of what they were doing and where they were doing it. They were the most important people in my life and this was their home. It was where I began to write, learned to play piano, and where I began to want to write songs.

Jackson was where I first heard music. It was what folks called "the blues." It was on the radio. It was on the jukeboxes. It was the music of Shannon Street in "Fight's Bottom" on Saturday night, when the music was loud and the bootleg whisky from Memphis flowed. The blues came from Memphis, too. Shannon Street was taboo at my house, something my grandmother didn't even think about. We never played the blues at home.

Our house was next door to Stevenson and Shaw's Funeral Home. The man who ran that business was Earl Shaw, one of the nicest men I've ever had the pleasure to meet. His wife was a good friend of my mother, and our families were so close that I related to his children as cousins for years.

Evidently business at the funeral home was good because I remember clearly when Mr. Shaw purchased another building in East Jackson and the movers came to take everything out of the place next door. And then the men from the junkyard came to put everything else in the back of an old truck. My grandmother knew the junk man and after a brief conversation with him he directed his two sons to bring an ancient and well-used upright piano into our front room and push it up against the wall. I was seven years old. Old enough to start learning to play. What she had in mind was that I learn some hymns I'd be able to play for her sewing circle meetings. That's how my music playing started.

There was no blues on the living room radio. My grandmother had that one locked on the station that played her soap operas in the afternoon and her favorite radio programs at night. When we got a second radio, it was quickly dubbed "the ballgame radio," and, sure enough, when a ballgame was being broadcast

I listened. But at other times I'd try to tune in WDIA in Memphis, the first Black radio station in the country, with on-air personalities like Rufus and Carla Thomas and B.B. King. Late at night I'd try to get "Randy's Record Show" out of Nashville.

I heard people talk about a music explosion in Memphis. I knew my favorite music, the blues, came from there, too. But I was living in Jackson, ninety miles east of Memphis, and had no desire to go anywhere else. Until I had to, when the family—my mother and I—moved to New York City. Though my mother and I left Jackson in the summer of 1962, I had known the move was coming from the time the new highway was announced. That had been a couple of years and a hundred rumors prior. The route the highway would take had sparked hours of conversation. In the end, it came through our neighborhood.

A lot of the neighborhood had already been cleared out when we left. Liberty Street Church, just behind us, and Rock Temple, the Sanctified Church a few blocks away, had already closed up. There had never been many commercial establishments in that direction and the four lanes were rolling through what had been blocks of aging residences. Soon it would all be gone. I could imagine the rows of gas stations and fast food joints lining what had been my backyard. Easier access for truckers and travelers going west to Memphis and east to Nashville.

In a way this was a prelude to a larger funeral. The Paving of America constituted a symbolic burying of the hatchet, a signal that the northern CEOs and southern See$s were at long last seeing eye to eye. The Confederacy had finally found cosigners for its hundred year loan and had negotiated its way

3

from Appomattox Court House through the gauntlet from apostate, around apathy, apology, appeasement, appeals, approbation, apprehension, and appropriation to approval. The southern quadrant of the contiguous country had done a century of icy isolation and by God a nig . . . a Negro had put a blow torch to the thermostat. Thurgood Marshall had thawed things, battered the last barricade with Brown v. Board of Education. The financial folks now faced the final frontier.

I had played my small part, a ripple in one of the incessant waves that were wearing down the mountain that had been segregation. Together with Madeline Walker and Gillard Glover, I had initiated school desegregation in Jackson. And factories would be built. And highways would uncoil like rattlesnakes from Maryland to the Gulf of Mexico. And Jim Crow, the bastard who had swung a thousand nightsticks and set a thousand crosses on fire, was not dead. But he'd been wounded. That time by three children: Madeline, Gillard, and me, civilians in a civil war.

Since those beginnings, I have not been proud of everything that has happened or that I have done throughout my life. But I consider myself fortunate. I was raised by two women—my mother and grandmother—who were both dedicated to my well-being and did everything they could to make sure I had every opportunity to succeed in life. They were dedicated to my book learning and were examples of what I should try to be as an adult and as a gentleman. The mistakes have been due to my own poor judgment both of people and circumstances.

I am the father of three children, regardless of rumor and comment to the contrary. My first born was my son Rumal, an anagram that makes use of the letters of his mother's first name. My older daughter is Gia, a soft sounding word for a very feminine delight. My younger girl is named Chegianna and goes by Che—pronounced *Shay*. This book is a chance to share some things with them and other readers, things I hope will be useful. Some of it is purely biographical. The central focus, however, revolves around experiences orchestrated by Brother Stevie Wonder, a true miracle of talent and concern for his fellow man. I was lucky enough to be with him when he set his mind and heart on doing something important, something that a lot of folks thought was impossible, and he got it done.

We all need to see folks reach beyond what looks possible and make it happen. We need more examples of how to make it happen. We will all face difficult circumstances along the way that will challenge our self-confidence and try to disrupt our decisions about the directions we wish to choose.

I hope this book will remind you that you can succeed, that help can arrive from unexpected quarters at times that are crucial. I believe in "the Spirits." Sometimes when I explain to people that I have been blessed, and that the Spirits have watched over me and guided my life, I suppose I sound like some kind of quasi-evangelist for a new religion. I am not and do not have a personal church to promote. I believe, however, to paraphrase Duke Ellington, that at almost every corner of my life there has been someone or something there to show me the way. These landmarks, these signals, are provided by the Spirits. This is not a subject I offer up for purposes of debate. Whatever you call the intangible influences that help direct you in your life is not the point. My contention is that your blessings derive from your positive contributions. But they must come from the heart. Not because of what you expect in return. Otherwise what you contributed was a loan, not a gift.

I am grateful to dozens of people who helped advance my work over the years, and who helped further the accomplishment I am trying to describe here. I hope that will become clear in the descriptions that follow. In the meantime, I would hope this book helps all of us remember to celebrate Brother Stevie Wonder, on his own birthday and on January 15—the birthday of Martin Luther King, Jr.—every year.

1

Words have been important to me for as long as I can remember. Their sound, their construction, their origins. Because of that interest, there are few places I could have been raised that would have provided more wonderful raw material than the southeast quarter of North America.

The word Tennessee means "land of trees" to the folks native to that part of the world three or four hundred years ago. Residents of the region respected the land and their attention to the details of their surroundings stands out in their descriptions. They examined their environment thoroughly, creating drawings of what they saw from a mountain that provided an unobstructed view for miles in all directions. South and east of the mountain, a blanket of treetops led to trails marked by the Seminoles. Due west, the Chickasaw people lived on the banks of the horseshoe-shaped Tennessee River that one encountered twice as it sliced the state into thirds. And everywhere stood dense forests. Tennessee, they say, was once 90 percent trees, the land of trees.

The natives from the heights of the Appalachians scattered when the new folks came into the mountains from the east.

These graceless, grimy intruders were more than a different tribe. And less. They were more than a different skin color and language. They had no respect for the land and its inhabitants. Arriving in waves, they attacked the mountains as if to level them. They slashed jagged holes and damned the streams before thunderous explosions collapsed the face of hillsides, leaving only the ugly scars to evidence their search for the black rocks they called *coal*. The natives charted their ragged trails of mutilation from the peak above Chattanooga. And they led their families west.

When I was a boy in Tennessee, our first class in the morning was geography and time was always dedicated to Tennessee and how it was connected to history. Tennessee was the Volunteer State. University of Tennessee sports teams were the Volunteers. I remember being shown pictures of Davy Crockett and Smoky the Bear. I also recall the slightly curved diagonal line I drew that linked Knoxville to Nashville to the city named after an ancient Egyptian metropolis, Memphis.

Memphis, Tennessee, was only ninety miles west of Jackson, my home. But Memphis was as far away as the North Pole in my mind. People in Jackson were always talking about somewhere else, mostly Memphis, because it was a close somewhere else and you could drink alcohol there, while Jackson was in a dry county. I talked about going to Chicago, where my mother lived. Some of my grandfather's relatives were in Memphis and I had visited them, but what I remember about the trip was getting carsick and throwing up.

The history that we were given about Memphis was done in light pencil that hopscotched its way to a semisolid landing with Elvis Presley on *The Ed Sullivan Show*. The city had started as a midway market, a meeting place on the banks of the Mississippi River that squatted in the muck almost squarely between New Orleans and Chicago. As such, it provided a perfect location for traders of all description and from all directions, who brought everything to exchange—from furs to furniture and cotton to cattle. As the steamboats and paddle wheelers sought the shallows of Memphis and St. Louis, they stirred great clouds of silt and sand, turning the surface of the waterway a burnished brown. The Mississippi became known as the Big Muddy.

The docks at the edge of the village were a magnet for hunters, trappers, farmers, and natives, who rolled up in wooden wagons to trade loads of tobacco, produce, and buffalo hides for guns, whisky, and farm implements. They all walked and rolled past the narrow, squalid shacks, no more than cages, where there were echoes of moans and rattling chains from human cargo.

The Memphis day was from "can see" to "can't see," and with the first hint of another sunrise the procession from the docks to the foul smelling mudhuts beneath the auction blocks began. There, nearly naked black men and women barely covered by rotting rags were led in, bound and shackled, with rawhide nooses around their necks. The least cooperative captives were hobbled with ankle chains that limited them to short, stuttering steps. They would be sold, these bucks, to the cutthroat Cajuns from the sea-level swamps. It was said that each year spent in the paralyzing heat of a Louisiana summer took five years off a man's life. When a slave was sold to the Lords of Louisiana, the observers lamented that he'd been "sold down the river."

Memphis matured from midway market to a major metropolis. Saloons and whorehouse tents, once soaked with the sweat of drunken sailors and reeking with the acid stench of swine, slime, sewage, and slaves is now better known for Graceland and the Grizzlies than for Beale Street and the blues. Its filthy foundation as a headquarters for whores and for humans sold to the highest bidder was obscured by the magic of musical melding. Sun Records considered itself the fuse that lit the 1950s with Elvis and rock 'n' roll. With Carla and Rufus Thomas and Otis Redding, Stax Records brought blues to the hit parade with hooks and horns and a solid beat, evolving into Al Green and Willie Mitchell. Memphis meant music.

And unless you stop to think for a minute, you might forget that it was in Memphis that Dr. Martin Luther King, Jr. was shot and killed on a motel balcony on April 4, 1968. That assassination is one of our starting points.

Stevie Wonder did not forget.

In 1980, Stevie joined with the members of the Black Caucus in the United States Congress to speak out for the need to honor the day Dr. King was born, to make his birthday a national holiday.

The campaign began in earnest on Halloween of 1980 in Houston, Texas, with Stevie's national tour supporting a new LP called *Hotter than July*, featuring the song "Happy Birthday," which advocated a holiday for Dr. King. I arrived in Houston in the early afternoon to join the tour as the opening act. I was invited to do the first eight shows, covering two weeks, and I felt good about being there, about seeing Stevie and his crazy brother Calvin again.

Somehow it seems that Stevie's effort as the leader of this campaign has been forgotten. But it is something that we should all remember. Just as surely as we should remember April 4, 1968, we should celebrate January 15. And we should not forget that Stevie remembered.

As Stevie sang on "Happy Birthday":

> We all know everything
> That he stood for time will bring
> For in peace our hearts will sing
> Thanks to Martin Luther King

2

Stevie Wonder could not see. He was blind. Blind was damn near part of his name. From the first time his name was broadcast and the tune's title was tagged, he was stamped "Stevie Wonder, the Blind Boy." I knew it was all part of programming, of selling Stevie to the public, but I still felt a little sympathy for the brother because it put something in capital letters he probably didn't need to hear.

I had never heard "Blind Ray Charles" or "Blind José Feliciano." It couldn't have been because Stevie played an instrument, because Ray Charles played piano and José Feliciano played guitar. What the hell?

There had been a stretch when brothers and sisters were taking on what they considered religious names. Cassius Clay became Muhammad Ali. Bobby Moore became Ahmad Rashad. In the old days guys named something else became Rock Hudson and John Wayne. Malcolm Little became Malcolm X. Ma Bell became Nine X. And Stevie . . .

Stevie started out carrying a tic-tac-toe of AKAs. He was known as "Little Stevie Wonder" when his first Top 10 tune turned the American airwaves into his one-man tidal wave. Had

12

I been around in those days with a microphone, it would have been a title wave. But since his real name was Steveland Morris, he had actually been riding the waves on a fictitious surfboard.

He might have been little when he was first spotted by the record executives at some show down in Motown, but by the time he played "Fingertips" on *American Bandstand*, he was clearly pushing six feet and looked like he could slam dunk Dick Clark.

I first had the chance to see Stevie Wonder at the Apollo on 125th Street when I was fifteen and living in the Bronx. The young man at center stage holding a harmonica and a microphone while urging the crowd to clap their hands was as tall as I was, and only the dark glasses that concealed his eyes reminded me that his hundred-watt smile from inside the bright spotlights was offered to a darkness that began behind his eyelids and not just beyond the footlights. The guy could flat-out play, and I hoped the "Blind" part of his introduction would be dropped rather than become attached to him as a professional name, like Blind Lemon Jefferson—as though plain old Stevie Wonder was an amateur handle.

Stevie continued to grow in all directions. To his full adult height of over six feet, but also in the public eye as a wonderful musical talent. An exceptional keyboard player, an enthusiastic percussionist, an inventive and challenging composer of both rousing dance numbers and thoughtful ballads, tunes that stuck with you and came back to you with fresh feelings. He demonstrated his full conceptual grasp as a composer and arranger with his orchestrated score of the movie *The Secret Life of Plants*.

The texture of his voice and vocal range made his every offering as a singer an individual accomplishment. His songs were sung by other artists, but not "covered." Throughout the 1960s and 1970s he remained highly valued as an attraction and was in constant demand.

I thought about Stevie often before I met him. Aside from his constant presence on the radio, he spent a good deal of time on my personal stereo. Along with the early look at him I got at the Apollo, I saw him again a few years after that, during a summer break from college when I stayed on campus to work as a sort of camp counselor. We took a bus from Lincoln University's Pennsylvania campus up to a New Jersey fairground for two hours of Stevie's songs and showmanship.

He put on an awesome display of virtuoso performances on a number of instruments. Seeing his growth since 125th Street on harmonica to the master of a variety of keyboards and percussion instruments and the ease with which he handled his singing chores elevated the brother to the top of my ladder as a performer and a talent. His playing, singing, and songwriting had expanded exponentially while he still retained the unrestrained joy that exploded like a physical force from his opening notes and lassoed everyone within reach of his frequency of freedom. I had never attributed to Stevie any supernatural powers or felt as though he was visited by aliens or touched by some witch waving a magic wand, but after seeing a couple of his performances, I was definitely captivated by the energy he always generated from the stage.

I was glad that by the time I met the brother—in the mid

1970s—he was just Stevie Wonder. Or Stevie. He had either lost or thrown away most of the ill-fitting descriptives that had been spread over him here and there like ugly coats of paint. Otherwise I could have ended up at thirty years old sharing the bill with "Little Blind Stevie Wonder." But things worked out.

A few years before the offer to tour with Stevie, Clive Davis had invited him to a show we played at the Bottom Line in Greenwich Village in Manhattan. After that Stevie would show up spontaneously at shows once in a while, at the Roxy, at the Wilshire Theater, but I never knew he was coming. That was what friends did. They could show up without a royal proclamation and know they'd be welcome. With the kind of schedules entertainers have, it's not odd that things happen spontaneously. You get a minute, you hear somebody's in town, and you want to see them. The bigger the celebrity and the more things they had to do, the more spontaneous things were.

I always called everybody "Brotherman" and Stevie had his own personal names for people. Soon after we met he began to call me "Air Reez," which was cool because I am an Aries.

Meeting him also sent me back to the Bronx for memories of what I had thought of the early "Little Stevie" and I felt happy for him. It has been a private joy of mine to have felt that kinship with the brother nearly all my life. Never caring in the beginning or now when someone might say, "He's blind, you know."

That meant the harmonica on "Fingertips"
Was no sooner settling on Stevie's lips

15

Than what inevitably came to their mind
For some reason was that the brother was blind.
Which obviously didn't mean a helluva lot
'Cause it said what he didn't have but not what he got.
His music hit a certain chord
And moved you like the pointer on a Ouija board
Your feet made all of your dancing decisions
And didn't give a damn if he had X-ray vision.
So why was it that people always remarked
"He's blind" as though Stevie was condemned to the dark?
Suppose you looked at it the opposite way:
They had 20/20 vision and still couldn't play.
And when they danced seeing didn't help them keep time
And things like that made me wonder just who was blind.

3

I'm going to have to ask you to accept some information on faith, the way I did. For instance, that on the morning of April 1, 1949, at Provident Hospital in Chicago, Illinois, a very pretty young Black woman named Bobbie Scott completed a roundtrip to and from the hospital delivery room. According to the information on the birth record, she gave birth to a child that was a legitimate-black-male, the tic-tac-toe of birth certificates in that day and age.

A lot of people's positions in life changed that day. Birth always directly affects far more people than is readily apparent. Everyone related to either parent gets an additional name to be called. My mother's mother became a grandmother, my late grandfather's sister became a great aunt, my grandmother's brothers became great uncles, their children became cousins again, and my mother's brother and sisters became an uncle and two aunts.

My father's family was affected the same way: his mother and father became grandparents, his seven brothers became uncles, and their children became cousins. My father, who was originally from Jamaica, and all seven of his brothers had the middle name "Saint Elmo." I'm not sure how many of his brothers named their children Saint Elmo, but my father decided he wanted to name his son after himself, name for name: Gilbert Saint Elmo Heron. This was cool with my mother up to a point. Using the same first name was cool. The use of the same last name was not only cool, but also fit with the legitimate-black-male of the birth certificate. But using Saint Elmo would have brought the known number of men on the planet with that middle name to nine, which was one too many as far as my mother was concerned. Not cool.

According to my mother, she had absolutely nothing against Saint Elmo or the fire that may or may not have been his responsibility. She did not question the veracity or the sobriety of the many seamen who had reported seeing this flaming phenomenon along the masts of ships at sea. She simply didn't like the name Saint Elmo, and she convinced my father that unless the saint came marching in, there would be no "Mo."

My mother suggested finding another name that started with "S" so the initials of father and son would remain the same. My father's problem was that he didn't know any other middle name that might go with his last name—all of the Heron men he knew had Saint Elmo as a middle name. Then my mother suggested "Scott," her maiden name. My father didn't think much of Scott—all the Scotts he knew had it as a last name—but he reluctantly agreed.

My mother had been named after my grandfather, Bob Scott. Everyone called her Bobbie, but her full name was Robert Jameson Scott. Her parents, Bob and Lily, obviously didn't care much about convention when it came to the names of their children. They gave them the names they wanted them to have. Bob Scott had died in 1948, after going blind ten years before. My grandfather had been an insurance man before and through the worst of the Depression and then began to break down. First, constricted veins blocked circulation in his legs. Then he went blind. He began to lose his grip, slipped, lost his mind, and later became violent and had to be committed to the hospital for the criminally insane at Bolivar, Tennessee.

Still, it was probably my father as a Caribbean version of Bob that made him attractive to my mother. Gil, my father, was tall, handsome, well-dressed, and well-mannered. So had been Bob Scott, who always wore a suit for business, with a white shirt and a tie, his hat cleaned and his shoes shined. (Later in life, I remember members of my father's old soccer teams telling me about the zoot suits and wide, striped ties Gil would be wearing when he arrived in the locker room.) When my mother talked about her youth in Jackson, Tennessee, and going places with Bob Scott, you could hear the pride in her voice and see her eyes shine. The strength of their relationship was obvious.

My grandfather had been "Steel Arm Bob," a pitcher who bested Satchel Paige's barnstorming team 1–0 when they came through Jackson. Reading the sports pages to him was how my mother got to know so much about sports and batting averages —the knowledge and real understanding of the details. My father liked that.

Gil Heron was young, exotic, and worldly, a veteran of the Canadian Air Force. He was also physical and athletic, and went

19

all out when he competed. The Aries fire lit up his face and made it glow. The joy of winning brought a smile that made you feel like you were standing in a bright, warm sun. Sometimes he was romantic and sometimes thoughtful, brooding over the quality of his competition and teammates who couldn't get the ball to him when they were pressed. He loved to talk about soccer, past games, teammates, opponents ridiculed as their pointless, desperate pursuit of him always ended the same way: *Goooooooaaaaal!*

Her honesty and curiosity, not naïveté, attracted Gil to my mother, Bobbie. My mother was the second of four Scott children, a scholar who graduated from Lane College, the Black university in Jackson, with an incredible 3.96 grade point average, and then moved north to Chicago. She was obviously a pretty and vivacious young lady, a college graduate with a soft drawl, and not a bad bowler. They had met at the bowling alley next to the Western Electric plant where they both worked in Chicago. She was slim but he could see the shapely legs, the firm hips, and the guileless smile. He'd known women who pretended to be sports fans, saying, "I'd love to come to a game and see you kick a home run." Not her. Not Miss Bobbie Scott from somewhere in Tennessee. She knew sports. She even knew about his "football." Soccer.

Gil would come home after soccer games and rub his legs down with alcohol. Only then would the cuts and scratches and bruises receive the notice they deserved. During games he was oblivious to discomfort; my mother would be appalled by his injuries. Opponents tried to deliberately injure him, with high tackles and tackles when he didn't even have the ball. It was inevitable when his team played groups from the surrounding areas. His skills would offend the opposition, often leaving them feeling foolish and flailing, victims of Gil's fancy footwork. There were scoundrels in places like Skokie, a suburb of Chicago then inhabited primarily by Europeans, who treated soccer like an ethnic heirloom. My mother talked about incidents when opposing players had felt forced to foul, going for his legs instead of the ball, not trying to tackle him but to injure; these were red flags to his temper. Bad move. Gil would grab them and either overpower them with the strength that could be generated by his powerful legs, or while grappling face-to-face he would suddenly jerk his opponent toward him, forcing their face into his forehead. Once he had been so upset with the blind-eye officials who ignored intentional attempts to injure him that he suddenly turned on the ball and kicked it over a wire fence into Lake Michigan, ending the game.

Bobbie was as worried about fights as she was worried about him getting hurt in games. And those were not related to the same set of circumstances. His reputation, or so the legend goes, was that he handled both of those very separate skills with equal dexterity and with equal enthusiasm. So she would go see him play, hoping that would be all.

My mother told me there was a certain grace and ferocity whether he was kicking goals or kicking ass. She didn't come up with that opinion just because she was married to him. Though she might have been biased, her belief in his talent was confirmed when the Scottish national team visited Chicago for a "friendly" match, an exhibition game, and were impressed. In fact, after the game members of the coaching staff spoke to him and made an informal offer for him to come to Scotland to play. He was, after all, already a citizen of the commonwealth.

My mother and father separated when I was one and a half years old, when Celtic, in Glasgow, Scotland, offered him a formal contract. My father decided to take an opportunity to do what he always wanted to do: play football fulltime, at the highest level, against the best players. It was, for him, the chance of a lifetime, the chance to play for one of the most famous teams in the British Isles. It was an opportunity to see who he was and what he was, to avoid sliding through fits of old age and animosity and spasms of "I coulda been a contender" that no one believed. That sort of thing can even make you doubt yourself, doubt what you know, doubt what you would have sworn if anyone was willing to listen. To play with Celtic was also a Jackie Robinson–like invitation for him. It was something that had been beyond the reach and outside the dreams of Blacks.

4

According to my grandmother, Lily Scott, I arrived at the house on South Cumberland Street in Jackson, Tennessee, in December of 1950, after taking the train south with her. My grandmother had come to Chicago to collect me from my mother after they agreed I would be better off in Tennessee while everything in my mother's life was restructured. Like where she lived, how she lived, and, to be blunt, who she didn't live with. She and my father had agreed to disagree and were to make this difference of opinion as official as their previous agreement. I was not needed as either a referee or witness to this action, and was sent on the Seminole with my mother's mother. According to the plan, I would be with her for six months. I was not consulted.

My stay stretched beyond those six months that had been planned, and eventually beyond six years, which landed me in the same school my mother had attended, St. Joseph's. The period from a skinny, chocolate, preschool-aged mischief maker to my short-pants uniform at Catholic school seems hardly a blink in retrospect. As I grew up I was blessed with the run of an aging neighborhood in the southern section of town where I was always near a "cousin" or someone who recognized me as a descendent of a family that was near legend in South Jackson. I was an heir of Bob and Lily Scott. My every appearance was a reminder of some hazy happening from the halcyon days before Cumberland Street was even paved, and before Jackson was large enough to show up on state maps.

All the Black folks lived in South Jackson. A substantial percentage of the community members were from my grandparents' generation. It seemed that the numbers were split between folks who were easing toward senior citizenry and those of school age. The hole was in the middle—people my mother's age. Those were the folks who had left Jackson and Tennessee for factory work and urban life in the north or farther west: St. Louis, Memphis, and Chicago. Somehow their children, like me, all ended up in Jackson with their grandparents, aunts, and uncles.

The most popular sport in the south was baseball, and the stands for the little league games were always fairly crowded with mature community experts. My game was somewhere between mediocre and all right, but my pitching reminded them of "Steel Arm Bob Scott," my grandfather, who once pitched for the local team. My ripping and running in general through the dusty streets brought back stories of the four Scott children who had run and ripped twenty years before I arrived. Everyone remembered them, so Jackson felt like a town full of parents and grandparents. I was welcomed everywhere. I was identified and respected in Jackson as a Scott: "Bob Scott's boy." I was identified as though the Herons did not exist.

I didn't mind being connected to Bob Scott. I just didn't know him because he'd died the year before I was born. Under consideration, I decided that most things that were important had happened just before I was born: my grandfather, the Second World War, Jackie Robinson, the things that were important to people in church or on the front porch at night. They had gotten all their living done, and their accomplishments were strung out behind them like pearls on a leash. Lazy evening conversations would allow us all to take figurative walks through the gardens where those highlights of their lives had been planted.

My grandmother had been born Lily Hamilton, in Russellville, Alabama. It was an appropriate name for a delicate, fair-skinned woman with raven-black hair that nearly reached the floor when she let it down to brush it. She was scarcely more than five feet two inches, and never more than a hundred and ten pounds. She was a laundress. Her first job had been for the railroad, cleaning and preparing the tablecloths and place settings for the club car diners and the uniforms for the porters and conductors who worked on the rail on the two passenger trains that shuttled between Miami and Chicago. To facilitate that job she had moved to Jackson, Tennessee, roughly halfway between those two points. Once I landed in Jackson, every summer I rode on either the Seminole or the City of Miami, back and forth to Chicago to see my mother.

By the time I came to live with Lily in 1950, she was "taking in" laundry for a living. She did her job at the house on Cumberland Street for individual, private customers who brought their clothes to the house and picked them up a few days later. I don't know how she started doing that job or how she got her customers, but among the people she provided this service for was the mayor (though he had started bringing his clothes before he was mayor), the chief of police (though his wife and son came more often than he himself did), and the owner of a large downtown department store.

I found out how she felt about quite a few things from listening to what she said to them, and about how much respect they had for her by the way they listened. I heard her address the chief about "the problem," what wasn't right, what was bothering folks, what needed to be done. He would nod his big bald head and in his half-growl he would drawl, "Aw, Lily, you know them kinda things take a while."

She would always speak her mind, and it took just the right amount of time for her to finish her points and to gather their shirts and other property. But she spoke her mind wherever she was. Like her evaluation of the waiting area reserved for Blacks in Corinth, Mississippi, a filthy, cave-dark backroom where we had to wait to change buses when we visited family back in Russellville, Alabama. She would be sure the white ticket seller heard her let loose a list of complaints. She seemed to make the other Black folks in there nervous. And I got the impression that she didn't care. There were no good racists and no places where you would prefer to be discriminated against. There was no best racist state; but there may have been a worst racist state—from my brief experiences, that dishonor would have to go to Mississippi. For whatever reason, I felt bad in Mississippi. I felt Black and mistreated. Maybe it was because of the things I heard about Mississippi, about the murders there, about Mack Parker and Emmett Till and Medgar Evers, who were all murdered in

Mississippi while I lived in Jackson. Maybe it was the size of the signs that said COLORED at the bus station in Corinth. Maybe it was the absolute stink in the bathroom of that bus station, which was unmatched in my experiences before or since.

My mother and uncle used to say they hated to go to the stores in Jackson with Lily because she would embarrass them. White cashiers at uptown stores always waited on white folks first; they would never ask, "Who's next?" If somebody white walked in they would go straight to the counter as if the Black people were invisible. But not with my grandmother. She was not in sync with certain facts. There were signs indicating some of the rules—like in that Mississippi bus station, with its "Colored" waiting room. But my grandmother didn't consider it a rule for her if there was no sign. And white people had their own limits as to how far they could or would push that "us first" bullshit. So in line at the cash register my grandmother would loudly say, "I was here before them" and hold out her money. It wasn't her stature that kept people off her; somehow her attitude and bearing brought her respect.

I would hear white folks whispering in stores in uptown Jackson when my grandmother would stand at their counters and say, quite distinctly, that she wanted to purchase something on credit. As a rule, colored people couldn't even ask for credit, but my grandmother did not follow rules like that. If she was speaking to a new employee, there would be a pause that hung in the air between us like a condor, not needing to wave its wings and disturb the air. The clerks would look at her—she was obviously unafraid to make eye contact with them—and feel their throats

27

tighten. They would excuse themselves to go get their bosses to tell her no. But the boss would approve it, and the clerks would return with silly grins tearing their faces up while they wrote down whatever it was she wanted to buy. I could imagine the bosses saying, "That's Lily, she's Bob Scott's wife."

There were regular gatherings on the front porch when the weather was warm. It could include any number of people from the neighborhood, but it always included Mrs. Cox, the school janitor's wife from across the street, and someone from the Cole family next door, as well as either cousin Lessie or Uncle Robert. And no matter where the conversations started, they would end up speaking on race. What was happening here and there. What they had read in the papers. What information had come through from the men and women who worked on the trains and knew what was going on from Miami to Chicago. I remember hearing about Emmett Till and Mack Parker on the front porch. A twelve-year-old and a truck driver, both murdered by white people. Mack Parker was lynched and Emmett Till was beaten to death. Inevitably, someone would bring up possible solutions, something that could stop folks from getting killed that way. The most frequent conclusion was that some organization, perhaps the NAACP, needed to do something. My grandmother was rarely too talkative on those occasions. She would talk when she had something to say and laugh a lot at the things the excitable Mrs. Cox would say.

What directed Blacks in Jackson was their belief in the Baptist church. We attended Berean Baptist church every Sunday. My grandmother did not like a lot of people. She wasn't one to be doing a lot of laughing it up with strangers. She was friendly with the church people and participated in all of their various to-dos. When she was in Russellville with Uncle Counsel or when her children were home for a while, she was visibly happy. But Lily Scott did not like people for no reason. She was not stuck up or snooty or snobbish. She was not narrow-minded, naive, neurotic, nosy, or negative. She was not combative, complaining, compulsive, or complacent. You could count on her. She was predictable, patient, perceptive, persistent, proud, private, and practical. She had a healthy respect for hard work and was not afraid to put in her time. She was a sane, sensible, settled, serious, solid, single-minded survivor. And she was a religious and God-fearing woman with high ideals, strong principles, and most of all, a belief in the power of learning. Though she did not have a lot of formal book learning herself, she had insisted that her children be educated. And she had scrapped, scrimped, scrambled, scrunched, scrubbed, scratched, scuffled, slaved, and saved until somehow all four of her children had graduated from college with honors.

She read to me and taught me to read very early. At four years old we were reading the funny papers on Sunday and a few chapters from the Bible each night. On Thursdays there was a man who delivered *The Chicago Defender*, the Black weekly paper. It was in the *Defender* that I first read columns by Jesse B. Semple, including his conversations with Langston Hughes. His column became the first thing I would look for. I cannot remember too many Bible specifics after Exodus, but I do know the Old Testament had a lot of long names to pronounce and that taught me phonetics.

The front porches of the Black folks in Jackson were where everyone sat in the cool of the early evening, and people always threw invitations our way if we walked by. But my grandmother rarely stopped. We would wave to folks we knew, naturally, and I would often hear, "That's Bob Scott's boy and Lily. Good man, Bob Scott." I never understood how they always skipped over my father to attach me to my grandfather, but I didn't mind or say anything because I knew my grandmother could hear them and she never turned around.

5

My grandmother would sometimes talk about her life back in Russellville, Alabama, before she moved to Jackson. She had several brothers and sisters, though I remember only two of her brothers; she would take me to see them in Alabama. She always noted the steady consistency of her brothers, how dependable they were, and how well they served as the decision makers for her generation. We stayed with Uncle Buddy, whose name was Morgan, after their father. He was the oldest and head of the family, a sober elder statesman who never said four words when three would get it said. There was also Uncle Counsel, a short, wiry, fast-talking man with a quick wit and dozens of new stories to tell.

The Hamiltons, my grandmother's family, were almost white people. The father of my grandmother and her brothers had been a white man who evidently could not marry their black mother because they were in Alabama. Apparently he spent most of his day in the large house at the front of the property, where Uncle Buddy now lived, and then came to join his family at the back in the evening. I don't remember ever seeing a picture of him, or them, from what would have been the early 1900s, but they were all named Hamilton and collectively made decisions about how the farm and livestock would be handled.

The Hamiltons came in two distinctive sizes. There was the small, economy size of my grandmother, with her energetic work ethic that carried her around the house and the yard from "can see" to "can't see," sweeping, dusting, digging around the flowers and the pomegranate bush; Uncle Counsel was her size and had the same type of irrepressible energy. Uncle Buddy represented the other size, extra large, and was always a comfort when he was near, this huge person in faded overalls and a sun-shielding hat. He represented stability, reliability, and security, and his size implied strength of both physique and character. It was darker than a thousand midnights just outside the bedroom window at Uncle Buddy's place in Russellville, but I knew he was around and I never had any trouble sleeping there.

It was always Uncle Buddy, with his long calm face and thoughtful eyes, who met us at the bus station in Tuscumbia, or less often met the train at Red Bay, Alabama. There was no direct anything to Russellville. My grandmother and I would crawl into the northwest corner of Alabama on a gas-choked, dusty Greyhound or a near lifeless locomotive. A trip of less than 150 miles took the better part of a day before braking at this cluster of clapboards or solitary shacks as though we had arrived somewhere.

As always, Uncle Buddy would come shuffling up with a welcoming grin for his sister and a nod for me. That was one of his speeches, that nod. After a long description of something by Uncle Counsel he would nod his head and smile. After an agreement was reached about things the family needed to have done, he would nod that it would be done. He could have been known as the Nodfather.

One of the more interesting stories I heard about the type of stock I came from concerned Uncle Buddy. One day he was down the path in the backyard while the rest of the family was gathered on the back porch. All of a sudden Buddy appeared holding his hand over his eye. When he got up close and moved his hand, the people on the porch could see that a bumblebee had stung him and left the stinger in the white of his eye. My grandmother said that everybody was screaming except Buddy. They helped him sit down and Lily removed the stinger with a pair of tweezers. When she finally had it, they gave him a damp cloth and he got up and said, "Thank you, I appreciate that." Then he went on back to whatever he'd been doing in the yard.

I used to think that under the word stoic in the dictionary there should be a picture of Uncle Buddy. But stoic isn't right, because it doesn't incorporate Uncle Buddy's smile and kind eyes. And having a bee stinger in your eye and saying nothing until you thank the person who removes it goes beyond stoicism. It's a wonder he didn't just nod.

I always enjoyed myself at Uncle Counsel's house, where we went for meals sometimes. He had children near my age and I could play with them. The meals were always great, with a lot of family members around the table and recollections by Uncle Counsel that kept everyone laughing. The Hamilton family was close, and I never felt left out of anything because of my grandmother's love and the love they all felt for her was partly mine.

Back in Jackson we had family around, too. The Scott house on South Cumberland was the second from the corner of Tanyard Street. Make a left on Tanyard and the third house was where Miss Emmaline Miles lived. I called Miss Emmaline "Aunt Sissy," and while there were a lot of folks identified like relatives in the south, like Cousin Lessie or Uncle Robert next door to us, Aunt Sissy was really my aunt; in fact, great aunt. She was Bob Scott's sister. I didn't always understand Aunt Sissy and the way she would hug me and call on African spirits. She would surprise me on her porch with fierce, emotional, smothering embraces and would run her bony fingers up and down my spine as she held me. She was also a virtual river of information that I could have used to find out more about the man I got half of my name from, Bob Scott. But I was too young to know to ask.

Everybody who talked about Bob Scott for any length of time brought up his love of sports. This alone was enough to make him my favorite relative, especially among the Scott men. My mother had a photograph in an album, a posed black-and-white family portrait that was taken in the late 1930s or early 1940s. It was the entire Scott family, three teenaged girls in Sunday dresses, a fresh-faced boy in a suit jacket and white shirt with no tie, and a short, fair-skinned lady with long dark hair. They were standing in a half circle around a well-dressed gentleman who sat at an angle. It was the only picture I'd ever seen of the man, Bob Scott, who was obviously tense at the center of the semicircle, holding a cane with large, strong hands, searching for the camera with sightless eyes.

I was struck by how tall Bob Scott was, reaching his wife's shoulder level while seated. I could also see two things I was

looking for in him right away. First, the athlete, Steel Arm Bob, the pitcher who bested Satchel Paige. The second thing was Aunt Sissy. I was looking for the family resemblance between him and his sister, and it was right out front. The tall rawboned physique, the African cheekbones, the bushy hair and eyebrows, the sad eyes. It was all there. Because of Aunt Sissy and the other older people in South Jackson, I was looking for myself in that old portrait, too. I was looking for what they saw when I passed by and they said, "That's Bob Scott's boy. Good man, Bob Scott." I was looking for what made Aunt Sissy hug me and call me her only blood relative when I dropped in after running an errand for her, for what made her say we had royal African blood in our veins, why she would invent words for illnesses that were allegedly attacking her, like "the epizootic," something that afflicted only special people—people like us.

"He was a gentleman and a gentle man," my grandmother told me about her husband. It was as nice a summary as I was likely to get. It told me something about the two of them that corresponded to things I had been told and overheard.

"Daddy never whipped us," my mother told me on a visit to Jackson. "But mama did. He would even try to talk her out of it."

"He never whipped any of you?" I asked.

"No. You see, he said that no Scott man would hit a woman or a child, that having to resort to that would mean he had lost control of his home and he would have to leave."

Maybe she sensed what I was wondering.

"Daddy was the insurance man," she added, "during the *real* Depression, when everybody was depressed."

I knew an insurance man in Jackson. His name was Mr. Fuller, and he came around once a week, though sometimes it seemed liked every day. He was a middle-aged balding gentleman who was always sweating and wiping his face and head with a handkerchief. He stood in the living room thumbing through his receipt book, waiting for my grandmother and sweating. And as he wiped his face, he would peek to see whether I was looking at him. I was. Mr. Fuller seemed ill at ease, but he was duty-bound to collect that little bit of change every week.

"Sometimes people didn't have it," my mother continued. "It was just small change, but they didn't have it. But during those times, with money being so short, you needed your insurance more than ever. Because you couldn't just skip a week and not be protected for that week. You would lose all of your money, your policy, and your investment to that point."

"He was a tall, big-boned man with brown skin that had red undertones like an Indian, and a wide, open face with a large nose. Solid. Honest. Thoughtful."

By the time I was eight or so, I could cross large streets and run errands. I went over to Aunt Sissy's every day. There were few disruptions to the quiet, organized life my grandmother and I lived, and one of the only people or things that could really get under Lily's skin was Sissy. She was too playful and unlike a sixty-year-old for my grandmother, who wanted Sissy to act her age. But hell, sometimes Lily Scott wanted me to act *her* age. Somehow Sissy's irreverence and disregard for quiet sanity irritated Lily; Sissy probably thought her sister-in-law took herself too seriously.

I would return with a daily medical report, typically

encompassing some new sickness I had never heard of. Of course, Aunt Sissy was entirely too knowledgeable to be any kind of serious about made-up African illnesses; she was a retired nurse. And anyway, Sissy was always up and tottering around in her room, an especially tall, bony, chocolate lady with a round face, a pleasant smile, and a head of gray hair cut close. Whether or not she needed me to run any errands, she would fumble around in her little purse for a couple of pennies for me for candy.

She shared her house with a short, silent woman named Miss Ora Boyd, and occasionally they would both sit on their porch in the early evening, though they didn't seem to communicate with each other much. If I went by after dinner, Sissy was immediately animated, always ready for a conversation.

"How come Aunt Sissy doesn't have children?" I asked my grandmother once.

"Sissy was married," my grandmother said, "and she had a son named Jimmy Doe who died."

"From what?"

"He had a very badly curved spine. It made him look like a hunchback, and it got worse as he got older until his spine pressed in on his heart and killed him."

I tried to organize a picture of that in my mind and failed.

"What is it? How do you get it?"

"It's called scoliosis. It's a curvature of the spine, a lateral curve. Sissy had a less disfiguring case of it."

"Aunt Sissy got the epizootic," I reported confidently. "From Africa. She said we come from Africa, me and her. Do we?"

"She came from Memphis and you came from Chicago," said my grandmother. She sounded exasperated, the way she often did when Aunt Sissy was the subject.

I thought it over quietly.

"The epizootic won't kill you, right?"

"Scotty, nothing will kill you if there's no such thing. I've heard all that foolishness from Sissy about what she's got and you know what it is? Nothing. That's what. Nothing."

You don't only get what you want from your ancestors. Or, you get everything from your ancestors. I didn't know as a child that I had scoliosis, and that it was something that would be a problem for me all my life, tilting me to the left like a six foot curiosity of Italian architecture. I found out years later, when I was given a physical in high school.

But Aunt Sissy running her bony fingers up and down my spine was not searching for our African ancestors. She was looking for Jimmy Doe, and happy he wasn't there.

6

I am very proud of the education I collected through seventeen years and ten institutions, from south town in Jackson, Tennessee, to Johns Hopkins University in Baltimore, Maryland. The easiest way to describe the total experience would be "different." Had it been a career I was describing, the word "checkered" might have come to mind, even though that word reminds me of an old taxicab company rather than what I'm trying to say: black/white/black/white, an extensive journey that covered all of the educational possibilities, including being taught at home. Because that's where my education began, in the center room of the house on Cumberland Street at Lily Scott's side. That is where I learned to read and count and where I acquired my respect for education. From a woman with only a little.

Maybe the whole black/white/black/white thing would be no more descriptive than saying, "like a nun rolling down a hill." But it worked out; from a Black and then a white school in Tennessee to the same things in New York high schools and through college, the alternating stops held true. And it all began with a black/white school, Black children taught by white folks in Jackson.

My grandmother took me over to St. Joseph's the day I turned five. Me and my grandmother, our short legs pumping purposefully, wearing some semi-Sunday clothes, down two blocks on Tanyard Street and past the projects to the three-story haunted brick residence of funny-looking clothes horses, employees and confidants of white folks' God—represented, it seemed to me, by a penguin (it was my first look at a nun). The white folks refused to let me in. I was finally admitted when I was confessing my true age of five and a half.

The school was in a dilapidated tenement-feeling building —purgatory for the few nuns and the red-faced priest sentenced to work there. It was a creepy damn place, and it provided an eerie and frightful voyage through shadow-cloaked hallways filled with an eternity of God-fearing intimidation for young Black kids like me imprisoned there. The proof of the school's physical condition gained validity after my second year, when it was closed and the building condemned.

Whether God himself actually lived there somewhere, I could not decide initially. I did, however, determine that in spite of the youthful appearance of these nun-women in dust-dragging black, they had been around St. Joseph's for years and remembered my grandmother and her children, and it turned out they had refused me until I was five and a half on purpose. They didn't let me in because my grandmother wasn't afraid of white folks. So I was punished, and made to feel uncomfortable.

There were lots of myths that other Black kids built up about Catholic school—like how they would wash your mouth out with soap. But I never saw any of that. In fact, I don't

41

remember getting a whipping until I got to public school two years later. The classrooms were upstairs, above the church part, which was on the ground floor. They held mass every morning before classes. If you were late for mass, you were considered late for school.

We studied the catechism. It was all taught by rote, so I could probably still recite the prayers. You remember them just like the Pledge of Allegiance; even if you didn't know what you were saying, it was understood that God was listening. I decided I couldn't be a Catholic. At least not right then. There were too many fucking rules and regulations about where to stand, where to sit, and when. At morning mass it was standing, sitting, kneeling, wheeling, dealing, silent, on prompts from occasional mumbling from the altar. Phooey!

The weird thing was what it did to the kids. How uptight and un-all right it made us. And that, too, became a life lesson about allegiance that I came to recognize as such. I had my introduction to the tattle at St. Joseph's. The rollover. And we were learning to do those things to ourselves for others who were not.

One early spring morning, I found an old rusty knife on my way to school. Later on someone told me it was a Swiss army knife, but that morning it was just a short, fat object of total fascination. As I crossed a corner of the grass part of the walk in front of Liberty Street Church, my foot touched it. Dislodged it. And when I bent over to see what it was, I could not believe my good luck.

It had been white at some point, a pearl or oyster color, and, man, was it cool. It had three or four different-sized blades, a corkscrew (for a very short cork), a bottle opener, a whittling blade, and parts so glazed over with rust that I couldn't pull them out. I was thinking about how I would remove the rust when I got home.

I got lost examining the wonders of my discovery, continuing on a path that my feet knew by heart. At the end of Tanyard Street, take a right to walk past the projects. Until about a block from St. Joseph's, I was still so intrigued by my find that I hardly noticed . . . Ann Morris. She was a classmate, but not someone I knew that well. She was already growing in her two permanent front teeth and reminded me of Bugs Bunny.

But today, this morning, anyone was a good friend because I needed to show someone my knife. So I showed Ann Morris as we walked through the gate and up the front steps of the school. And I dropped my prize into my coat pocket.

By lunch time it was forgotten. And after lunch, during recess, when a whole posse of first through fourth graders ran after each other and from one another in dizzying purposeless circles, I felt and became aware of, without any actual signal, a change in the tenor of the game playing and each-other chasing. When I turned to check out what was going on, I saw a gathering, a ragged huddle of small black and brown faces turned upward to the chalk white face that seemed stuck halfway through the "habitual" cowl, scowling down earnestly. In the midst of this forming circle was Ann Morris and the subject of her earnest speech.

They were coming my way. All of them, with Ann Morris appearing even smaller and shrinking next to sister whatever-her-name-was holding her hand.

43

I don't really remember how the interrogation began, but it had been about Ann Morris telling the woman that I had a knife, making it sound like a machete and me a midget Zorro. I said I didn't have one, that I'd thrown it away. And then Charles Dawson, on orders from the penguin, was designated to rummage through my pockets until, beneath a tissue and two gum wrappers, in the coat lining . . .

I felt a wave of religious irony then: when you needed help you called for God. When you got it, you thanked Jesus. When you didn't get it, you cursed God. But I didn't. I cursed Ann Morris. And Charles Dawson. And sister whatever-her-name-was, who used this drama of the search and discovery incident after my denial as a God-sent lesson that, (1) Thou shall not lie because, (2) God will be sure thou art caught, and, (3) you will be punished. Sister whatever-her-name-was took charge of (3), and to illustrate it, I was sentenced to stand up against the fence every day during recess. And I hadn't reached seven years old at the time. But every day during recess, I felt like I was a thousand years old.

I did get several positive things out of St. Joseph's. For one thing, I got an education that was good enough for me to be skipped a grade when I got to public school; I did the third and fourth grades in one year. And for another, I got to make my debut as a vocalist in the second grade at St. Joseph's during one of the many talent shows. I did an unaccompanied version of "Jamaica Farewell," by Harry Belafonte. It was number one at the time.

"Down the way where the nights are gay . . ."

Hell, it was a hit.

7

When St. Francis was condemned, I landed at South Jackson elementary school. I didn't do a lot of singing there, but every once in a while my best friend Glover and me would call ourselves doing something that was supposed to be singing. The prettiest girl in our class was named Wanda Womack. She had two sisters and they were all fine, but Wanda was the one in my class. Somehow in fifth grade the word around school was that Wanda and I were "going together," like girlfriend and boyfriend. It seemed as if people looked around and put people together, just like that.

Ritchie Valens had just put out the song "Donna," and Glover and I were fooling around and I was switching the words so that it was "Oh, Wanda" instead of "Oh, Donna." Glover dared me to sing it in class. I said I would if he'd do the background. The crowd went wild! Naturally, we tried another tune right after that. We went into "All in the Game," and it was awful.

Wanda and I ended up going together for a few years, until seventh grade. Though back then you'd have to stay up all night to be up early enough to know much about sex. I guess we might have kissed once or twice when I walked her home from

45

school. I went on one date with Wanda, if you could even call it a date. There was a banquet held at our church in honor of our basketball team. Usually we were lucky to finish the season; that year we finished first.

To be honest, Wanda and I were competitors more than girlfriend and boyfriend. There was a stiff competition for grades between the three top girls and the three top boys in our class, and that meant Wanda, Dorothy Nell Bobbitt, and Alice Bonds against me, Glover, and John Odom. I was still a report card Scott in Jackson, and was an A student through sixth grade.

Though I did well, I didn't have good study habits. I depended on my memory of the classroom discussions and the notes I would take from the blackboard while the class was going on. But grades were important, and I took pride in getting good grades. I had a lot to live up to. My mother's sister Gloria was already teaching English overseas. She'd been in Indonesia and Israel, and sent me a camel saddle from Egypt. It was the only one in Jackson.

Despite the lack of mementos and photos from those early years, I can reach down into a barrel, it seems, and bring up scraps of yesterdays once tossed aside like gum wrappers. The raw feelings, like shock or sharp pain, or fear suddenly grabbing your heart, are closest to the top, easiest to reach. They return to me unbidden at times.

I burned the back of my right hand badly on the coal and woodstove that sat like a cast iron Buddha in the living room, my grandmother's bedroom. Another time I needed a dozen stitches in my left leg from a frantic slide into third base. I played little league baseball and football and basketball. Shortstop, pitcher, quarterback, pass catcher, guard, imagining I was preparing for Merry Lane High and Lane College. I remember playing nearly all sports. Except soccer, which we scarcely knew about in Jackson.

I can see other disconnected pieces of my childhood life in Jackson. I remember Harry Caray announcing the St. Louis Cardinals games from all the neighborhood radios. I remember going to Sunday services at church as regularly as a deacon. First flashes of what I thought was love, sensations close to shock each time I saw the prettiest girl I had ever seen. The memory frozen like an ice sculpture as I stood with barely a heartbeat; a "don't let her know" grin shattering like a windshield all the "be cool" I was reaching for. Stacks of these images sit neglected in the barrel—fascinating, nearly faded slices of my life.

There were things growing everywhere, and a lot of talk about what folks were planting and how various crops were doing. That part of the country is known for its black, fertile soil that was "good to grow," and people did some growing. Outside of town there was cotton by the bale, tobacco by the pound, and strawberries by the quart box, plucked from the bushes that grew shin high. But the farmers out in the "country," which is what we called everywhere outside of town, weren't the only ones growing. In the front and backyards of the houses in town were displays of the yesterdays, displays that showed these townsfolk's roots were not too solidly city; that only their houses were planted in town while something within them drove them out to dig and hoe and rake and dirty their hands in the dying sunlight, to plant if only a single row of vegetable memories, to turn full spades of the thick black soil over

47

and slice it with their shovel tips to a depth of eight inches. Then they could reach into the pockets of their gardening aprons for seeds to sprinkle among the decapitated worms.

In the backyard on South Cumberland Street, my grandmother and I were an unlikely farming duo. There was an annual yield from a peach tree, and a grape vine weaving its way along the south fence. Half the backyard space was cleared one fall and flattened near where a basketball backboard was erected with a netless orange rim, but otherwise there was a row of tomatoes, a couple rows of thin spring onions, and an attempt at cabbages one year. In the front yard there were roses and snowball bushes and the prize of the yard, a pomegranate bush that grew in season with its branches loaded down by the pale red apple-looking fruit bursting with tiny, juicy buds.

It was in the backyard that I first encountered and defeated a snake, hoeing an arm's-length nonpoisonous chicken snake to mince, slashing at the earth with such unaccustomed energy that my grandmother came to take a look.

"I knew you were doing more than weeds," she said, trying to assess the danger and confirming that there was none.

"Aw, boy," she chided, "this was harmless."

"It is now," I told her, trying to catch my breath.

Just knowing that there were several species of poisonous snakes in Tennessee, most notably water moccasins and cottonmouths, put me in no mood to check on pedigree before deciding that the state could do with one fewer.

I had a black cat with a small patch of white at its throat. I didn't like most animals. I didn't like dogs, showing their attention with wet tongues and cold noses. I did not like fish or birds because there was nothing to pet. I loved cats and still do. But somebody poisoned my cat, and my grandmother didn't want me to see the cat dying under the back porch.

That's how I became acquainted with cruelty—and with the fact that death doesn't always just happen, it can be caused. The memory is of me sitting and crying on the back porch with my grandmother holding me by my shoulders both to comfort me and to keep me from looking beneath the porch where my cat had crawled away to die.

I had felt somehow like the prince of the neighborhood, who knew everyone and was cared for by all. But evidently not, because I had to be shielded and warned away: someone had poisoned my cat. Someone killed Snowball.

Other images of death follow on from that: Mr. Spann's funeral, when they should have kept the casket closed after he lost control of his car and burned up inside it. The services for a little girl of seven I knew who had a heart attack and died. I hadn't known that death took people that you knew and children so young. And once I knew that, I knew what it meant when I saw an ambulance in front of Aunt Sissy's house, which I could see from the window of my school. She was brought out on a stretcher and I knew she wouldn't be back.

The images—of relatives, good friends, and the neighbors who were close enough to be called cousins and uncles and aunts even though they weren't kin—are clear. Some of them are animated, moving through the parts of their lives where I saw them most often. Some of the ladies are dressed up and

49

clean like Sunday mornings; the men are covered with the dust and grime of a day's work like a second skin. Most are smiling, enjoying something, but others are bent to nearly broken in half, crying in front of my grandmother, who is lying in a coffin surrounded by flowers.

I found Lily one sorry Monday morning in November, during seventh grade, cold to my touch. I'd gotten up to make her breakfast, and I knew it was strange that she wasn't stirring. I slipped quietly down the back hall to the kitchen to get the food going and saw her laying there, her profile clear in bed in the shadows of her darkened bedroom. When I dropped a pan, I took another furtive glance but she still hadn't moved. I went on frying strips of crackling bacon and eggs in the skillet, and as they were sizzling I took a wash pan of heated water and a washcloth to her room and placed them on the nightstand. I called her name softly and touched her wrist to wake her. She was as cold as ice and so stiff with rigor mortis that I could barely lift her arm.

I called next door, and the kid picked up the phone; I was so wild, he dropped it. I went outside and saw the woman from the house going to work, and she came and took over.

At the funeral, my uncle sat at the end of the pew crying, tears seeping from under his glasses and staining his shirt like sweat. I can feel myself almost falling into this image, beaten up again and nearly blown over, stunned and stomped on, pushing against a gale force wind to close a door I never meant to open. But I remember as I turn away from the images and the barrel that I did not cry. Not that day.

I had run out of tears.

9

Up to that day in November 1960, my mother had seemed more like an aunt, just like her sisters, like Sammy was a tomboy aunt and Gloria was a bookworm aunt. But on that dingy gray morning my mother and I had been brought together like cymbals in some ill-coordinated band's clanging climax. It wasn't only that we were unprepared to be put together then, it was that we had both just lost our mother.

Immediately after my grandmother's funeral, I spent six weeks in New York with Aunt Sammy and my Uncle William. New York City was as cold as a whore's heart that December. Every fucking day. I couldn't ever remember a day in Tennessee as cold as an average day in New York. And there was snow up to your ass, or at least well over the rubber overshoes I wore. At the school I attended for a few weeks, the teachers talked funny and I hardly knew what was going on because I came in on the offbeat. Since I knew I was going to be leaving again soon, there was no incentive to listen up and catch up.

Aunt Sammy, born Sam Ella Scott, had been a hell-raiser as a child, and was the biggest sports fan in the family. And no wonder, since she had played basketball through high school and college, and worked as a physical education teacher. On previous visits to New York, Sammy had taken me to my first live baseball games, to see the Dodgers play at Ebbets Field and to Yankee Stadium for a game against the Indians. She had taken me out on her motor scooter, not just around her neighborhood on 225th and White Plains Road in the Bronx, but out to Coney Island and to Yonkers Raceway. Sammy loved to gamble, and when she wasn't on the rail watching trotters, she hosted all-night "rent party" poker games.

William was no shrinking violet either, though he was an obvious intellect. He had majored in math and graduated early from Lane College. Like his sisters, he had been anxious to leave the rural reality of Jackson behind. Unlike the three ladies, who headed first for Chicago and its booming postwar economy, William signed an agreement with the U.S. Air Force and was stationed in Wiesbaden, Germany, before settling in New York City and taking an upper-level position with the Social Security Administration. I'm not sure where the name William came from, but it didn't matter because everybody called him "Baby Brother," which got shortened to B.B. or just B.

I enjoyed hanging around with Sammy. The best thing about being with Aunt Sammy was that she liked to go places that I enjoyed. It was not like spending time with someone who would rather have been anywhere else. And when she talked to me, she looked directly at me, not faking interest. She talked to me as though I had a brain and could understand English. It was refreshing. Often she had to preface whatever we were doing with a conspiratorial, "Don't tell yo' mama where we went!" And I didn't.

Back in Jackson, my mother, who moved back from Chi-cago, and I spent the next year on South Cumberland Street together like the first two people at the rail watching the life boats lowered as our lives took on water. Even if my mother cared to live in Jackson, where the roots of everything Scott were planted in the yard, and secure her teaching position at Lane College, notices were being served throughout that section of South Jackson: there was a four-lane highway coming through from the south that would connect to Interstate 70, and it would reach us by the end of 1962. Everybody had to go somewhere.

My mother and I stayed put and picked up our mail there, but my mother was already firming up plans, in touch with her brother, Uncle B., in New York. She and I lived together and I started eighth grade back at South Jackson primary school. But something else was happening, too. My mother, far more perceptive and far more committed to me than the other way around, was obviously making up her mind about her son. She knew she loved me because mothers do, but she had to decide whether she liked me. I think she decided we could be friends as long as I was honest. The best way to do that, she decided, was to let me see that she was honest. No hype and no hurry. What she showed me as time passed was that her faith was unshak-able and her love unconditional.

There was a brand new junior high in town, an all-white public school called Tigrett, for students from the seventh to ninth grades. There was also a lot of talk about desegregation, as Brown v. Board of Education crept across the south and school boards started to understand the ramifications of what Brother Thurgood Marshall taught the Supreme Court. In November 1961, a petition circulated through South Jackson primary school, a list of "who's willing to go to a white school?" or "who wants to go to a white school?" I signed up; so did a lot of other people. But the crackers down there still felt a certain obligation to the Confederacy, an inherited allegiance to the memory of Robert E. Lee and Jefferson Davis—even though all they had to relate to were the names of highways and the battlefields that had been turned into tourist traps. I knew the list was just something that had to be done according to the law, to demonstrate a need for transfers to be approved. It's possible that some folks only signed up because they thought the NAACP lawyer who was preparing a court case to challenge the segregated school system needed to demonstrate substantial numbers. I don't think anyone thought it would happen anytime soon.

One night just after New Year's Day 1962, when the second half of the school year was just starting, my mother came into my room. When something was serious, my mother would take a pen and twist it through a curl in her hair while her voice got deep and she said things very clearly. Loud enough to be heard, but soft enough that you had to listen. A tone of anti-panic, like she could be heard actively being calm. A kind of calmness that made the hairs stand up on the back of your neck. It used to really get on my nerves when I heard that tone of voice. But I was also still getting to know my mother—it had been only a year since my grandmother died—and I didn't know how to interpret her tone of voice and how serious it was.

That's how she sounded that night. And it sounded serious. It sounded like I was in trouble. Or somebody was. I waited for her to get to the point as she started to explain that the negotiations between the NAACP lawyer and the Jackson City Council had been settled. That is, settled in favor of the NAACP. Then my mother asked whether I still wanted to go to a white school. She never said I *was* going. She just asked whether I wanted to go. And if I wanted to, I had to start *the next day*.

She said forty students had signed the petition when it first went around in November, but now that they were ready to integrate the junior high school, there were just three making the switch. And that was if I decided to go.

I asked her who was going.

She said Madeline Walker, who I'd gone to St. Joseph's with, and Glover, who was my man, were the other two students.

I think part of why her jaw was so tight that night was because she was upset that so many of the other kids had backed out. But she didn't say anything more except that I should think about it, that nobody would look down on me for not going, that in fact no one would even know anything in particular. All they had ever announced publically was that there had been forty names.

Did she want me to go? I thought she did, but she also wanted to be fair. She knew when I signed up there had been a long line in front and behind me, a lot of people. I figured the city council was calling our bluff: "Okay, y'all coloreds, let's see how many of these signatures are just autographs."

I decided to go to Tigrett, and started the next day.

I didn't know what to expect. All the books were the same, and the syllabus was the same, too. We were in approximately

55

the same place in the syllabus as we'd been at South Jackson. They always said the schools were separate but equal, and the books weren't the difference. The school was very different physically. Tigrett was departmental, and we went from classroom to classroom and had different classes with different people. That was new to me. At South Jackson we stayed in the same class with the same folks all day long.

It may sound strange, but I didn't look ahead. If I had, I might have realized we would get to the Civil War in American history. That was going to come up. But I swear it snuck up on me, and the ramifications snuck up on the class. When we did get to the Civil War, it was like reviewing it from the loser's locker room. I don't know how many classes I'd had about the Civil War up to that point, but none of them had ever been from a point of sympathy with the South. Okay, so now the South was the home team.

We landed on a page with a picture of a Black man in chains, a slave. It was as if nobody knew it was coming. Everyone froze for a minute. Then this one guy, Steve, who was a real pain in the ass, snickered. The teacher chastised him and took over again and we moved on.

I have come to the conclusion that "The Spirits" played a part in integrating Tigrett, in making it work so smoothly. I found out later that right after New Year's Day the city council wanted to make a deal. It was a secret that stayed that way until we were already in classes, leaving no chance for opposition to build. If they could integrate the schools quietly, without confrontation, they could save money, avoid any bad publicity for the city, keep down the potential for rednecks to stir up trouble if the question had gotten into the news. The council had some specifics when striking the deal with the NAACP lawyer: only junior high students, and Tigrett would be the "test school," in part, I'm sure, because of its location, far from Main Street. The council also wanted to go immediately, with as close to zero noise about it as possible.

I suppose they must have sat down and said, "Hey, it's coming—like tomorrow morning, and judgment day, and color TVs you can afford," and decided to get a jump on things. I don't want to prop up the Jackson City Council as societal visionaries, but their plan worked pretty smoothly. And it was a move that advanced the city's economic potential a thousand fold: it made clear that Jackson's politicians knew the Civil War was over.

9

By the spring of 1962, as eighth grade at Tigrett finished up, the bulldozers and road graders working on the new highway were just over the rise to the south, only a few miles away. My uncle B.B. had organized a three-bedroom place for us to share with him in the Bronx. My mother and I were moving to New York.

The night before we were scheduled to leave Jackson, I went around to see some people one more time. I had known that we were going to New York for months, but held on to the hope that before we left something would come up, something that could save me from the big city. I didn't think about what had happened to my grandmother. I didn't consider what my mother wanted, or what my uncle had planned. Nobody else's life mattered but mine. I realized what that was: it was terribly selfish.

I recognized my feelings for what they were. They were my sight, my hearing, my senses of taste and touch and smell, all together. They were my sum total and I didn't look for this total to give me answers because somehow no single sense of what was happening to my life could make sense of it all. Only when I asked myself how I felt could I relax as though I knew something. I knew that "how do you feel?" wasn't the right question to ask most people. It was rhetorical, irrelevant, a question as mundane as it was insignificant. To most people. But not to me.

I could blame it on geography. The move to New York wasn't something that my mother or anyone else was responsible for. We *had* to move. Somewhere. If not to New York then to some other new somewhere. The "urban renewal" project that had been rumored for so long as part of Jackson's future was literally just over the hill. From Church Street I could see the bulldozers. For years it had been vaguely rustling offstage like a coming storm, but now it was starting to rain.

Jackson's urban had become renewal
Political concessions made things suddenly doable
A six lane highway paved the way with mass approval
And the house on Cumberland Street faced imminent removal
And all my old side streets were asphalt memory lanes
And in July of 1962 I left on a 4 a.m. train

I didn't want to go. But I came to the conclusion that there was no villain, no one who should be the target of my disappointment. I was just one of a thousand people from South Jackson who had to get the hell out of the way. And I felt better about myself by the time the train reached Chicago, halfway to New York.

When we arrived in New York, we moved into the apartment my uncle had found on Hampden Place in the Bronx. Our street was only one block long, and just two blocks from

59

the 207th Street Bridge just over Fordham Road. It was within walking distance to Uncle B.'s job at the Social Security office on Jerome Avenue, and only a fifteen-minute walk from what would be my new junior high, Creston. This new place seemed a long way from the place on 225th and White Plains Road where I had stayed a year and half before, after my grandmother's funeral. Both addresses ended in Bronx, NY, but that's all I knew that connected them. My six weeks at the other place were not long enough for me to have lost my rookie status.

The apartment was different, for sure. It was pretty nice: it was on the second floor, which was the top floor, and my room had plenty of room for all my junk and a window that let in a nice breeze. Our things from Jackson had arrived before us, and our black-and-white TV was in the living room. B.B. had a color set on a stand in his room. And I was allowed to watch his TV when he wasn't there. That ended up being a couple of nights a week and most weekend nights. But I didn't feel comfortable, that's all. I felt stupid and awkward around my uncle and at the store and everywhere else. It was disquieting to move from a place where you knew every blade of grass to a place where there was no grass. And New Yorkers made you feel that you were beneath or beyond their notice. I wondered whether I could or should adjust to that, to try to be like that, or just to try to ignore it. That's what they did, just ignored everything.

Living with my uncle was a great benefit for my mother. She had someone she trusted and respected to share the expenses with and, once school started, someone to challenge me on what had become a mediocre academic performance and question the silent hours I spent in my room writing short stories and essays. Beginning the year before, in eighth grade, I had wanted to write: stories, songs, poems, essays, whatever. I read and I wrote. But what I read was not my homework or lessons. And what I wrote was primarily practice for myself. The time I spent on it was nonnegotiable.

My uncle's position was that there was no excuse for my doing less than excellent work in my classes, getting less than the straight As all the Scotts had worked for and gotten. The fact that I had finished Tigrett with no As was not up to his standards.

I remembered my mother reading to me from letters Uncle B. wrote us before the move, saying there were a lot of kids Scotty's age in the neighborhood, that he saw them all the time. But either they had all moved away in the meantime or B.B. had been drinking too much. There didn't seem to be any young people around. After going out every morning and afternoon and not seeing anybody younger than the hill that went up to the dead end at the end of our block, I was miserable.

I finally gave myself a break and started looking at the advantages. The main one seemed to be that I was returning to New York at the same time as National League baseball. The new New York team was a collection of old New York players from old New York teams that made the new New York team's games like an old timer's day every day. I became a follower, if not exactly a fanatic, of New York's Metropolitans, who were slickly and quickly transformed, shortened, to the Mets, probably for back page headline convenience. There were thirteen letters in the long way to say Mets, and sometimes the whole back page

61

headline was thirteen letters. Something like METS LOSE AGAIN fit perfectly, and often, that first year. They were firmly ensconced in last place by the time I got to the Bronx, with no dream of advancing. I gloried in headlines like METS WIN 1 IN A ROW.

Eventually, I also found the kids my age B.B. had sworn were around. There was a small fry, a kid about eight years old, who I met one day when I was out throwing my rubber ball against a wall. I asked him if there were other kids around, any guys my age, any kids who played ball, real games. He said yes, yes, yes, and yes, and explained that games of stickball and softball were played at "the Deegan." He was too young to have left the block, though, so he couldn't tell me how to get to the Deegan. He headed home.

But the kid, the first New Yorker I'd met who didn't know it all and admitted it, returned a little while later with a thin white guy in his early twenties, known as Jimbo to his friends on Hampden Place. Jimbo knew quite a bit. Within fifteen minutes I had told my mother, gone back out, and walked the five minutes it took to reach the Deegan.

It really only took the New York kids one quick look
From the time that I got in the game
They can tell right away if you can or cannot play
A player or just one more lame
After an inning or so when one kid had to go
I agreed to right field in nothing flat
And I didn't make a play because no balls came my way
I did nothing until I came to bat.
And I really don't mind saying I was so glad to be playing

That the moment they threw me the ball
The mix of raw anticipation and my two weeks of frustration
Helped me hit a double off the wall
The smile on my face told the kids from Hampden Place
That a player had moved to their street
They would all mock my drawl, but knew I could play ball
It shows how much I need to compete

My aunt Sammy went with me on my first day at Creston Junior High. I had been thoroughly saturated by then with stories that might best be titled "Tales of Creston."

Certain actual events
With semi-factual incidents
In retrospect make no damn sense
But at the time seemed real intense
The mythic and the legendary
Exaggerations seemed so scary
Life feels extremely temporary
When you're headed for the mortuary

Well, needless to say, Creston was not fatal. Aside from the fact that it was all-male and that Aunt Sammy signed me up for a vocational program that had me taking metal shop and electrical shop. My mother straightened that out, but her motivation to become a presence at my school wasn't because of my lackadaisical absence of enthusiasm for the simple-minded remedial courses I was taking during the first months at Creston. She went to Creston because I never had homework, and she finally saw a report card listing the courses I was in.

63

The day after the first report cards were issued, I was called down to the vice principal's office. There was a murmur of respect for me when the announcement went out during after-lunch homeroom. His office was responsible for discipline.

I had been there before. Related to his real job. When something went down at Creston, or if Creston students were suspected of something in the neighborhood, including a two or three block section of Grand Concourse, reprimands or an investigation and a suspension might be in order. These punishments were administered by the vice principal. I had seen him after I engaged another ninth grader in a slap fight.

This time he opened with his taking-charge voice.

"Heron," he said, tossing out a soiled paper plate and hanging up his coat. "Your mother is a very impressive lady."

He turned into my surprised expression with a shark's grin and reclaimed his seat behind his desk.

I knew now this wasn't about his usual business. He left me standing above him, a position he would never have conceded to an adversary or someone who was about to receive bad news or bad treatment.

"She was here this morning," he continued, opening a folder. "And she's got an unusual complaint. She says remedial courses for you are nonsense, ya know? That you could have handled remedial before you were enrolled. That the time you spend in the classroom probably feels like detention and that even in her worst nightmare she never saw you at a vocational high school."

He leaned back and appraised me, as if looking at me for the first time. Perhaps he really was. I looked at him for eye contact. He looked back at the folder.

"I went to talk to your teachers, ya see? Your mother wouldn't have been the first one to suspect that her son was more Einstein than Frankenstein, ya know?"

He liked that one.

"More seminal than criminal," I muttered, tiring of being played with. He started eyeing me suspiciously.

"Well, it was damn near unanimous, and they agreed with her. Ha! When I told her I'd look into it, she said she'd wait. Ha! I don't think she necessarily believed me. So I assured her I'd have a response today that you could give her when you got home. I was really beginning to think she knew what she was talking about. Her dress and bearing and vocabulary, everything . . . anyway, there was a bit of a discussion with Mrs. Kaufman, and she said you'd have to work on your math."

I nodded. He stood up, folding the folder on me as he rose.

"So we're moving you to 9-2. Mrs. Kaufman will be your new homeroom teacher. Mrs. Katz has a note from me and everybody else will be informed by tomorrow and have their class rosters amended."

I nodded again, like Uncle Buddy.

"You can move now, but be sure to give my regards to your mother."

He reached for my hand.

I also advanced my music career greatly at Creston. Actually I had no musical ambitions at the time. I liked to sit down at the piano and play the chords to "Ooo, Baby Baby" by Smokey Robinson. But that was about it. Until I got a break. A little red-headed music teacher at Creston summoned me to her classroom one day. When I got there, she asked me to read to her, to read a part of a script. I didn't know it at all, but it turned out to be from *The Mikado* by Gilbert and Sullivan, and she had me read the lead role, Ko-Ko, the high executioner.

I found out later the guy the teacher had wanted to play the role had rejected the part, so she had asked around for ideas about other candidates who might have some musical inclinations. There was only one play a year, and from what I understood, the guy had been a smash hit the year before. It was almost taken for granted that he'd star in *The Mikado*. I guess he was playing hard to get. I ended up getting the lead role as the executioner who doesn't want to execute anyone. Seemed like I was getting typecast.

10

I don't know what to read into this, but there have been a lot of Jacksons in my life. I lived in Jackson, Tennessee. The guy I wrote songs with, later, was Brian Jackson. In 1984 I voted for and did a fundraising benefit for Reverend Jesse Jackson. My road manager for a long time and a good friend for a longer time was named Earnest Jackson. And while living in the Bronx—before all the Jackson people—I worked at a place named Jackson's.

The place we lived with my uncle on Hampden Place looked like the private driveway for someone who lived on Fordham Road just east of the Major Deegan Expressway and the 207th Street Bridge from Manhattan. If you continued east on Fordham Road, you faced a left turn and a sharp incline that led to University Avenue, Jerome Avenue, the Grand Concourse, and the Fordham shopping district. Halfway up that incline on the right-hand side was an attractive-looking restaurant, Jackson's Steak and Lobster House. A prime attraction of Jackson's was a huge picture-window lobster tank where customers were invited to select the lobster they wanted for dinner. Great. I saw the lobsters in the tank scrambling over each other desperately, as though they knew what fate awaited them.

I was not motivated by "things" that dipped into my mother's finances. I was not worked up about my wardrobe and didn't mind taking a little teasing on the basketball courts because I didn't wear Chuck Taylors—Converse All Stars were the Air Jordans of that era. I had inherited a couple of nice jackets and a good assortment of sweaters from my uncle, but unfortunately my uncle didn't have any Chucks to hand down; we didn't wear the same size shoes anyway.

It benefitted my mom that I was not on her for this or that, but that wasn't why I didn't ask. I knew her expenses expanded when my uncle left, but I hadn't been after her for stuff before he left, either. I had what I needed to get by: a good selection of broom handles that served as stickball bats, a good leather basketball, an expanding collection of Marvel comics, and a radio that kept me on the field with the Mets, my adopted baseball team.

I managed to hold myself together by hustling. I made deliveries up the hill to old ladies on my bike, the same one I'd brought along from Tennessee. It had a basket on the front where orders from the corner grocery rode while I peddled. In the evening I met the newspaper trucks for the night editions and rolled them back to a corner candy store on Fordham Road and Sedgwick. In those days the *Daily News*, the *Mirror*, the *Post*, and the *Herald Tribune* all had night editions that were dated as the early edition for the next day. There were no individual deliveries to the stores. Instead, there was a central drop on Fordham Road where the trucks were met by youngsters with wagons, who hauled the various copies back to the neighborhood shops where huddling groups of retirees waited for them. Between what I covered with the wagon and peddled up that hill, I kept pocket money that I often doubled by betting on stickball games at the park in the afternoons.

But then came a job. Or rather, *the* job. That was when I was called to replace the man who was the dishwasher on the night shift at Jackson's. I was actually too young to work there, too young to be in a place that sold cocktails past midnight. But while laughing, I had smeared some of my mother's eye shadow across my upper lip where there were so few hairs I knew them all by name. The owner knew I was too young. The manager knew. Not how young I was, but how old I wasn't. But they called when they needed somebody suddenly.

At times I might do an 8 p.m. to 1 a.m. shift, their heavy time. The time when I would ordinarily be studying or listening to the radio or working on one of my stories about a private detective with a comic book name and five pages to catch his man. Instead I was in the "pits," in the elbow of a dishwashing machine that mostly moaned and groaned as it trudged along on a conveyor that mostly conveyed how hot and how tired and how thick with grease everything was.

From the moment I walked in there, it felt flat-out awful. I went to the back, through the swinging doors that separated the dining area from the dying area. It was hot, unnaturally so. You dig? The kind of heat that changes your mood and your attitude. A nondiscriminating hope-to-God-some-cold-beer's-waiting-that-I-can-bathe-in hot. Like a combination microwave and a dame with big tits on Spanish Fly rubbing up against you like she wants to melt you hot.

It had something to do with the combination of heat from the grill, with all the burners blasting, and the steam at my post, the dishwasher corner where these two flaps were located, reminding you of the tunnel of love. When I raised a flap to my right, I could shove a wooden square about my size into the darkness that always roared over the sweating dishes. To the left the dishes emerged with a whoosh of steam that literally seemed to smack me dizzy every one and a half minutes.

There was a young Italian waiter who came through our work area as though he was on roller skates with some customer's lobster, headed for a huge pot of scalding water, always singing, "That's your fucking ass, baby!"

At Jackson's, I came to understand the term "sweatshop," though this wasn't one and they never treated me bad for even one second. But I also came to understand why they have child labor laws wherever they have them.

At about 11 p.m. it was as if the Spirits whispered my name to the manager just as the big hand of the steam release struck me full in the face and made me so nauseous that my knees literally wobbled.

"How 'bout a steak, kid?" the manager asked.

"Right through your fucking heart," I croaked back.

And everybody howled and somebody slapped me on the back and I almost vomited. I stumbled and bumbled my way to the back window, where the change in the taste of the air, the smell of it, the feel of it against my face and chest like water after a desert trek, made me feel nearly ecstatic.

I praised the steak and potatoes and veggies the cook fixed especially for me. He was a gigantic Jamaican who always sang off-key and could handle a half-dozen orders at once and still keep his grills spotless and his platters looking as if he pulled them from an ad in a magazine. I ate every bite of everything, finishing with nothing but butter on my fingers from the rolls.

I soon learned how to beat the heat by walking to the open door after every second tray of dishes, about once every five minutes. I learned how to flog the smog, joke about the smoke, and to pour a cool glass of water over lettuce leaves and put them in my hat. I made it through every shift because my mother and I needed that money. The five hours I put in should have earned me about seven-fifty, but they always gave me ten bucks. The men I worked with called me "man," and they treated me like one, so I went back every time I was called, usually once or twice a month.

After finishing junior high at Creston, I had to decide which of two Bronx high schools to attend. Benjamin Franklin or De-Witt Clinton. After a year of all-boys education at Creston, I had sort of figured I'd go to the coed Franklin. I was not aware of any intellectual advantage professed by Clinton. The basketball team there was good, but there were no girls.

My mother did not weigh all factors, I'm sure. She had heard some derogatory comments about Franklin, and that convinced her that I was not going there. Based on where I was not going, I ended up enrolled at Clinton, an education factory of eight thousand boys who attended classes in three shifts: 7:30 a.m. to

71

1:30 p.m., 9:00 a.m. to 3:00 p.m., and 10:30 a.m. to 4:30 p.m. My first semester I drew the middle shift.

Registration for classes at Clinton brought my greatest fear of New York—being swallowed alive. In my mind I had seen myself as one of thousands of people stampeding down a boulevard like a human tidal wave, unable even to break stride, running both one step ahead and one step behind the next person. The worst aspect of this was that it wasn't an emergency, not an escape to anywhere away from anything. It was just everyday survival.

I felt as if I was signing up for work on an assembly line. I felt like I had imagined New York would make me feel: a struggle against becoming *nobody*. That was the difference I should have been able to express from my first stay in New York. I had been looking for that at Creston, but walking or riding to and from school with other guys from the block had calmed that strangeness I dreaded. It was back at Clinton. It came back on the registration line; I was an insignificant cipher, a six-digit dimwit with no connection to this concoction, with no place that was mine. In Jackson I had been somebody, recognized and respected. Maybe my problem was ego. Maybe my problem was being spoiled. But I felt otherwise, I felt that how successful you were depended on how comfortable you were. Some people were just small town people, and there was nothing wrong with that.

In the middle of that afternoon's line of fires I felt completely anonymous, as though I was being erased, as though I was losing contact by making contact, resigning by signing in. By joining I became disjointed; by taking a number I became one. I was in New York because my mother wanted this. She was here because she wanted it for me.

I had all kinds of problems at Clinton. It's no good to point at a general malaise, like a depression, feeling stressed or full-court pressed by a crowd in New York—it's too common. So I attributed it to the teachers.

"It's the teachers' fault," I told my mother. "I can't relate."

She blew up. I could talk about serious things with her for as long as I needed, but Saran Wrap problems, problems she knew I should have seen through did not fly.

"You don't like your teachers? Awww, that's too bad. The teacher isn't there for you to like her. If you do, that's all right. But that's not what she's there for. What you need to do is read the books she read. Just ask her about supplements she would recommend, added to her syllabus. And remember to take your weakest courses in the morning and your strongest classes in the afternoon. That means for you the math and science is in the morning and English and history are late courses. Right? Right."

That was an important conference, and the suggestion she made about when I should sign up for which subjects was crucial. The next semester I decided I would sign up for a last period English class, which was how I met Miss Nettie and got the opportunity to go to Fieldston. And I almost blew that.

11

During that first semester of high school, my mother and I headed to Alabama with Aunt Sammy to see the Hamiltons. And we stopped in Jackson, Tennessee, on the way.

The visit came at a time when I was really desperate, unable to get comfortable in the Bronx. I went through periods of time when it was all right to be in New York, and other times when I just knew I didn't belong there. That perhaps nobody did. I thought during those times that I belonged in Jackson.

Arriving back in Jackson felt curious, a revelation I needed. After following the Smoky Mountains down, past the point where Bristol, Virginia, bellies up to Bristol, Tennessee, we came into Jackson on Interstate 70, which now cut a five-hundred-mile, eight-lane diagonal route across Tennessee. The completion of Route 70 had brought about major change in Jackson: there had been growth I could see from the highway. Industry, jobs, money.

We pulled in to the house of a friend of my grandmother after midnight. I hardly slept before I was up at what the Amish would call early. I bathed and was dressed to go out immediately. I was anxious to walk on *my streets* and breathe *my air*. It was midweek, a school day, and I made my way out to Merry

High School, the Black high school, and arrived just after the opening bell.

All of my old gang was there. Even Glover, my best friend and lifelong rival, the guy who had integrated Tigrett Junior High School with me and Madeline, was there. I found that he was king of the hallways. I had grown in the eighteen months since I'd left, but he was still an inch taller and about ten pounds heavier. And now he wore a social maturity that made me feel like I had been left way behind. Perhaps I had been. Glover said he'd had sex. I still had only ambition. But what I really envied was how loose and comfortable he was. They all were. They were home. I hadn't been comfortable since I left. I wanted to feel that way again.

The real joy, what I thought I missed most, was seeing and talking to girls. They felt good even without touching. In New York I spoke to girls with a mouth full of doubt, trying to see the words I spoke and sap the drawl off of them. This morning all the girls were as pretty and soft as I remembered, but now with added bulges in their blouses and hips that made skirts dance as they walked. I used a month's worth of New York smiles as we strutted around and I threw "Hey" and "Hi'ya doing" every which way like a politician.

I went back to join Aunt Sammy and my mother for dinner and eagerly reported on my day as a celebrity from New York City. After dinner I got cleaned up and dressed up to go back out to Merry High for the Southern Serenaders, a school-wide talent show with students singing the latest tunes. I knew I would have been doing something solo or with a group if I had still been around. I wasn't doing any singing at Clinton.

75

Something strange happened. Somewhere near the end of the show, it all got tired. Jackson. Merry High. The Southern Serenading. Even the girls. They were still soft and cute, yes, but that was what was wrong with it. They were the same. I imagined that in twenty years I could walk in and nothing would have changed at all. Without leaving my seat and while the music played and somebody sang, I imagined myself back up the highway in the Bronx. And I wasn't called "country" anymore—or not without a smile. And everything I could imagine in the world was a subway ride away.

I would be all right when these few days were over and I was back in New York. I didn't live in Jackson anymore. You can go home again, I thought, but only to visit.

12

The tinny school P.A. system at Clinton made voices sound like they were talking from the bottom of a well, and I can still remember the principal coming on there as I walked into history one afternoon in November 1963, still damp from swimming class. He was saying something about a terrible event in Texas. "The president and some other people have been shot . . . not yet clear about the extent of the injuries . . . awful thing to have happened . . ."

The history teacher was watery-eyed and red-faced, blowing her nose, not saying anything, not taking attendance. I edged sideways around some folks to my seat in the crowded room. Hell, I thought to myself, this is a real shame. Is my whole high school life going to be this way?

After a while the voice was rising up from the well again.

"May I have your attention, please. I regret to inform you that your president is dead." There were more words, but our teacher had heard enough. She took a step or two backward and sat down, waving toward the door. School was over. Somebody had killed the president.

I did not recognize all the implications of a presidential assassination. But I recognized death. This one took over everything.

It came into everyone's house and sat down. It squeezed into every radio on every station. And every television station had the same pictures at the same time. Pictures of Oswald. Pictures of Johnson, formerly the vice president, being sworn in on an airplane. Pictures of the governor who got shot. Pictures of Kennedy's wife. Pictures of the book repository. Empty again. The third floor window. The policeman who arrested Oswald. More pictures of Oswald, the parkway . . . a replay of the motorcade from the other side of the parkway, opposite the book repository, elevated, squared up on the space where the cars will first appear. Not a lot of area open because this hill obstructs, and there's a viaduct with bare-headed men wearing raincoats with what are probably sawed-off Uzis. Glints of chrome and movement, people turning. The midrange drone of the crowd lining the route rises in volume as the lead car appears and enters a patch of sunshine. People wave and applaud and from inside the applause, distant but distinct: Crack! Crackcrack! Three shots with the second and third sounding as though they overlap.

Theories, speculation, inquiries, explanations.

Oswald being led in handcuffs off an elevator into a crowded hallway lined with the curious, the furious. There's a deputy in a white hat who seems disturbed by the glare of the lights and looks down to his left. The group pushes its way through the taut rows of bystanders, forming a parade-like path for the lawmen and their prisoner. Then an awkward intruder produces a gun and fires point-blank, belt high. Oswald crumples forward as his assailant is wrestled down. *I've just seen a man murdered.*

78

When I started the second semester a few weeks later, things did not look good. I walked into my English class at 2:00 p.m. and found a young white chick who looked like a student herself. Naturally she didn't look like a Clinton student, but there was an all-girls high school down the parkway and she could have gotten by as an inmate from there. I figured she must be a temporary replacement or a tutor or someone doing a field project for a sociology class. She was short, wore glasses, had a small voice, and maintained a counterfeit all-business front. If I had known the Mormons had an off-the-compound work program, I might have pegged her for a missionary.

She did not look like someone who had been destined to pull faculty duty at an institution for eight thousand mostly Black and Latin boys in a joint laid out more like a penitentiary than a school. On top of everything else, her name was *Nettie Leaf*.

What I came to enjoy about Miss Leaf was the way she took herself and her classes so seriously. It was far better to have a teacher who cared, about the class, about the material, about you, who cared about something, than another ho-hum hour of holding on and trying to stay awake. English was not number one among the half-wits at DeWitt Clinton. But it was cool with me. If Miss Leaf thought English was number one, how could I complain? So I showed up and didn't fuck with her. Maybe I stood out because I read the damn homework: *The Lottery* by Shirley Jackson and *A Separate Peace* by John Knowles.

That homework was a real clue about Miss Leaf. Wherever she came from, the students might have really been into those stories, but this place was the exact opposite of wherever. I didn't ask the other students how they felt about it, but I thought *The Lottery* was justice. For once. *A Separate Peace* was the book that got me to the point where my communications with Miss Leaf turned into static. I thought the book was white noise about white people; about her, not us. I don't know why that particular book was the last straw. It was no more irrelevant than anything else I read in school. At Creston I had read *Great Expectations* and Leon Uris, for crying out loud. I had performed in *The Mikado* without delving into the inherent racism of either Gilbert or Sullivan, neither of whom had a fan club in the ghetto. But this was not an ethnic protest or part of the "Up with Harlem" movement. Hell, I didn't even live in Harlem. And aside from Langston Hughes's column in *The Chicago Defender,* I wasn't familiar with a lot of Black literature.

> For two or three days in a row
> I sat there like I didn't know
> Two or three hours went past
> And I didn't say nothing in class
> She thought that I didn't read it
> So when she pushed me about where I was at
> I said I could write better than that
> And when she said she didn't believe
> I gave her some of my stuff to read.

Miss Leaf apparently liked my writing. Or thought she should. Or something. A few days later Miss Leaf asked me to stay after class. She asked where I came from and what else I had written and whether I had heard of Fieldston and would I be willing to meet somebody?

The answers were Jackson, Tennessee, a lot of stuff, no, and meet who?

When she explained that Fieldston—not Feelston, as I heard it—was a school, I joked with her: "Is that your auld lang syne?"

Fortunately she got the joke. You had to be very careful about joking with white folks. They took everything, especially themselves, very seriously. And at the same time, they resented a brother taking himself that same way.

"Yes, that's right," she said. "It's in Riverdale and it's a private school. I think it would be good for you. What would you think of that?"

What did I think of that? I'd never thought about it. I didn't think I would be eligible, so I didn't say anything. But the more I listened to Miss Leaf, the more I thought she was the type of person people always thought I was: a hick, just off the Trailways bus from some town where the bus stopped at a combination general store–post office three times a week and who thought everybody on TV had to be *real short* to fit in there. When she suggested a meeting with an old friend of hers who was a teacher at Fieldston, I thought, what the hell? After all, if I could last a few more months, I might get an A in her class.

Which is how I ended up in a Howard Johnson's on Fordham Road across from the Bronx Zoo. I had already had a cheeseburger and was dealing with a strawberry sundae, sitting in a booth of either leather or linoleum, opposite Miss Leaf and a short, sandy-haired man with glasses, named Professor Heller. He was studying me like he wasn't studying me. I watched him

81

watching me and tried to watch out. I also took my time with that ice cream. I was enjoying it, which was what they suggested, though I was wondering why they were just having Cokes.

I was getting curious as it went along, though. When Miss Leaf had brought up the possibility of attending Fieldston, I thought she was either kidding or just trying to be nice, which is what some white folks did when they were kidding. I hadn't taken the idea of this meeting too seriously. First of all because I didn't think anybody who was plugged in that well to Fieldston would be trying to get thirty thugs to pay attention in a last period English class at Clinton. If so, she must have committed some kind of felony for which she was paying penance. Maybe she had to recruit someone as part of her penalty. But I didn't see her as a top recruiter any more than I saw Clinton as prime recruiting territory—or anymore than I saw myself as a good recruit. I was a long shot. How long? How about the odds against a jackass in the Kentucky Derby?

That meant that nothing happening there at HoJo's was more important than that strawberry sundae. I was in a hell of a position. If I paid too much attention to the sundae, I would ignore the people who bought it. But if I didn't stay on it, it would melt, which would be unfortunate and also make it seem as if I didn't want it. I did.

The meeting had put me between a rock and a hard place at home, too, with my mother. It had been a good move to say I was interested. My mother had heard about the school when she worked at the library on 231st Street. She knew Fieldston was real, and was a real good school. My uncle, who was real sarcastic, said he didn't believe in fairy tales unless they included a real fairy. I got it.

So there we were, me, Miss Leaf, and Professor Heller, whose eyes seemed magnified behind his glasses, flicking a look my way every now and again. The two of them were good friends, and as the time eased along I went from uncomfortable and irritable to amiable and agreeable. What I figured out halfway through that sundae was that nothing was happening that day. No matter what they said or thought, unless I said I definitely would not do it, or got smart-alecky. I decided not to ask them whether it was true there were no Black people in Riverdale.

Professor Heller asked questions. He was a nice, soft-spoken gentleman who made me feel a little ashamed of my suspicions. I was looking at him like New Yorkers look at everything, like it's fake and he couldn't possibly be a nice person appreciating my writing.

"And you're from West Tennessee?" he asked.

"Yeah, Jackson," I admitted.

"What did you come to New York for?"

"For good." I was joking, not indignant.

"No, ha, ha. I mean, did your mother have a job opportunity here?"

"She knew she could get a job," I said. "She's got her masters."

The conversation went on with small talk like that.

"And you think you might like Fieldston?"

83

"I don't know if I'd like it. I understand it's a good school."

"It's a very good school, with smaller classes and more intensive study, and better college opportunities come from that," he said. "But you'd have to take an examination."

I decided he could probably take, or at least understand, a joke.

"A physical? I could pass that."

I had reached the end of my strawberry sundae.

So it was arranged. Sort of. The procedure, whatever it was, that would gain me admission to the Riverdale equivalent of Valhalla would be handled by Professor Heller. I understood this to be a unique benefit, a lock, a guarantee—or as close to fact as yesterday's *New York Times*. Like having a high-wire act done for you by Joseph Wallenda. Like getting The Amazing Kreskin to pick your daily number. The only thing remaining was the mere formality of the admissions test. It was rarely an obstacle, I was told; it was more used like an aptitude test to gauge what courses I needed to work on. So I went back to completing the year at a school I was now certain I could get out of, DeWitt Clinton, to working on my basketball game at whatever local gym was open at night, and to picking up whatever work I could on Fordham Road.

Just before the exam, though, I took a sort of field trip to Fieldston to visit the place and audit a couple of classes. I really hated it. You needed to be rich just to drive past their campus, which resembled a New England college, with all the buildings handsomely connected by walkways and gray stones encircling well-tended lawns. There was enough ivy on the walls to redo the outfield at Wrigley Field. So when it came time for the test, I took a dive, threw it. The room where I took the test was like a college lecture hall. It was half-full, probably seventy-five people. They might not have all been trying to get in for free like I was (Miss Leaf had said the tuition was about $2,200 a year) and it seemed unlikely they were all trying to get into the eleventh grade. I doubted there would be more than a dozen openings in a Fieldston class in five years, unless a bomb was dropped on Wall Street. I spent the full three hours on the English section, but once the math section started, I gave straight answers on thirty-five or forty questions and left after about an hour.

Two weeks later, the phone rang at our apartment. It was Professor Heller. I hadn't been expecting a call, figured they'd send a letter. But maybe it was good that the professor called: I owed him an apology or a thank you. It needed to be something like, "Thank you for the chance I kicked away, sir." Saying that I could have done better on the test wouldn't sound any more convincing to the professor than it sounded rattling around inside my head, and I knew it was true. But if I couldn't convince myself . . .

". . . somewhat disappointing test results," he was saying.

That was a slick way of putting it.

I can't say I didn't know how much my mother wanted me to go to Fieldston. I can say that as I listened to Professor Heller, I *thought* I knew how much she wanted it. I didn't know again.

". . . and the committee was not enthusiastic about it. But if you're willing to meet . . . I need to ask you again, however,

85

if you really want to come here, Gil, because if you don't, then we're wasting our time."

"Yes, sir, I'm interested."

He said he would try to arrange a meeting with the committee. This was starting to sound like extra things I didn't want to do, but that was the whole point. To go somewhere with your hat in your hand is to go through things you don't want. If you want the scholarship, you have to reveal this and reveal that, test for this and test for that. Man, there was a lot of shit to go through. And now, some kind of committee.

But hadn't I stood in line after crowded line to sign up for classes at Clinton? And stood around registering for the wrong fucking classes at Creston? Waited 150 or 200 years to get into Tigrett, back in Jackson? At least what I was going through now was supposed to be for something valuable.

The meeting was set up, and then one morning a week or so later, I heard four sharp raps on my door. *Bam, bam, bam, bam.* That was not the way I was used to getting up. I rolled over groggily onto the book I'd been reading the previous night and my bare feet hit the floor. Not quick enough.

Bam, bam, bam, bam.

It was my uncle.

"Scotty! It's eight o'clock!"

I opened the door. My uncle was moving toward my mother's room.

"Get yourself some juice," he said. "And go to your thing."

He went into her room and closed the door behind him.

86

I knew my face looked like a question mark as I washed up. I could hear my mother through both doors, moaning, and saying things with a thick voice I did not recognize.

"Tell Skaa-dee go 'head to the mee-din', o-kaaay?"

What was wrong? What was going on? Uncle B.B. came out of her room and again closed the door, a tense, uncomfortable expression on his face.

"Go on and get dressed and go to your meeting," he said with serious eyes. "She'll be all right. Get moving now. You don't need to be late for this. She's going to the hospital where Sammy was. Call when you get a minute."

Then he was back in my mother's room and I was adjusting my jacket collar and quick stepping down the stairs. I could hear my mother slurring loudly to tell me to go to the meeting and B.B. saying, "Okay, okay."

I heard the doorbell buzz and click open as I reached the first floor and I recognized my mother's harried, hurried, horrid doctor as he came in with his shirt sleeves rolled halfway up, his wrinkled striped tie hanging limp and off-center, and his forehead sweating.

He frowned and sniffed, "Acidosis," as if answering a question from me. Then he hurried past me and up the stairs.

Soon I was scurrying onto a bus, clattering across the 207th Street Bridge, and switching to the Broadway train in Manhattan. I was heading to a committee meeting and my mother was sick.

I had not been in the administration building during my campus visit. But I had passed by it at the top of the long, curved driveway that led onto Fieldston's campus. There was only a sprinkling of youngsters rushing across the quadrangle as I entered the administration building. I went upstairs to the designated floor where the principal's office door was. A smiling secretary nodded me through another door. Inside were roughly half a dozen jacketed gentlemen and one lady in a smart business suit, all standing at a long serving table. There were thin cookies on china plates. There were dainty china cups, a sturdy sterling tray supporting a sweating silver coffee pot, and a slightly smaller pot of hot water. There were tea bags, lemon wedges, sugar, packets of saccharine, instant creamer, a small bowl with cream, and an unopened pint of half-and-half.

To my right, chairs sat in a half-circle facing a solitary chair that sat isolated, with its back to the wall. I was just about to get disruptive when Professor Heller rushed in from behind me and clapped me on the back as a greeting. He was wearing the same jacket he'd had on at Howard Johnson's, with elbow patches, and his glasses had a strip of tape on one hinge. He hustled past me and began glad-handing the others, all white, all prosperous looking, all obviously executives or administrators.

Soon I was sitting in that center chair facing the folks Professor Heller called the committee, meaning the committee that decided who got in. I was flattered that I got to see them, and didn't know enough to be intimidated. I wasn't disrespectful; that wasn't in my nature. Besides, I assumed that since I had failed the test, I was only there because: (A) Professor Heller recommended me; (B) they would like to have a reason other than a poor test score to reject Professor Heller's choice and this could be it; and (C) I had asked for it.

> So no matter things that I might sense
> I need to be civil in my own defense.
> Sitting in front of these folks seems silly
> But I owe it to the Prof to stay chilly
> If this is judgment day more's the pity
> That I have to come in here before this committee

I kept wondering about the verdict of this six-person half-jury, and as far as I could figure it, two of them—Professor Heller and the lone woman on the committee—seemed to lean in my favor; three seemed against my admission; and one seemed neutral—the head of the committee, who was politically savvy enough not to want to take a side. That meant, in my mind, I wouldn't make it in.

Some of the questions were meant to reveal how I would feel about being around people with more money than I had. I explained to them that currently almost everyone that I knew had more money than I did, but that with a good education I might well be able to catch up. My point was that Fieldston students weren't the only people in a better financial shape than I was.

The questions about how I would feel in the middle of all these kids with money were questions they struggled with. They stood between me and the Fieldston community, Fieldston folks. But they were closer to my financial status than to that of the members of the Fieldston community. They may have been good at whatever they did, teach or administrate or whatever. But they were more like tutors with offices.

One asked, "How would you feel if you saw one of your classmates go by in a limousine while you were walking up the hill from the subway?"

"Same way as you," I said. "Y'all can't afford limousines. How do you feel?"

I could hear fear in their voices, and it was really there. They sounded intimidated, not by me but by their surroundings.

And all of their degrees can't get them on their knees
And their mastery in classes never gets them off their asses
They're always tiptoeing and elbowing
As loud as ghost whispers and as quick as grass be growing
Their spoiled students must be pampered,
Moving around like snails in amber
Their disciplinary instincts are all the way dead
Smiling at this, patting that one on the head
On fire with midnight sunburns that take root under the collars
But "little lord have mercy" here is worth a million dollars

At a quarter past ten, they decided to break for a few minutes. I confided to the head of the committee that my mother had possibly been hospitalized and that I wanted to make a call. He directed me to a secretary in an inner office. I called Metropolitan Hospital and asked to speak to Mr. William Scott. After a short wait, B.B. came on the line. He sounded winded.

"It's okay, sport," he said quietly. "It looks like we're going to have to bachelor pad it for a few days. Your mother is in a diabetic coma. She's going to have to take insulin like Sammy. We have some things to discuss, so you need to come down here."

That was all I needed to know. There was somewhere else I needed to be. Now.

The members of the committee were hovering over their chairs when I got back to the main room.

"Excuse me, lady and gentlemen, I have to say something. I have to go. My mother landed at Metropolitan Hospital this morning. She's in a diabetic coma and I have to be there with her. I know you folks were having this meeting especially to talk to me, and I appreciate that and want to thank you. But I'm leaving. If you all vote to allow me in here, I'll appreciate that. If you vote not to let me come, I'll understand it. But whatever you do, you're going to have to do it with the information you've got so far. I hope it's enough."

I turned to Professor Heller.

"Thank you, sir. You did a great deal for me and you stuck with me. I thank you, but I'm about to go see about my mother, okay?"

I didn't feel like smiling, but the man deserved one. I nodded and acknowledged the other individuals around the room respectfully. Their somewhat stunned faces wore expressions that didn't know what to be, caught between words, slapped without malice into another person's reality far from the insulated isolation of their Riverdale routines.

I shook hands with Professor Heller in case it was the last time I would see him. Then I walked out the door of the well-appointed chamber, away from the silver and the china and the cookies and committee. Down the stairs to the door that led to the curving driveway. From there to the Broadway local train. I dropped a token in the slot. I had to get downtown.

13

I suppose I arrived at the hospital before either the doctor or Uncle B.B. expected, because all of a sudden I had walked up to where they were talking outside my mother's room and stepped between them to look. There was a nurse standing at the head of my mother's bed adjusting tubes the size of cigars inserted in her throat. There was a surgical cap covering her hair. She was on a gurney with her eyes closed and the small room where she was being treated was filled with the sound of her assisted breathing. The nurse was working in half-light dimness, walking quickly around the gurney, covering my mother carefully with a sheet, and examining every angle and aspect of the connections to a machine the size of a short refrigerator that expanded her chest and cleared her mouth of saliva. She was the color of cigarette ash. She was lucky she was in a coma and couldn't see herself, because seeing herself like this might have scared her to death.

My uncle seemed to feel as though I was in danger of that same fate. He was staring blankly into a space unseen by others, focusing on instructions or recovery processes or excuses the doctor was giving for missing my mother's decline into her current condition. She had been in his office just a week before.

When I stepped past them, I broke into my uncle's attempt to believe whatever this son of a bitch was lying about. B.B. reached out to bar my advance into the room. I understood that he didn't want me to see her. He didn't understand that I already had. I turned away from the two of them and walked a few steps back down the hallway. I could still hear the machine. A tense two or three minutes later, the doctor scurried past me and B.B. was quickly at my elbow. He was an inch or so taller than me, and thirty pounds heavier, but he looked exhausted and appreciably smaller than usual today.

"A ninny," he spat at the doctor's shrinking form as the nervous little man departed. I told myself I would never forget the doctor standing in the light of that forty-watt bulb at the bottom of our stairs, sniffing the air like an allergic albatross and hissing "acidosis."

But we should have known. And I guess the fact that I knew that, was the reason I didn't chase the little man down the army green hallway and kick his ass like a stuffed toy. I felt too much like kicking my own. I knew the little bird-beaked doctor should have averted this tragedy, but I should have too. And I saw beneath the shallows of my uncle's expression that he felt the same way I did. As though that lady in the hospital bed there had two men at her elbows whose responsibility was to look out for her, and we blew it. We blew an easy one.

Shopping for the family groceries, making that Saturday run, had been one of my jobs since before we moved to New York. Not just for my mother, but for my grandmother before that. It was one of the ways I legitimately earned the two pennies

93

or a nickel Aunt Sissy gave me when her budget expanded to include a cut of meat or some other extravagance from the A&P or another uptown market. Uptown was five or six blocks up Cumberland Street, easier and quicker once I got my red truck bike with a wire basket in front.

In the Bronx, I just looked at restocking the refrigerator and cabinet as my job. My Saturdays automatically included an hour or so of carrying a list and rolling a shopping cart. I knew sometimes as clearly as my mother what we had and what we needed. I not only knew what our regular brands were, but the weekly quantities. In a special week, when something was going on, the six-pack of soda might clone itself on the list. In recent weeks, though, I had regularly brought back two six-packs of soda on Saturday and another one or two six-packs during the week. I wasn't drinking any more soda than usual. My mother was. I knew now that she had been fighting off dehydration and sugar imbalance with direct deposits of syrup and water.

She had been tired, listless, and dehydrated, and couldn't figure it out. Uncle B.B. had lived with Aunt Sammy, who'd had diabetes for ten years by the time I stayed with them briefly after my grandmother's death. I guess it was different being around someone who was controlling the debilitating aspects of diabetes with tablets or injections of insulin. B.B. hadn't seen the onset of the illness, what their Tennessee neighbors called "sugar diabetes."

B.B. and I left the hospital and went for hot dogs at Nathan's, a late brunch B.B. called it. I liked Nathan's most of the time, but this hot dog was like a rubber cigar. Not happening.

My uncle went into "normal" mode, treating the outing like one of our haircut trips or once-a-month movie trips. Those were his contributions to normal, since he was supposed to be a father figure or male role model or some such, to teach me how to cope with things like my mother going into a coma.

"How did your interview go?" he asked halfway through the meal.

It was the first time I'd even thought about what had happened earlier that day.

"Okay, I guess," I said. "It seemed like they were asking me stuff they already knew, either from Professor Heller or from the long questionnaire you filled out."

"Just wanted to see if you remembered what lies you told?" he said, trying to crack a smile.

I wouldn't have been the only one in that room who'd told lies. Or the first one, or even the main one. Sitting in that room with the committee I'd felt like I was at one of those theaters where the actors hold the face of the part they're playing in front of themselves on a stick. It's a play that's not even like a play. You're not even asked to suspend your disbelief like in an ordinary movie or play. They're holding the masks in front of them. That's what the committee hearing had felt like, I realized. I'm sure somebody reviewed all prospective students, but I was willing to bet they didn't have meetings like mine for the students paying full tuition, meetings where you sat there like a bug under a microscope, pushed and poked, taken like a joke.

When B.B. and I got home, I heard him talking to his sisters and other relatives, bringing everyone up to date. I stayed in my room and he stayed in his, as normal. I could tell he wanted to keep things as close to normal as possible, not making any radical declarations.

Then, around 7 p.m., the phone rang. It was Professor Heller. The first question he asked was about my mother, and the second was about how I was doing.

"Very well, thank you," I said. "But a hell of a day."

"I wanted you to know that you're to be granted a full scholarship."

Evidently my silence said a great deal to him.

"I really believe that your handling of that call and the way you spoke to everyone before you left was crucial. You handled that very well, with decisiveness and maturity, with the proper attitude concerning priorities."

14

My mother quickly adjusted to being a full-fledged diabetic and went back to work. She had been moved to a desk job in the Housing Authority and spent her days at the Amsterdam Houses on 61st Street. She claimed it was not a bad change.

Our refrigerator held a tray of insulin. She had learned how to measure out her doses and inject herself with a needle. She made me watch the process one day, from how to jab yourself in a fingertip with a short silver needle and put a drop of blood on this paper that turned colors to tell you how much medication to take, to shooting herself in the hip and swabbing the injection point with alcohol. Then she came over to me with an orange and a fresh needle.

"You need to know how to do this," she said half-seriously.

She knew that when it came to being brave the world did not turn to me. I declined the opportunity to squirt some water into an orange right then. I told her I appreciated the vote of confidence, but that I was concentrating on her not needing me to do any injecting. She laughed and told me that even her brother would do it and he was definitely an old scaredy-cat. I told her that my fear took precedence because it was young and had to be nurtured. We laughed some more. My mother knew good and damn well there was no chance of my using the works. I had a thorough needle phobia.

By the time I started at Fieldston that fall, in September 1964, my mother and I had also moved to the Robert Fulton Houses—in other words, the projects—down in Chelsea, living on our own in a two-bedroom place on West 17th Street between Ninth and Tenth avenues. The project buildings covered five square blocks and were the center of a regeneration of that section of Ninth Avenue, with a small town's worth of barber shops, bodegas, pizza shops, record stores, and clothing stores. I quickly learned I was a minority within a minority—the neighborhood seemed to be 85 percent Puerto Rican, 15 percent white, and me. I did what I could to blend into Little San Juan without trading in my connection to Black America or the Temptations.

The good news was that the rent for our new apartment was seventy-three dollars per month; the bad news was that what would have been a twenty minute ride from our old place to Fieldston would now take at least an hour each way and involve switching trains. I had to take the train two hundred and thirty blocks uptown to reach school.

One look around the campus was enough to remind me how expensive the school was. The classroom buildings seemed to be held together with interlocking stones, like medieval castle walls. The green lawns looked as though they were trimmed with scissors. There was a new gym with glass backboards and room for two full-court games side-by-side. There was also a well-kept quarter-mile oval track and a manicured football field separated by a fence from a soccer pitch. The stage in the auditorium could handle full-scale productions for five hundred viewers. There was a split-level art building for painting beneath skylights that always let in a lot of natural light.

Music classes were taught in a cozy tower room you reached by climbing a spiral stone staircase above the auditorium and the student recreation room with its vending machines and ping-pong tables. There were three pianos in the building: an upright for the theater stage that was available only when there was no class being held, another one in the music room up in the tower, and, in a separate room next to the auditorium, a beautiful Steinway. It was an absolutely marvelous instrument. And not only was it the best piano around, it was the one that was almost always free and thoroughly accessible. Unfortunately, it was also the one the music teacher, Mr. Worthman, had established a rule against playing. Since I was the main one playing the kind of music Mr. Worthman objected to, I felt he might as well have called it "the no Gil rule."

Mr. Worthman headed the music department and the glee club. He reminded me of one of the villains from the *Spiderman* comics I read. He had the same hooked beak, the same pale complexion, and most of all, the same horseshoe of white hair around a light bulb shaped bald spot. We were opposites in appearance and in musical taste. But while I would never have tried to shut down his choral group, he showed more than mild disapproval of my music. He hated it.

The first time I played the Temptations on the Steinway, when I had just arrived on campus, the wild dancing made enough noise to raise professor Worthman from his crypt. He arrived in the music room to see it looking like a dance hall. I was just starting into a Stevie Wonder tune when I got busted.

I felt like there was something personal going on between Mr. Worthman and me. Nobody could remember exactly when the "hands off the Steinway" rule had been posted, but I somehow connected it to something unreasonable and attributed the whole fabrication to Mr. Worthman. Maybe it had something to do with the songs I was writing; maybe it was because I performed around school with other students but never joined the glee club. If all else failed, I could always play the it's-'cause-I-come-from-the-ghetto card, though that didn't seem to apply to Mr. Worthman—he didn't seem to care that I was from the ghetto.

You have options when you decide something is unfair. You can say to hell with it and play anytime and anywhere you see fit in open defiance of the rules. You can challenge it legally and carry it all the way to the Supreme Court—or the high school equivalent. Or you can pick and choose your times, hit and run, try to avoid a showdown. I did that.

I opted for a melodic form of guerilla warfare, floating in and out with stealth and style. I mixed in a little black magic so that my fingers would be quicker than Mr. Worthman's eyes. I used clock management, and stopped playing just before and just after lunch, when my classmates had a few minutes to watch me get in trouble. I stopped doing all the flamboyant finger snappers from the radio. I stopped playing requests for the latest top ten tunes by the Beatles and Rolling Stones, any of which would bring in a dozen unwanted singers. I stopped doing tunes that would inspire kids to unreasonable facsimiles of the dances from the new TV shows like *Shindig* and *Hullabaloo*.

I didn't love confrontation, and I had been frequently warned that Mr. Worthman really enjoyed confrontation, that at times he was known to say it was one of his most effective teaching tools. There were times I would have challenged the professor if I'd gotten caught, times when I was working on my own songs. I had adopted a New York attitude since starting at Fieldston, and I had certain spaces that I didn't want rolled over anymore. But my scholarship also depended on being able not to react to personal injury, to getting pushed around, to personal restriction and harassment. Not that the scholarship was a big deal to me, but it was a big deal to someone who was a big deal to me: my mother.

Still, I was in a good writing groove and Mr. Worthman was in my way. He might snatch all the younger students sneaking in to play "Stand By Me," but I planned to be the guerilla he missed. I was successful for a while. Months, in fact.

Then in April, I was sitting alone at the keyboard during a free period of mine that I often spent playing ping-pong. I'd had a sudden creative inspiration. I often heard tunes in my head. But this one arrived with words attached like bright bulbs on a Christmas tree. No sooner had I sat down to play than Mr. Worthman arrived with a short, pudgy gentleman in overalls with a handlebar mustache and a tool box.

The mustached man ignored me and slid a metal box beneath the Steinway, walked gingerly to the side, and pushed up the flat top. He propped it open at a forty-five-degree angle, exposing the mechanics of the piano's wires and pads. There are few things more beautiful than the strings of a Steinway. I watched every little move the piano tuner made under the hood.

Mr. Worthman, meanwhile, was making sweeping motions with both hands, directing me toward the door, too distracted for a protracted lecture.

"Heron, you know the rule!" he barked.

He was also talking to the other man about what needed to be done. "Total A-440, with a pad that needs to be changed on the F-sharp in the third octave. It sounds like it got damp or something."

Then again to me: "I'll deal with you later."

He was sweeping again, like "Out, out, damn Scott."

I wanted to stay and watch the piano tuner, but I left—and forgot the song I had been just about to capture. If I was able to play a song once, I would have it; this one had gotten away.

Things were still cool for a while. I didn't see Mr. Worthman at all for a few weeks, and his not seeing me kept anything from triggering his memory.

I should have left well enough alone. I should have left the piano alone. But not having been able to remember the song pushed me toward a point where I thought I wouldn't mind a confrontation. So I did what I wanted to do. I had a plan. The choral group had their big spring recital coming up on the quadrangle, and there would be extra rehearsals after school; meetings during class time would be scuttled. The piano would be sitting there all day every day without anybody coming in to play it. That was almost obscene.

My strategy seemed to work. For the next three weeks I stopped by the Steinway every day for a few chords or a verse or two of my latest song. I was starting to get comfortable. One afternoon at the end of April, Mr. Worthman landed in the Steinway room as if he'd leapt from the tower in a parachute. I was too astonished even to show surprise.

When he caught his breath and his face started to regain its natural pallor, he said, "You're in a lot of trouble this time, young man. I hope you know that. I've got a good mind to have them take you up before the disciplinary committee. We'll have your parents in."

When the letter arrived at home a few days later from the disciplinary committee at Fieldston, I had forgotten Mr. Worthman's threat. I expected it to raise my mother's blood pressure and her voice, but that wasn't her way. When she called me into the kitchen, I didn't know what to expect. But her flat tone of voice raised the hairs along the length of my arms.

"You want to tell me what this letter's all about?" she asked, holding it in front of her face like a fan.

"What does it say?" I said, taking a seat at the kitchen table opposite her.

"It says that I need to appear with you in front of the discipline committee next Monday for a 9 a.m. meeting."

I took a breath.

"I played a piano," I said quietly.

"That's what this is about? You played a piano and I'm supposed to come up to your school about it?"

"Yeah. This music teacher said they might call you up there but I swear I thought he was joking."

She paused for a beat.

"So you played a piano and then what?"

"Then nothing. That's all I did was play the piano."

"You usually tell the truth," she said, "but I don't hear it."

She sat for another moment.

"Did you hit someone—like the music teacher?"

"No, ma'am."

I had heard from other students that Fieldston had a "no suspension" policy. They believed that suspension gave the students a vacation from classes. I had told my mother about that.

"We'll see about this," my mother finally said, as though she were really exhausted. "I don't need to be going up there and getting a surprise. You may as well tell me the whole thing."

The next Monday we trudged up the hill after the long subway journey I had told her about many times. She was surprised but pleased to see the cookies and tea service and coffee pot and the discipline folks engaged in pleasant conversation and sipping coffee from good china and munching on dainty cookies. I didn't have much of an appetite.

The face-off was called to order and my mother and I sat side-by-side facing a similar semicircle to the one I'd met a year prior when she was ill and I left early.

"Mrs. Heron," the principal began, "we're facing something of a problem here and we need your input. You see, Mr. Worthman here caught Gil playing the piano."

My mother's reaction was almost imperceptible. She

relaxed her shoulders and recrossed her legs. Her expression was pleasant enough, a little smile. And she looked critically from face to face as though waiting for the punch line of a joke.

The principal's voice droned to a close and I saw Mr. Worthman stare with energy and focus at me. He had been waiting for this moment, and now he was speaking too loudly with certain emphasis as though it was a prepared speech that he had rehearsed. He talked about how valuable the Steinway was and how he had caught me playing it before and how the rule had been put in place to prevent students from playing "boogie woogie."

I didn't notice the transition when Mr. Worthman had finished and suddenly collapsed in his seat as the principal started speaking again. He said something about how it would be easy for the committee to mete out the punishment but that at Fieldston they thought it was important for the parents to be involved and that what they wanted was my mother's recommendation.

The pause between the principal's question and my mother's response fell on each member of the committee like a guillotine. She took a long breath before turning in my direction.

"Expel him," she said crisply and clearly. "I understand that you don't suspend students and I understand why. I agree with you. I don't believe in suspending students either. So if you believe playing the piano is high on your list of offenses, expel him."

She was dominating the room now. Her voice was clear and her diction was perfect.

"I'm going to work now. If you expel him, he'll tell me when I get home."

It was an amazing piece of business. There hadn't been a second when she seemed shaken or awkward or the least bit uncomfortable. She looked every bit the well-dressed business-woman perfectly at ease, and as she gathered her bag and scarf, she could easily have been heading out to a waiting limousine instead of to the subway, as was actually the case.

Finally she turned to the committee members as we were leaving. "When he told me what this was all about, I didn't believe him. I thought he had finally done something that he was too embarrassed to tell me about, that he had lost this wonderful opportunity and we would both be humiliated to sit here when I heard the truth. He told me the truth. He said he had been playing a piano. I will only add this: when something goes wrong on Seventeenth Street, I don't call you. Because that's my responsibility. And this is your school. If he has done something that merits punishment, don't call me. Send him home. We'll understand. I need to have him show me the way back down that hill. You can tell him whatever you decide."

I resisted the urge to look back at Mr. Worthman.

We walked down the hill without saying much. That was another thing I appreciated about my mother. She wasn't afraid of silence. By the time we'd arrived at the base of the stairs that led up to the subway, she had come back to herself.

"I want you to leave those people's things alone," she said. "You're up here to get an education. Get it and come on home. I'm sorry I didn't believe you. I learned something today, too."

I think she and I got a lot closer that day.

15

I am extremely pleased to report that I only had one session with the Fieldston disciplinary committee. That does not mean that I committed only one infraction. That would be ridiculous. I guess it's a little like being charged with a first offense even if it's the tenth time you've done something. It's the first time you got caught.

In that respect, I can never accuse the people of Fieldston, neither the students nor the faculty, of being racist. I can accuse the students of knowing each other for years and preferring to hang out with each other instead of some guy who just got there. I can accuse the teachers of having taught my classmates for ten years and me for ten minutes. But I can't say they never took the time to tell me that I was doing as little work as I did.

So there were students and faculty members and executives who did not like me. But to their credit, I honestly believe that they just *didn't like me*. What's wrong with that? There were a lot of Black folks who felt the same way over the years. They were just less anxious to let me know it.

Most of this wisdom was acquired over my three years there. As a tenth-grade rookie, my first year there, I was working overtime at Jackson's or wherever the hell I could to make ends meet and stay afloat in Spanish class. I felt more comfortable as the years went on. It was just a school, after all. I had probably set some sort of poverty precedent by receiving a scholarship to cover books as well as tuition. The books at public school were free, but at Fieldston I found the cost beyond my legal reach, and mentioned the possibility of a heist, which inspired Professor Heller to get me a voucher that I used for sixty-four dollars' worth of knowledge.

My mother and I didn't have enough money for it to be one of my issues. I took every opportunity that showed up on Seventeenth Street. I managed to catch a run at the A&P supermarket on Eighth Avenue three nights a week, and since I had improved a great deal on piano and still kept up with the top tunes on the radio, I looked for jobs as keyboard player with some rhythm and blues or rock and roll bands in the city. I managed to hook up with a few groups for weekend jobs at schools, in hotel bars, and at birthday parties. There was a whole culture then a few levels down from the bands we were imitating. The bread was short, twenty or twenty-five dollars a night, but it beat the hell out of nothing.

Every summer from the time I was sixteen I took a job as a seasonal worker for the Housing Authority. I spent one summer at the St. Nicholas Houses on 135th Street in Harlem, one at the Dykeman Houses on the Upper West Side, and one at the Housing Authority's central office at 250 Broadway. That turned out to be a very good summer. Aside from the nine to five I was doing, Monday through Friday, I signed up as a referee for four or five games of basketball every weekend. The New

York City Housing Authority had a summer basketball league and furnished uniforms, score books, time clocks, and balls for two teams in every set of projects. The Authority also made up a schedule, made sure the court was available, and assigned a referee to officiate the game and turn in a report to the central office at 250 Broadway.

That's where I came in. Refs were paid ten bucks a game, so I could make an extra forty or fifty dollars per weekend. My shelf work at A&P started at 7 p.m. and ended between midnight and 2 a.m. I would send inventory upstairs from the basement, or stand upstairs with a hand truck snatching crates of canned goods, bottles, and cans. Dairy products and meats needed to be stacked weekend deep before the Saturday deluge. All the weekend sales specials and new product displays had to be stacked and stamped. All the summer work ended up paying for college tuition.

I had decided to attend Lincoln University after my 1967 graduation from Fieldston. I wanted to go to Lincoln because it seemed to be a place where Black writers had come to national prominence. Perhaps because of its location: if not exactly the middle of nowhere, at least on one side or the other. It was outside of Oxford, Pennsylvania, about forty-five miles from Philadelphia, fifty-five miles from Baltimore, and thirty miles from Wilmington, Delaware. Perhaps that isolation and absence of urban distractions had allowed the creativity and intellect of Langston Hughes, Melvin Tolson, Ron Welburn, and others to flourish. Whatever the reason, I thought the place was extraordinary. Its students had made noteworthy accomplishments in a number of areas. Kwame Nkrumah got his degree there in the

1930s and went on to become the leader of independent Ghana. Cab Calloway had gone there. And my candidate for Man of the Century, NAACP lawyer and first Black on the Supreme Court, Thurgood Marshall, went to Lincoln, too.

The school was founded as the Ashmun Theological Institute in 1854 at the insistence of the Quakers, who formed a powerful political force in Pennsylvania. In an era when it was still illegal to teach Blacks to read and write unless they were ministers, Ashmun was not only a tool of political appeasement for the Quakers, it was a double blessing for Blacks who now had both an institution of higher education—a first—and a safe house across the Maryland line that could be used as a rest stop and hiding place on the Underground Railroad.

In 1869, four years after the "war between the states" and four years after the assassination of Abraham Lincoln at Ford's Theater, the small school for aspiring Black theologians in Southeastern Pennsylvania was renamed Lincoln University. Abraham Lincoln was not a factor in my decision to go there, though I obviously knew the place had not been named for a luxury automobile. Black Americans have always held to the idea that Honest Abe was a friend of the downtrodden and mistreated slaves in spite of his Kentucky birthplace and pragmatism on the slavery issue—as in, "If I could save the Union and allow the institution of slavery to continue . . ." The fact was, he couldn't have allowed slavery and still hung on to abolitionist support, so he authored a document that was politically expedient, the Emancipation Proclamation, that is credited with "Jubilee" as the news slowly spread through the South causing the celebrations Blacks refer to as "Juneteenth."

The Lincoln of Langston Hughes and Thurgood Marshall was not the place it had been when I got off the bus in September of 1967. School leadership had jettisoned a 112-year tradition as a male institution the year before. There were a large number of coeds unloading their trunks and bags from family station wagons. The general attitude of Lincoln's executives was notably animated; their conversations centered around how necessary it was for Black schools to be open to change, and how good it was that in spite of diminishing funds and contributions to Black schools because of the disturbances on college campuses across the nation, Lincoln was growing; that in spite of the destruction of a century of traditions, Lincoln would be a stronger institution in the end.

Certain old-schoolers seemed unsettled by all the change. Juniors and seniors as well as veterans returning from service in the armed services found the rapid expansion and coeducational system distasteful because of new restrictions and rules of conduct at odds with their lives before the admission of women. A lot of the upperclassmen grumbled that they were glad they'd be leaving, and the vets that they were sorry they had returned. I felt fortunate to have arrived when, through these older students, there was still a shadow of the tradition that had been so much of an influence on the Lincoln men who helped shape Black America, but the place felt like a campus in flux.

The years before a conflict never receive the micro-scrutiny
But the fuses are lit then for future upheaval and mutiny
Because small events in corners no one cares to see as critical
Become defining moments, later underlined as pivotal.
Pennsylvania's Quakers knew a lot about persecution
And to their credit tried to find acceptable solutions.
Speaking out about the Northerners who wallowed in hypocrisy
Continuing to discriminate from behind walls of bureaucracy
So few cared in 1854 when some religious dignitaries
Founded a school for "colored folks" called Ashmun Seminary.
Each state politician would congratulate himself
For preserving the reputation of the entire commonwealth.
They successfully stopped the Quakers from raising so much hell
And kept them from putting another crack in the Liberty Bell
"Off the beaten path" was nearby when compared to this school's
    isolation
Overlooking how perfect a place it would be for an underground
    railroad station
To get back to Philadelphia back then took the best part of a day.
There was a small village called Oxford but that was more than
    three miles away.
There's no one to disturb, no one to object, just farms and farmers
    out there
Fifteen miles from the "mushroom capital," a marketing town, Ken-
    nett Square.
For one hundred years the school progressed in relative obscurity
Its distance from any place known as a place provided some both-
    way security
Another "Lincoln" university out in Missouri helped to keep folks
    confused
As to the ground shaken by American giants like Thurgood Mar-
    shall and Langston Hughes

But the 1960s brought "Black Power" and then student
    organizations
From colleges became involved leading the "sit-in" demonstrations.
Suddenly schools like Lincoln with Black student populations
Suffer corporate backlash and diminishing donations
They bring in a white president despite laughter from Black schools
And Marvin Wachman comes in with a thick stack of new rules.
He says changes are the cure for the financial condition
And overnight erases Lincoln's hundred year tradition
Becoming "state-related" and instituting "coeducation"
"Old school" alumni and returning vets resent the alterations
They had made their own rules out there in the wilderness
And isolation of the location had built a strong togetherness
Lincoln's reputation was already going down in flames
When I got there in '67 the place was filling up with dames
I didn't resent the women but there weren't enough to go around.
I didn't resent the "state related" kids from nearby towns
But something else was happening and students weren't supposed
    to know
Lincoln's state relationship included "COIN-TEL-PRO."
As now that you've got background and a certain point of view
I'm awarding you a scholarship to go with me to Lincoln U.

113

16

I was not immediately sorry to be at Lincoln. I spent a lot of time from the day I reached Lincoln's campus becoming familiar with the outstanding collection of Black American literature.

It took a few days to organize my class schedule and find out where the holes were in my week that would permit extra time among the "Black stacks" in the ancient library. Lincoln had a collection of Black books and special editions of literature that were exceeded only by the tremendous amount of material available at the Schomberg on 135th Street in Harlem. In becoming a state-related school, Lincoln had opened itself up to a larger proportion of area students whose fields of interest were a far cry from the course load Thurgood Marshall found to be such a strong foundation for his career as a lawyer. But that material was exactly what I was after.

Soon, a lot of the time I was supposed to spend on biology or math I spent at the typewriter or in that back room where they kept the books too precious to check out. You had to read them there, so that was where I was a lot of the time.

Every Wednesday evening the noted authority in Black American literature Professor J. Saunders Redding drove up to Lincoln from Washington, D.C., and delivered a three-hour seminar on the subject. My first year there I audited his lectures. He did most of his lectures without opening a book; he was a walking repository of Black American literature. He had personally known a lot of the people who connected me to where I came from creatively.

At some stage during my first year, I had the idea for a novel and wanted to write it. I thought I could find the proper rhythm and could balance my schedule between class work and work on the story, but it proved difficult and I was getting nothing done on the novel. There's a story I heard once about a jackass that was set down squarely between two bales of hay and starved to death. I was just like Jack. When I opened a textbook I saw the characters from my book, and when I sat at the typewriter I saw my ass getting kicked out of school for failing all my subjects.

Still, in the fall of 1968 I was back on campus, having put up all the money I had earned over the summer plus a small grant from the school to follow up what had been a less than scintillating freshman year. Six weeks into sophomore year, though, the same thing that had brought my first year crashing down around my ears began to threaten my second.

I asked the school for a leave of absence so I could devote myself to writing *The Vulture*. I would remain on campus for the rest of the semester since I had paid for room and board. I would be at work on the novel and would receive incompletes for all my classes rather than a complete set of failing grades. That would make it easier to apply for readmission to Lincoln or elsewhere.

My advisor was the head of the English department and a thoroughly decent and sympathetic man, but he had no intention of endorsing any plans I had for leaving school to write a book. He respected what writing of mine he had read, but there had been nothing in any of it to suggest to him that I was the next great Black writer to come through Lincoln. And as he reminded me, "the novel is a *most* difficult form."

I knew how difficult it was. That wasn't why I was writing a novel, to show how tough I was. I was simply tired of school. But when the truth wouldn't work, my advisor was not above or below getting rid of some pesky interrogator by assigning him a task somewhere else. The good doctor told me that if I was really serious about leaving Lincoln, the man to see was the dean.

The dean reacted to my proposal as though I had taken leave of my senses and asked me to get the school psychiatrist to approve the plan. The dean must have thought I was crazy. It certainly seemed crazy that someone as poor as I was would bet his last money on a first novel.

When I told my mother, she said, "Well, I don't think quitting school was the smartest thing you could have done, but go ahead and finish writing it and then come home and get your job. Promise that you'll go back and finish school. You're going to need to go back and you're going to need a degree, okay?"

"Yes, ma'am."

I really felt good after our talk. She was always able to be both critical and encouraging. My mother had proved once again she loved me unconditionally. She had kept her faith in me. Again. I wanted to make her proud of me, and I wanted to prove that she had taken the right tack.

She was not unaware of my flawed makeup as a person. Nor did she turn a blind eye or ear to the things I lacked as a writer or singer. But her criticism was always constructive, and offered in a manner that let me down easy. When she read or heard a problem, she would say things like "what I might try instead . . ." or "rather than . . ." and avoid just saying something didn't work. That's why I had always taken my ideas—my prose and poetry, my melodies and lyrics—to her, even before I felt ready to share them or even show them to other family members. I just knew I would learn something from her comments; she gave me another way to look at what I was doing.

My mother actually provided the punch line for "Whitey on the Moon," and also suggested mimicking Langston Hughes by repeating the opening line of the poem—"A rat done bit my sister Nell"—after the bridge-like middle section.

When I called my Uncle B.B. to tell him I was taking time off to write, he jumped all over me. For a family that had sent an entire generation to college—my mother and all her siblings, including B.B.—I was setting quite another precedent by being the first one of their line to "take a sabbatical." I had to stand in the hallway at a payphone listening to him and his opinions on a whole variety of choices I'd made up to that point in my life—the marijuana, the late hours, the guys I chose to hang out with. He saved his worst blows for the last; he spent five or ten minutes that felt like an hour criticizing my style and talent. We were both almost out of breath when he finished.

I planned to finish my novel before the start of the second semester in February 1969. That showed how little I knew about what I was doing. By January, I had little more than I had when I saw the university psychiatrist in October and gained his approval. But that month, January, brought me the idea for the ending of the book and a method of connecting the four separate narratives to the book's opening. Now all I needed was a chair and my typewriter.

That was damn near all I had. For the next two months I worked in a dry cleaners about a quarter mile from campus. With their business struggling, the owner and his wife both needed to work elsewhere and wanted someone to mind their property and take in and hand out the dry cleaning during the day. A guy in a van stopped by around six each evening to pick up what I handed him in a large laundry bag and return finished items previously collected. I slept in the back and took meal money from the small income generated by the students. A few friends would read pages for me, including one student who was a regular customer at the cleaners. They saved me from being pulled into the discouraging blank pages that I faced occasionally when a scene or an idea about the plot, the characters, the connections, something, would not work. The experience of writing *The Vulture* was my way of doing the high-wire act blindfolded, knowing that if it didn't work, if it wasn't published, there was no safety net that I could land on and no hole that I could crawl into, no way to face the other folks at Lincoln and no money to go anywhere else.

17

Since I have lived in the United States of America all of my life, I have seen too many deliberate distortions of events and too many slanted pieces of our history and lives to feel that I can correct them all or even put a good sized dent into them. All I can say is that if the truth is important to you, understand that most things of value have to be worked for, sought out, thought about, and brought about after effort worthy of the great value it will add to your life.

It will come at a great price. The time and sweat invested in that pursuit may cost you in hours and days you cannot use in other directions. It may cost you relationships that you would give almost anything else to develop, with someone who cannot stand to come in second to anything. The passion with which you commit yourself to something intangible may well turn away the very support that could sustain you.

What you will need is help that exceeds understanding. There may be disruptions on every level by those you try to touch, who shy away from you because understanding is not what you are looking for. Your only hope for stability on the levels of togetherness beyond understanding is trust. Anyone who claims to love you knows they will not understand every element of these things you need and that is where trust must carry you two the rest of the way. The truth you are seeking to write about, to sing about, to make sense of for others is something that you pursue not because you have seen it but because the Spirits tell you it is there.

Quitting my classes altogether in October 1968, at the start of my second year at Lincoln, was one of those moments in time that test how thoroughly you are trusted beyond understanding. It was one of the active places that all relationships will have to face to overcome before they move securely into love. I hate to get into Oedipus, because most of my life I have driven the wrecks. My grandmother would have died again when I quit school. But my mother went there with me.

And in April 1969, I had a finished manuscript of *The Vulture*. I had stayed at the university cleaners, sitting in a folding chair in front of an ancient Royal typewriter, and now used fifteen of my last twenty dollars to get a bus to New York City.

I bluffed my way past a stern, stiff-haired secretary at the front desk of a publishing company and managed to meet the man whose name I had picked up in a magazine—the man who edited *Soul on Ice* by Eldridge Cleaver, which had been published the year before. I lied and told him he had been recommended to me by people "in the organization" and presented him with the completed copy of my novel and agreed to come back in two weeks.

When that day arrived, I was waved right through the reception area to the editor's office, where the person I saw was shuffling through a file cabinet with his back to the door. My heart skipped a beat when I saw my manuscript on his desk. Even upside down, I could read what was written in red ink: ACCEPTED.

I was still trying to look like I was on furlough from "the organization." I had on a blue dress shirt tucked into pressed black jeans with razor sharp creases under a zippered black leather jacket. I was carrying an attaché case to look more businesslike than thug. It might have looked like a carrying case for large handguns or a breakdown shotgun, but in it I only had my shaving kit with personal cosmetics.

He was into business that day. It was just past noon but he was looking end of the day. His tie was loosened and his sleeves were rolled up. There was a cigarette burning in an ash tray that held a quarter pack of half-smoked butts, crumpled and twisted.

"Hi there, Gil," he said, dropping another stack of folders on his desk. "Have a seat. I've got myself a problem here. A book I thought we had rejected was accepted somehow and I can't find the contact information for the author. You know how that goes. So many scripts come through."

He sat down heavily opposite me at his desk and lit another cigarette. He had a good-sized office with three leather chairs, including his, at angles around a huge ebony desk. With the paperwork and folders scattered across the desk, the open file cabinets, and the fog of cigarette smoke, I felt like I was in a closet.

"I went to bat for you on this, Gil," he said, leaning back and making a steeple with his fingers. "It's interesting, but it's not at all what we had expected. We're handling almost ninety percent nonfiction, especially in, uh, the ethnic arena. A mystery story is a hell of a departure from *Soul on Ice*."

"We didn't think it was too smooth to bring you another autobiography right away," I said with a straight face. "A big chance of getting redundant and getting hung up in that 'cry from the ghetto' crap. You know what I mean? It's important that we be seen as well-rounded people who like all kinds of music and literature and all."

"Well," he said, fingering the corner of my manuscript, "they're giving me a shot with this on two conditions. Actually three. Number one is that we can agree on an advance of $2,000."

With that, he pushed an envelope forward on his desk.

"Number two is that we rewrite all the ghetto-speak dialogue into English. And number three, we need to switch the order of character number two and character number three. Two sounds too much like one. Do you agree?"

He sat back heavily, trying to read what I was thinking.

I was too shocked to change expressions.

I wasn't deliberately disguising my feelings with a poker face. I found out later what a good idea that was, but at that moment, sitting across from the editor, I was frozen for a minute. What I had just heard was like one of the "good news, bad news" jokes that were going around at the time. "The good news is that there's a check for $2,000. The bad news is that you have to undergo radical surgery to cash that check."

I couldn't remember what I had expected just moments before. The most exciting thing to me was that there was a check right in front of me. A huge check with my name on it. I was excited. There was more money sitting there than I had ever seen outside of a bank. There was more than three months pay from all three of the summer jobs I'd worked the previous summer getting together money for Lincoln. That check would cover tuition, room and board, books, everything—even after I gave my mother a 25 percent commission.

The money for the surgery. There must have been a contract somewhere on the desk that would make it official. Cash the check. And what about the surgery? Of the three conditions, two and three were a drag. But if I could talk this man out of two and three . . .

"You want to change character two and character three," I said with a question mark hanging off the end of the sentence.

"Well, Junior, character two, is so much like your lead character, Spade. I think the readers will get them crossed. They sound really close in some ways. If you just put three between them . . ."

"The way that Junior idolized Spade and imitates him and tries so hard to impress him is what I'm playing with," I told him. "The similarities are intentional. I think if I separated them, what I was trying to get across would be lost. Plus the whole mystery thing . . ."

"Yeah, you know what?" the editor said, reaching for his cigarettes and giving me a fake smile. "I think our readers are going to be into the ghetto experience more than the mystery angle. I mean, the opening scene with the body, the murder victim, those documents, ha, those are great literary devices. But what people should be grabbed by is the atmosphere of danger, that something dangerous could happen at any moment."

123

"Well, the atmosphere is all a part of it," I said without energy. "But I'm not looking at the mystery as secondary. That's what holds it . . ."

He cut me off again. I was beginning to see getting interrupted as more a matter of his style than just happenstance.

"I know that you authors tend to take everything you write as the holy grail, but the most important person in these discussions is the one who isn't here, the reader. That's who editors represent. I've been at it quite a while, and rather successfully."

"I'm not questioning your résumé," I said, "or the positive contributions you make to your writers. I'm just not that anxious to throw the mystery away."

I tried to make it sound like a joke, and found a way to smile. "You know, I got two or three bodies I gotta do something with. I can't just leave them laying around the neighborhood."

There was a noticeable change in the atmosphere in the room. Things had chilled. As if I needed more proof, the editor began straightening the various folders and papers on his desk, leaned back in his seat, and lit another cigarette.

"I'm gong to give you time to think about things," he said. "Right here we have a two-thousand-dollar check made out to you. And over here we have your manuscript. I've been clear about the changes we need to make to get it published. Now you have to decide if you want it published."

Yeah, that had been pretty clear. I remained seated with my thoughts focused on the five-dollar bill that was pretty much all I had in my pocket, and in the world for that matter. It was so amazing to consider how far things had changed in the year since I had started writing this book. First I just wanted to see where the idea led me. Then, when I came back to school, I just wanted to have a clear schedule, uncluttered with classes to go to, papers to write, text books to read, and exams to take. I quit school for this. All the time, I just wanted to finish something. I had a list of ideas as long as the road from Jackson, Tennessee, to West Seventeenth Street, all unfinished and blowing along the highway, scraps of paper, pieces of thoughts I never developed. So, more than I needed to compete with the hall of fame school records of my mother and her siblings, more than I needed to stifle the snickers of my Lincoln classmates who called me crazy, I needed to finish one thought. And I had.

But, since I had never finished anything to speak of, never had anything in print beyond a line or two in this or that school publication, I had never projected my work beyond the hoots and hollers that were tossed my way by Lincoln's hardcore "Rabble Crew" who insisted my disappearance from class was due to my complete dedication to smoking marijuana and that the only writing I did was scribbling apologies to everyone I had lied to when I said I was writing a book. And on this desk in front of me was not only a chance to slap them in their faces, but a check for $2,000. Imagine that? I could walk back onto campus next year showing the benefits of a two-grand advance, and have the opportunity to shove copies of a book with my name on it down the throats of the big-mouthed jokers in front of the student union, guys who'd made me look like a reefer-smoking idiot for months. And a chance to see my mother smile and justify her faith and squelch my uncle's scalding critiques. All I had to do was sign that paper and walk out.

125

Walk out and leave my manuscript. Leave my manuscript like leaving a pet at the vet to have it neutered. Leave a deer on the taxidermist's table to have its guts ripped out and replaced with sawdust, its head removed to hang over this smug, smirking egotist's fake apartment fireplace. I tried to add it up again while I sat there feeling cold and clammy, poker-faced, like some leather-jacket-clad form of dead.

I got up slowly with what I'm sure was one of my worst attempts to look like I was smiling. The editor had turned away in his swiveling chair and was concentrating on not looking at me. So he probably didn't see me pick up my manuscript and walk out of his office.

18

People speak in a certain key that's similar to a musical note. When you talk to people naturally, it's comfortable because there's no strain or stress on your vocal cords. Sometimes when people speak too fast or make vocabulary choices that don't ring true, it occurs to me that something is wrong with what they are saying. That was what I heard at the editor's office in New York.

I have always told folks that I left with my manuscript that day because of a feeling. I did have a feeling. But I got it from a hearing. That day in the editor's office I was so full of myself that I might have missed most of the discussion if every word had not been so momentous and magnificent to me. What I missed instead of words was meaning.

I heard every word. Almost as individual elements, isolated as though they had nothing to do with me or with each other. But I didn't tune in on his meaning until the middle of a solo about Junior imitating Spade. I heard him hit a false note, a note that shouldn't have existed in this conversation. Something like an F-flat. There is no such note. Not for a musician. And not from one musician to another. Not from people playing the same tune.

The editor wasn't just testing me. There were more notes that didn't belong. His voice went totally out of tune. I can't read minds, but it sounded like he was establishing his domain over a rookie writer who wouldn't be a factor after today. His intention was to hurt, to insult. Not to pay me, but to pay me off. For me to disappear and be grateful for a couple of grand.

I took the subway to 23rd Street with some semblance of a plan pushing its way through alternating pulses of panic. Plan B felt like what it was and what I didn't want it to be, what I had never seen coming, had foolishly not even considered. Here's some other shit I can't talk to anyone about, that probably nobody but my mother would believe. An offer of two thousand dollars. An opportunity to have the book published that I'd thrown together on a beat up old Royal typewriter at the university cleaners.

A gritty Manhattan mist felt chilly and uncomfortable on my face and bare head as I emerged on the northeast corner of 23rd, one block west of the bakery where I would spend my remaining dollars before going to 17th Street and taking ten bucks from my mother's cold cash, a coffee can in the fridge. I would leave her a note, a lie, and catch a bus back to Lincoln.

In front of the 23rd Street YMCA, I ran into Freddy Baron, a guy who had been a classmate of mine at Fieldston. He was with his father. It was good to see Freddy, and I had always liked his father, too. Freddy and I had played on the football team together our senior year, a team that finished 4-4. My favorite memory of the season was a game in which Freddy and I scored our team's only two touchdowns in a 14-8 victory. Freddy scored his when he intercepted a pass from his defensive end position and ran it back forty yards. Mine was a bit more complicated. I was standing about ten yards in front of our punt returner, ostensibly to serve as a blocker. The kick, however, was high but short, and the would-be tacklers went past me, angling toward our return man. I fielded the punt and took it back seventy yards past the opposition's massive right tackle.

Recollections of high school heroics were a relief at that moment, but none of us was feeling too good about standing there in the rain. The Barons had just finished a workout that included a mile run and a few laps in the pool. They were both flushed and looked fit and healthy. But within the thickening wall of April gloom, they proposed that I join them at their home for dinner and assured me that Mrs. Baron, who I'd also met, would be happy to see me again. I couldn't have sworn I had better plans, so we got on a crosstown bus going east.

I caught up with Freddy, heard how unbelievably cold the winters were in Madison, Wisconsin, where he was adjusting to college life. I talked about Lincoln and how I'd finally dropped out of school and what had just happened at the publishing office that day. We had a pleasant dinner and Freddy and I went downstairs to the rec room to play table tennis and shoot pool.

When we got back to the apartment, Freddy ran directly into the bathroom and I was about to collapse onto the sofa when I saw that Mr. Baron was seated under a reading lamp in the corner with his reading glasses on and my manuscript in his lap. He read on for a few minutes after I took a seat near him. Then he closed it up and put it carefully back in the plastic cover.

He smiled, folded his glasses carefully, and put them back in their case. Of all the Fieldston parents, he had always been the most approachable, the most available to drive guys to a band rehearsal or stand on the sidelines alone to watch a lightly attended football game. He spoke with my mother fairly often. I had stayed at their house a few times, too. The Barons lived in Stuyvesant Town, on East 23rd Street, which was practically next door to West 17th by Manhattan standards.

"Gilbert," he said in his rich baritone, "I've read about forty pages here and I must admit I don't know a lot about the life you are describing. But I know more than I did because you know it so well. I've got two friends who write commercials and they're always talking about the art of telling a story in one minute. That's what they do. I'd like to show this to them and see if they couldn't put a few things in the margins."

When he stopped, Mr. Baron took a furtive look toward the bathroom, reached into his breast pocket, and pulled out a fifty dollar bill and handed it to me. I understood that he didn't want Freddy involved, but I hadn't said anything about the current state of my finances. I appreciated his perception.

"Look," I said hastily, "I've got a tax refund due . . ."

He cut me off.

"No," he said seriously. "Let me tell you a story. When I was just getting started, I almost didn't make it. I had rented a space and had my whole line of dresses and everything there. And I had made arrangements for everything to go out, most of the pieces had been ordered and I was confident that they would be moved. But my rent was due on the warehouse and if I paid it

I wouldn't have money left to ship the pieces out and all of my outlets had thirty and forty-five day leads before money would be coming in. I had cut every corner imaginable and it just wasn't going to happen. It was about midnight and I was writing my landlord a note about getting everything out of there and a little about what else had happened when I saw him walking down the hall. When he saw my light on, he stopped by."

Mr. Baron said the landlord came to his space and after hearing the situation, told him to hold off on paying the rent, said they could work it out when the money started coming in. "I tell you Gilbert, I'd only talked to the man when I rented the space and seen him a few times going in and out. Very businesslike, short on conversation. But he raised my spirits. And I never forgot what he said then. 'If you ever get a chance to help someone else get started, do that for me and tell them to pass it on.' Then he waved and was off again. I believe in that, Gilbert. I don't want this back, but I do want you to remember it and pass it on."

Mr. Baron smiled and got up. "I'm going to hand this over to my friends and have them get in touch with you at this number." The number on the manuscript was the pay phone at the diner across Route 1 from the dry cleaners where I worked.

I still felt washed out, but the kind of help Mr. Baron gave me was help in its purest form, when somebody does something for you for nothing. But I still intended to get him back that money in two weeks, three at the outside.

About ten days later, before I'd had a chance to square that debt, I was wrestling with the day's dry cleaning load when the niece of the owner of the diner called me from across the road.

"It's the telephone, Spider," she said in her soprano. "It's a call from New York."

The lady on the phone was named Lynn Nesbit. She was a literary agent with a firm on the Avenue of the Americas. A week before, a friend had dropped a manuscript by and asked her to take a look. She had read it all in one sitting. The following day she'd shown it to a friend at World Publishing. They agreed that it needed some work.

"But would you be willing to accept five thousand dollars as an advance?" she asked.

I don't remember whether I accepted before or after I fainted. Whichever it was, I agreed to meet Lynn Nesbit in her office in three days. I was so happy I could have peed in my pants.

World Publishing also bought the rights to *Small Talk at 125th and Lenox*, a volume of poetry released simultaneously with *The Vulture*. That one I dedicated to my mother, because she always appreciated the poetry so much and had helped me with some of the lines and ideas. The novel I dedicated to Mr. Jerome Baron, "without whom the bird would never have gotten off the ground." And I have tried to follow his advice and pass it on every time I have the opportunity.

19

After taking what would have been my sophomore year off from schoolwork and grades, I was registered to return to Lincoln in the fall of 1969. That summer, though, with the books in the process of being published, I used some of the advance money to buy an old Nash Rambler convertible, a 1965 with 100,000 miles on it. Before heading back to school, I drove to Fayette, Mississippi, with a friend of mine from Lincoln named Steve Wilson to witness the election of Charles Evers, Medgar Evers's brother, who was about to become the first Black mayor elected in the south since Reconstruction.

First we spent a slow-moving day slogging through nearly tangible humidity in my old home of Jackson, Tennessee. I spent a couple of evening hours with a girl who was starstruck over a New Yorker; Steve drank.

I was going to Mississippi looking for something else to write about. I was afraid to think about being back at Lincoln with nothing to write about. I'd always wanted to write novels, but I had come to think that a writer was writing all the time and, after my mystery, I didn't have any idea what I would do. There was no doubt that my state of mind had been attached to finishing *The Vulture*. And my ability to pay for returning to school had been connected to earning some tuition and room-and-board money. My personal credibility had been saved when I got the deal but I honestly didn't know what I could do next.

Back on campus I hung out with a lot of guys who were into the jazz heavies, the ones you didn't hear too often on the radio. We spent a lot of our time supposedly doing our homework, but really in each other's rooms checking out the jams—Coltrane, Dexter Gordon, Herbie Hancock.

I also met Brian Jackson that Fall semester. He was a freshman with classical music training. I was playing keyboards one day and having awful trouble with the sheet music for "God Bless the Child." Brian could play that stuff like it was easy. We hooked up in the music room; he showed me some music of his own and I started writing lyrics for it. He and I started writing songs for a group called Black & Blues, and worked together for quite a while doing songs for this group.

I'd been writing short stories since I was a boy, but it took until I was nineteen or twenty before I got my thoughts together to do a novel; in the same way, I was writing songs all along but they weren't very good. But I continued to work on them. By the time I met Brian I was getting more of an idea of what I was going to do.

I managed at least one trip per month to New York City. The Last Poets had their East Wind thing going on, and a couple of guys I knew—the percussionists Charlie Saunders and Isaiah Washington—went with me to see that whenever I visited. I got to know all the Last Poets, too, because Abiodun Oyewole's cousin went to Lincoln with me. I thought that they were bring-ing a new sound to poetry and to the community, and I enjoyed it. I was a piano player and played with different groups still, and the songs and poems that I had written had a musical tilt to them because they were compositions as opposed to just poems over rhythms. Their things were a cappella without music. I always had a band, so it was a different sort of thing. But we were trying to go in the same direction.

One Sunday night in November 1969, as I pulled in through the arch to campus after a weekend in New York, I was met by three guys before I'd even gotten near my dorm. It was Brian along with two guys from his jazz combo, Carl Cornwell, who played sax, and Leon Clark, the bassist. They were visibly upset and wanted to talk to me.

It turned out the drummer for the band, Ron Colburn, had died Friday night. They'd had a rehearsal that lasted until about midnight, and Ron, who was asthmatic, started having trouble breathing at the end. His inhaler gave him no relief, so the guys walked him to the infirmary. It was closed. Someone went to the security guard's office and explained the problem and the guard let them into the infirmary. There was no oxygen. That meant they had to call the fire department in Oxford, three miles away. Though the ambulance hurried to Lincoln, there was no oxygen aboard the vehicle, and on the way to the hospital in Avon Grove, Pennsylvania, Ron died.

Brian and the other members of the band saw his death as unnecessary and felt something needed to be done.

So I did it. I closed the school down.

135

In all honesty, I could never have closed Lincoln by myself. But with equal honesty, I will confess that had the school closing ended in disaster, the blame would have been laid squarely on me. And I would have accepted it. Not for the sake of heroism or martyrdom, but because it was my idea, and because without the benefit of any elected campus position the pressure brought to bear on the university administration came from my direction and without any more formal constituency than the one I threw together that Sunday night.

On every campus there are key groups and special people that don't necessarily hold offices in student government or any organizations but that command respect from the student body. On Lincoln's campus at that time, there was one such group I wanted with me and felt I could not move without: the vets.

Lincoln had a group of brothers who were vets on two fronts. These brothers straddled the two Lincolns—they'd begun their quest for a degree under the old-school, all-male system, gone away to the armed services, and returned to a coed, state-related system that most of them agreed had diminished the tradition of their school. Most of them had chosen to return for sentimental reasons and because a degree from Lincoln still meant something to them. A lot of them had obligations and responsibilities placed on hold while they closed out the unfinished business of a degree. In short, they were folks with a lot at stake during this particular school year.

I went to see them first.

Having withdrawn from Lincoln for a year and returned with two books on my résumé gave me a veteran's image, if not the military service the term implied. I was at least looked at like something of a Lincoln veteran.

Along with the respect afforded the vets, there was one other tangible advantage to "old head" status. You got to live in Vet Ville, a cluster of barrack-like buildings at the far west end of the school grounds, behind the old gymnasium, often lost in evening fog.

Meetings were not commonly held in the Vet Ville bunkhouses, but news of Ron's death and my visit got an interested majority to gather. The wardrobe varied, with some men in pajamas and bathrobes and others in jeans and the familiar green jackets.

I described as best I could the events that preceded Ron's death. I also reminded them that during my first year, my next-door neighbor in the freshman dorm had died from an aneurism, and that another student had died after an accident. I reminded them of "Beaucoup," an upperclassman who'd had a hernia misdiagnosed, and "Bird" Evans, whose badly broken ankle was treated as a sprain. My main point was that Lincoln was twice as large as it had been when the current facilities and medical provisions had been deemed adequate. They no longer were.

"So what are you after, Spiderman?" asked a brother standing near the door, using a nickname that had accompanied me from Chelsea.

I passed around a few copies of a list of what I labeled "requests." There were seven items on the list:

1. We request that the on-campus medical facility be available twenty-four hours a day.
2. That the infirmary undergo a thorough examination by competent medical personnel and security representatives who can quickly assess its status.
3. That the recommendations of the person(s) conducting the inventory be accepted ASAP and that a schedule be adopted for bringing our facility supplies up to current community population requirements.
4. That Dr. Davies, current on-campus physician, be dismissed.
5. That a schedule be organized among all the available medical supplementary personnel to cover the campus responsibilities until a permanent replacement can be found.
6. That a fully equipped ambulance be purchased and placed under the jurisdiction of campus security, with a competent driver always on duty with an appropriate license.
7. That a new on-campus physician be aggressively sought and hired, whose primary responsibility will be the entire Lincoln community and who therefore will also be aware of coed treatment and sensitive to our new diversity.

"Hell, you ain't gonna get all a this," somebody said quietly and passed the sheet on. "Numbers five, six, and seven."

"We need them," I said.

Brian and Carl agreed.

"So what do you want from us," said another vet.

"I want you guys on the doors to the classroom buildings after breakfast," I said. "I want you to tell folks there are no classes in the morning and that there's going to be a campus meeting in the chapel at ten o'clock. It's for everybody: teachers, day student commuters, administration folks, everybody."

I finished with, "I can't get started without support from down here."

"And what about after the meeting?"

"There will be no classes until these requests are met."

"You may get the first."

"Is it agreed that we need these things?" I asked.

"Well, yeah, but you know what they gon' say about money."

"Fees are up, enrollment is doubled. We're supposed to be state-related," I cut in.

"All right, Spiderman," came a baritone from the back of the room, "we'll work with you in the morning."

It was one in the morning when I left Vet Ville and headed slowly back to the main campus. I had to consider whether the issues I had numbered were as succinct and well-stated as they needed to be. It was all kinds of ironic that after a five-hour emotional roller-coaster ride, everything boiled down to my ability as a writer.

As I walked back, I heard the vets chorus of comments ringing in my ears: "You can probably get them first four, maybe, but you can forget them last two or three."

Well, we'd see. Because none of them were expendable. I knew that good negotiators always included points they could afford to concede. But I wasn't putting together a package to negotiate. The whole thing was shaky. There were only thirty students or so out of more than six hundred who knew anything was going on. And only thirty who recognized me as in charge. This was a hell of a thing, no doubt.

I tried to put together a list of things to do in order of priority. I started to realize what I hadn't done since I arrived back on campus. I hadn't eaten. I hadn't had anything to drink. I hadn't cracked a book—but that was okay because classes were cancelled at least for tomorrow. Hell, I just plain old hadn't shaved, showered, smiled, or sat down to really consider what I was going to do tomorrow. And now, at 1 a.m., it was already tomorrow.

Arriving at the regular dorms, I took the stairs up to Eddie's room two at a time. There was a whisper of marijuana squeezing its way down the hall, mixing with the dampness of two thousand rainy nights that had soaked into the floor and the walls of the old dorm like that forgotten first coat of paint, now inseparable from the wood. I heard something by Miles on the box, something slow and thoughtful and lonely. Something Miles could do without trying, maybe because he was that way.

I knocked, entered, flipped out a cigarette, and passed Eddie my list on my way to a chair in the corner. The room was full, like on the nights when the NBA was playing or a Monday night football game was on. Eddie's room, with a larger than usual common room, had become the meeting place. Eddie passed the paper on and nodded at me.

"We need to organize how this chapel thing is going to go," I finally said.

Everybody shifted in their seats. I could see tired and seri-ous and thoughtful and sad on brothers' faces. I could feel it in the room.

"We need to get in touch with Ron's folks, too. See what we can do. Anybody talk to them yet?"

Carl said yes. That was good. I'd rather have fought the vets than do that.

There are so many divisions and subdivisions on a college campus that it is probably a social miracle when the whole com-munity is pulling in the same direction, everybody wanting the same thing. The next morning, when I walked to the podium at the chapel, it was way over its capacity of two hundred. It was standing room only, with people jammed all along the back and in the aisles.

I was as brief and devoid of drama as possible. This was not an occasion to try to whip up waves of emotion. The truth was dramatic enough. The third brother to die in two years at Lincoln was being buried in a couple of days. These deaths served to highlight the fact that the facilities at the isolated old school had not kept pace with its growth.

I reviewed the incidents that had magnified the shortcom-ings of Lincoln's health services. I described the three young men, two classmates and a fellow musician. I took care not to attach blame for the tragedies. But then I listed the specific mistakes made in diagnoses and treatment, and said this pat-tern was no longer acceptable. I then suggested that a complete boycott of classes would minimize the potential for injury or illness while allowing the administration to concentrate on our requests. I announced that this boycott would remain in effect until further notice. In conclusion, I read the seven requests, told the assembly that they could collect a copy on their way out, and assured them that everyone would be kept abreast of progress made in these areas. Then I expressed a confidence—that I did not feel—that these adjustments would be made quickly and that we would all be back on our regular schedules soon. Then I asked them all to leave the chapel slowly—repeating the need to avoid anyone getting hurt.

Obviously I could not and would not even try to handle the responsibility for the entire campus. The more positions I delegated to other people, the more folks would participate. Let me note that there was no formal student government, and if there had been I'm sure folks would have been more focused on what would have been seen as my coup d'état than on my list of requests. As it was, I had to admit that I had no mandate, and that there had only been the vets standing at the doors of the classroom buildings and my standing on the chapel stage to suggest I was in charge.

Finally, however, it was the reaction of the powers that be that cemented my precarious perch as the voice, if not the head, of the student body. A schedule was posted that afternoon listing the nurses who would be in the infirmary from midnight until the regular 8 a.m. opening. On Tuesday morning Dr. Warren Smith, the school psychiatrist, arrived and let it be known that he would be conducting a review of the infirmary inventory and making recommendations for upgrading the supplies. One, two, and three.

I resisted the opportunity to ring the chapel bell and announce that we were almost halfway home. I went to dinner instead and then back to Eddie's room. After all, the vets had conceded the first three points would be met. The rest would be more difficult.

I went to talk to Dr. Smith as he moved around the supply room in the infirmary, opening first one cabinet and then another, noting what he found. He was a large, friendly bear of a man with a bald spot and graying hair. I hadn't seen him in more than a year, since he had approved my request to take the year off. I wanted to ask him what he thought of what was going on; I wanted to ask him for suggestions on how best to approach the top people, the university president and the dean. He would also know where the money was and who had it. In the end, this was always going to be about money.

But Dr. Smith kept talking, controlling the conversation as though we were being monitored. I sincerely doubt that we were. It could have been that he was offended by the criticism of the medical facilities. Perhaps he had been reminded by administration officials that his letter from the previous October had made it possible for me to return. Or it could have been that he knew the conflict was only beginning and that Ron Colburn would not be the last casualty.

In fact, there was another one that night.

There are casualties in every conflict. It gave me no pleasure to include the request that the campus physician be dismissed. The timing of the request, in the wake of Ron's death, implied a connection—that the doctor had been at fault. Actually, he hadn't

143

been involved in any of the three fatalities I had discussed in the chapel. The doctor was an old-school Lincoln man, a graduate with a practice in nearby Oxford who lived on campus with his family and was available day and night. But I really had no choice. The doctor was having a battle with the bottle; he won some rounds and lost some. A couple of his losses took place at the wrong time and influenced his examination of patients. One of those patients led a group of students into the doctor's front yard on Wednesday evening. He was carrying a papier-mâché dummy with a rope around its neck. The student threw the rope over a limb of a huge tree in front of the doc's house and set the dummy on fire.

The school doctor came out of his house to confront the crowd, screaming at them about his innocence, swearing that he had nothing to do with the deaths.

That's when I arrived, walking slowly into a position between the excited group and the tearful doctor, standing alone in a T-shirt and dark slacks. I could see the doctor's tears of rage and sadness behind his glasses. So could everybody else. We had to look into the eyes of the man being burned in effigy, and see the wide eyes of his children staring out of the front window behind him, watching their father's impotent humiliation, perhaps fearful that their lives were in danger.

A cold flash scampered across the back of my neck. The whole scene had me spinning. I didn't begin to relax until the students started backing away, scattering toward the dorms. I knew now that the doc would resign. I got no joy from request number four.

As the week wore on, I saw Dr. Smith and others coming and going with supplies, taking packages of meds, crutches, bandages, oxygen tanks, halogen lamps, updated medical dictionaries and books on the latest treatments, and even a few pocketbooks for patients needing to stay overnight. There were also new curtains, carpeting, and a new eye chart. And the infirmary was staffed every night.

It was generally agreed that the highlight of the week, the most dramatic moment, came after the student body decided to continue the boycott. The last three points were not done. There was no schedule of doctors beyond a day or two in advance, there was no ambulance, and there was no line forming to take the newly open position of campus physician.

On Thursday afternoon, I was wondering what I could do to pacify certain factions grumbling and mumbling about returning everyone to class. The rumor was that if we reached the weekend without further progress, there would be no real reason to continue the boycott. People were warning: "We got all we could after the doctor quit. Extending this boycott thing is all about Spiderman. He need to quit."

It might have worked. Negative talk can produce a negative mindset. Which is why my heart did a little jerk as I stepped out of the lunch room. Parked at the bottom of the northside incline as though just waiting for my nod of approval was a blood-red ambulance with a fresh coat of wax. The shine was strong enough to be seen by the blind, and the dishwater gray sky was momentarily shocked into retreat by the energy of the red radiating from that vehicle.

145

The weekend passed and we reconvened in the chapel on Monday. This time I called for a vote, and the students voted to continue the boycott.

On Tuesday—day seven without classes, day nine since what was feeling more and more like a daring game of chicken began, day eleven since Ron Colburn had died—I was sitting in the front seat of an administrator's car, riding around the perimeter of the campus under a light rain. It was day one of the administration focusing fully on me as their problem.

"What is it you want, Spider?" he asked.

This brother, light skinned with glasses and a moustache, was one of the younger administrators, one who tried to relate. I'd gotten to know him when I stayed on campus part of one summer to work as a counselor for a summer program. He was probably eight years older than I was, married, a ball player, and a Lincoln man.

"Just what it says on the paper, man," I said, lighting a cigarette.

"No, Spider," he said, slowing the car. "What is it that *you* want out of all this?"

"You think I got . . ."

"Well, you know," he cut in, "me and some others know you. We knew you when you were down here in the summer with the kids and there wasn't none . . ."

"I was a friend of Ron's," I said. "As I am a friend of yours. There's six or seven hundred . . ."

He nodded his head sadly, looking ahead through the grayness.

"You should have let it go last night," he said.

Last night had been dramatic, and I had gotten the impression from a lot of people that there should never have been a vote; that I should have simply walked into the chapel, thanked the students for their cooperation in applying the pressure that got us six out of seven of our objectives. Victory, essentially. Six out of seven was two more than the vets had foreseen, and nobody thought we'd get it all. Therefore I should have come in last night and said, "We won, so go to class tomorrow."

I hadn't done that. And maybe it was somewhat chicken-shit not to do that. Forget about the fact that on Monday night we were no better off than on Friday morning. There had been a feeling of suspended animation on campus from the time after the tomato-ketchup, fresh-blood, fire-engine red ambulance had been parked so conspicuously in front of the student union building. That was a real surrender.

"I couldn't do . . . "

"Yeah, you could have, Spider," he said. His use of my nickname somehow reduced me from student leader to comic-book caricature. "And you should have."

"I was supposed to just announce that, right? Some son of a bitch would have accused me of being a dictator."

I felt like I was talking to myself.

"You started it by yourself and kept it going. You gave it the shape and strength nobody else on this campus could have. Anybody popular enough wouldn't have had the guts, the nerve."

He paused and dropped his voice to tell me a secret.

"They spent last week with you kickin' their asses," he said, laughing. "They were kickin' their own asses for letting you back in here. But other folks kept saying that it wasn't bad, because it wasn't wrong, what you were saying. There was a mix of admiration and self-recrimination. We were students here, too. And we knew."

Then he finished: "They're over being scared. They're gonna get you out of here."

The question of who "they" were was never put to him. I got out of the car and trotted to shelter. He drove off.

I was still sitting in the basement of the student union building as night closed in around the campus, filling all the spaces between the few naked trees and colorless, spartan dormitories. The classrooms and buildings where all the knowledge was stored and stacked were hidden behind fog. I was virtually inside a private one of those myself, focused in and fogged up when a young coed, a freshman I recognized, walked up to me. I don't remember enough of what she said even to paraphrase it, but as quickly as I could I was up the stairs and walk-running south between the administration building and the security house. I crossed the street and went quickly to another house there, usually dark but now well lit.

Inside there was a smile for me from a handsome middle-aged lady. She introduced herself as "Dr. Mondry" as I reached to shake hands. She was interested in the job opening we had, she said, but she would only take it with my approval.

Dr. Mondry saved my life.

INTERLUDE

May 1970

The laws of chance got bitch-slapped for sure one night when the
artist had his back squarely against a wall. He'd been knocked
out, and as he slowly, swimmingly came to, there were the anxious faces of the six-foot-seven Robert Berry and G.I. Joe Sheffi
staring down at him with wide eyes.

It started to come back to him.

They'd been about four miles north of Lincoln University
on Route 1, a couple of miles from Avondale, Pennsylvania. One
of the old Isaac Hayes—bald, dig?—tires on his ancient, rusty
Rambler, the left rear tire, had committed suicide. (Evidently it
shot itself. They'd heard a loud *boom*.)

Unfortunately it developed into one of those domino-type
incidents. With the death of the admirable left rear, now a candidate for becoming a million rubber bands, the Rambler convertible was converted. From a '65 white Rambler into a white
Rambler with a black vinyl top and innumerable rust spots going
into a skid at sixty miles per hour. Without benefit of brakes

he dared not even tap. And with a panoramic view of more or less rural America sliding sideways across his windshield as the two-lane blacktop changed to four lanes and they slid like a three-legged whale across the double yellow lines and the soft gravel shoulder on the opposite side of the road, through a sizable piece of the parking lot of a local insurance firm, and soon after into a sixty mile-per-hour collision with the corner of the insurance company's local office.

More came back as the artist continued to come to.

The driver's-side door handle was still in his outstretched left hand, though the car was now some twenty feet away. The door was behind him, serving as both a back rest and an explanation as to why he had not become a smear along the local office wall. The car was smashed beyond further mobility. The artist was not.

By the eyewitness accounts of Berry and Sheffi—and sobriety was never an issue with those two—he had used the door as a shield when the old Rambler smashed and crashed against the corner of the insurance company wall. The hinge of the door snapped like a number-two pencil and the artist went airborne. First the door and then his back slamming flat against the smooth plaster.

He was conscious quickly enough to direct the removal of the rifles and shells from the car and trunk and have them hidden across the highway behind a barrier on the shoulder that resisted, though did not restrain entirely, vehicles intent on plunging down a steep embankment on the east side of that two-lane entrance into Avondale, Pennsylvania.

He had not been bothered by the trickle of blood that was tip-toeing its way down an uncharted path from the long scratch two inches left of center on his forehead, which miraculously was the only visible injury among the three of them. There was the truth that he had been knocked unconscious, but he overlooked that when he told the state trooper he was all right.

He was.

The three of them got a ride back to campus and the artist got a butterfly bandage for his head that made him look like a warrior wounded in the turmoil of college unrest when he appeared two days later on the Washington, D.C., evening news, being interviewed by Max Robinson. They were all laughing about the expression on the state trooper's face as his eyes flitted back and forth between the door and the artist, who was denying the need for medical attention as blood soaked through the napkin he had pressed against the scratch.

"He was bug-eyed," Berry exclaimed, folding his long frame nearly in half. "When he said, like, 'You're all right?' It was supposed to be a statement, but it came out like a question—with a little squeak on the end of it!"

"I was just glad he didn't say, 'Could I see your license and registration, sir?'" said the artist, chuckling.

Maybe the laughter was 75 percent nervous tension. The aftermath of an incident that could have had a lot more tragic consequences: the run they were making, the guns, the shells, the speed, the beginning of a soft rain greasing the roads beneath the well-worn tires of the Rambler, the explosion of the left rear tire when it blew out, and their uncontrolled slide sideways

151

across Route 1, the calm discussion as they sliced the chain-link fence in front of the insurance building, the tension, bracing themselves with the artist's death-lock grip on the door handle, and then . . .

He had to admit that the thing had almost gotten out of hand. And almost is a valid operative because the great "March on Oxford" never became a real road show. It would have been a real walking nightmare. And the artist had still been debating whether or not he could have, would have, gone along with the marchers if he hadn't been able to turn it around, if somebody hadn't.

He understood that agreeing not to do anything was not the answer that satisfied searchers at the close of the symbolic sixties. During a peace rally at Kent State University in Ohio, the National Guard had been called to campus to maintain order. When the marchers turned in their direction, they panicked and fired into the crowd, killing four. Then two students were murdered at Jackson State University, a Black school in Mississippi, shot through dorm windows by members of the Mississippi State Highway Patrol.

The problem the artist had was the muted reaction from Attorney General John Mitchell. Well, muted was generous. Zero is not mute. It is as silent as a stone. A statue with limitations.

Okay, the feds were responsible for the National Guard in Ohio and had no direct jurisdiction over the Mississippi State Highway Patrol. The problem was that nobody in Mississippi had control over them either, and as the nation's top cop, Mitchell had authority over whoever was not exercising authority in Mississippi. Zero.

So the artist made a move at Lincoln, asking the students to shut down all campus activities in protest of the shooting of Black students and the resulting national silence. It worked, but only by the hardest. He found out how difficult it was to contain all elements resulting from a mass response.

The students at Lincoln understood the implications of what was happening on the other campuses; they could not ignore shit like that and say nothing because every nothing you say and do makes it just that much easier for the next incident of that nature. A campus-wide agreement at Lincoln would show solidarity with Jackson State and Kent State.

But just as the artist was about to say to himself that it had gone down a lot more smoothly than he had anticipated, somebody shouted, "Let's march on Oxford!"

Suddenly the idea of a march bounced around the chapel like a badminton birdie, helplessly rocketing off the rackets and raising a ruckus that rolled out of the old meeting hall to recongregate beneath the arch that welcomed you to the university.

The artist hadn't known what to do first: send a group ahead to Oxford to try to alert the citizens of that sleepy, primarily agricultural hamlet that this was not a realization of the fear that many of them had always held in their most secret places, like a town with a penitentiary on its outskirts.

And what about the Pennsylvania Highway Patrol? There had never been any publicized friction between the "state boys"

153

and the hundreds of Blacks tucked away in this corner of the Quaker state. But then again, there had never been three or four hundred students turning Route 1 into a bumper-to-bumper parking lot, crawling along the three miles into town, a line of frustrated, confused farmers and good old boys trying to ease back into northern Maryland in four-by-fours with shotguns in the shotgun racks.

Maybe their grains of common sense surfaced there beneath the arch. Maybe something flashed on them at the threshold of Route 1 and nothing but three miles of open and exposed Pennsylvania fields. Maybe it was the cameras and the earrings and the platform shoes and halter tops and sunglasses that showed them that what they were thinking about—this proposed demonstration—would signify no more than their agreement to close the school had. That they were not prepared, hadn't planned, and that Oxford was not the problem. The only things that could have happened were bad.

Their decision not to go had the artist smiling that lopsided grin of his again in the back of the cluster. They didn't go.

The artist did. Two days later he was on television in D.C., speaking on the evening news about a meeting held earlier that day with Attorney General John Mitchell, where, along with Howard University student government president Michael Harris, he took Nixon's right-hand man through everything from the infamous "No Knock" law, used in Chicago in the attack against the Black Panthers Fred Hampton and Mark Clark, to the illustrations on the walls of his office showing eighteenth- and nineteenth-century punishment scenes, including Blacks in chains and overseers with whips in hand.

They explained why they had closed their respective schools, which ignited a wave of closings on the East Coast, and watched as John Mitchell boarded a late-afternoon flight to Mississippi.

20

At the end of that tumultuous school year, two or three people from Black & Blues graduated, so Brian and I had a chance to write things not strictly for that group. And when I went home for the summer, I went to see a man named Bob Thiele, who had started his own record label called Flying Dutchman. Bob had produced Coltrane and knew Archie Shepp; he had made major contributions in the jazz world. And even though I was never really into the Beat poets, I knew he had also produced some Jack Kerouac recordings.

When I opened the door to the Flying Dutchman office, Bob was standing there at a desk that faced the door, talking to his secretary and leafing through some papers. That was really cool—the first moment in my life when a photograph came to life. I'd seen his picture a hundred times, and there he was. The surprise grabbed my throat and lungs, and fright held me for a second and a half. I hadn't expected the president of the company to be standing in front of the door, but I quickly gave Bob the spiel I had prepared for the secretary or secondary.

I told Bob I was a songwriter. I told him that I had a partner, Brian Jackson, and that we thought that he was recording the kind of people we thought might be interested in what we were doing. Bob said that he didn't have any money to do an album of music at the time. But he had read my book of poetry and said, "If you do that and make any money, maybe we can get some money together and do an album of music."

The thought of doing an entire spoken-word album had never even crossed my mind. But aside from continuing to record the types of jazz musicians that had been the foundation of his recognition and reputation in the 1960s, Bob Thiele wanted to create a recorded chronicle of the era. Many changes in our society that took place in the 1970s were credited to the 1960s and Bob wanted those sounds on wax. These were often albums that had no commercial potential, but that were enormously insightful as slices of an age and invaluable as snapshots of a period that reshaped America first and everywhere else later.

Often these albums were not music. There was an album of a speech by the first Black mayor of a major U.S. city, Cleveland's Carl Stokes, that was followed by questions from the press; there were several speeches by H. Rap Brown and Ms. Angela Davis; there were readings by the DJ Rosko of articles and columns by Pete Hamill and Robert Scheer, among others, including a chilling rendition of "A Night at Santa Rita" with music by Ron Carter and James Spaulding; there was the thoroughly hair-raising "Ain't No Ambulances for No Nigguhs Tonight" by Stanley Crouch. And as the summer of 1970 was drawing to a close, I went into the studio with a small group of folks on folding chairs and did poems from *Small Talk* and a few songs I had done on pianos in coffee houses.

Up until shortly before I made that first album, I was just one of nine in a group and arguably not the most important voice of the group. From the standpoint of how much original music I contributed, I was important to the group's fabric and character, but I wasn't the lead singer very often, and I wasn't ever responsible for carrying a show.

When the LP came out, I didn't think we'd get any airplay. I never thought about how much reach the record would have. As it turned out, FM radio was starting to be kind of necessary right around this same time because of a few popular stations, especially in Philadelphia, Washington, Los Angeles, and the Bay Area. And those stations began to play a lot of the stuff from *Small Talk*: "Whitey on the Moon," "Brother," and "The Revolution Will Not Be Televised" got picked up. The success of *Small Talk* was only regional, but they were good regions and it was labeled a "breakout LP" because of those sales.

At some point during the next school year, Bob Thiele called me up and said, "Who do you want to perform with?" By that time Black & Blues had completely broken up, so Brian and I decided to work with Ron Carter, Hubert Laws, and Bernard Purdie. We knew Purdie because he played with King Curtis, and King Curtis played with Aretha. Ron Carter wasn't known as much for bass at the time, but he played great bass.

We entered RCA studio in New York City in February 1971. When everybody came in and didn't know us and didn't know the songs, Ron Carter spoke up.

"We can work this out," he said. "Let's try a song about some of my favorite people."

So we worked out "Lady Day and John Coltrane," and it went from there. All I'd had for that song at first was a bass line and a chord thing with it. I never would have been able to really hook up that progression properly if Brian wasn't there when I got into it; he opened it up, picked it up, and took it to where I sang it. I didn't know anything about suspended fourths and all that, which is what the song is based on, so Brian was integral.

I had an affinity for jazz and syncopation, and the poetry came from the music. We made the poems into songs, and we wanted the music to sound like the words, and Brian's arrangements very often shaped and molded them. Later on when we wrote songs together, I'd ask Brian what he had on his mind, which sometimes I could more or less intuit from the music, because it carried an atmosphere with it. Different progressions and different chord structures brought a certain tone to mind. Sometimes I'd ask him and he'd convey in words what sort of feeling he was trying to bring about with that particular chord and that helped me get into it.

The new version of "The Revolution Will Not Be Televised" that emerged from those sessions tended to be the focus of talk about the album, *Pieces of a Man*. But it was followed on the LP by a song called "Save the Children," and that was followed by "Lady Day and John Coltrane." Then came "Home Is Where the Hatred Is" and "I Think I'll Call It Morning."

When people picked "The Revolution Will Not Be Televised" to decide what kind of artists we were, they overlooked what the hell the whole album said. We didn't just do one tune and let it stand, we did albums and ideas, and all of those ideas were

159

significant to us at the time we were working on them.

But none of that would matter too much, for two reasons. First, because one of the main ideas behind recording our songs was to get them out there for other people to hear and cover. That plan started to work immediately, when Esther Phillips covered "Home Is Where the Hatred Is." She got the song via Pee Wee Ellis, who was then working at our label, Flying Dutchman, but who had been brought in to work on Esther's first album for another label called Kudu.

"Home Is Where the Hatred Is" seemed to run parallel to Esther's own life, since she had openly overcome a serious drug problem. So the heroin thing was something she could communicate with in terms of a song and, to this day, I'm desperately proud of the way she performed the song. It brought it to life and that's a helluva thing for a writer to be able to hear in one of his songs.

The other reason it didn't matter was that despite having a second album on the way, as far as I was concerned I was still a student. And if I tried to picture myself doing something professionally, it was as a novelist, not a musician. I was working on another novel, *The Nigger Factory*, and I had come up with a plan to get the credentials that might allow me start a career as a writing teacher.

21

If you don't believe in the Spirits—and I didn't understand what they were at the time—then let's just say I was "lucky" that I didn't mail my application to Johns Hopkins University, where I had decided I wanted to go for a master's degree in writing; lucky that I didn't go down to the school on a day when the head of the writing seminars was not there; lucky I didn't go down without taking my accomplishments with me; and lucky I didn't take no for an answer. That last one almost played me, however.

It was not a day I'll ever forget, but I had long since started a habit of writing about days when things I thought might be important happened. Believe me, the day I was to apply to Hopkins was one of them. Aside from the fact that I was delivering the application personally and would need some kind of receipt noting their having gotten it, I felt like taking the trouble to go down there might make a better impression. And yeah, I didn't have a lot of faith in tossing books or LPs in the mail and just hoping it would get all the way through. There was no reason for me to supply a mailroom or mailman or secretary or whoever-the-fuck with *The Vulture* or *Small Talk* or *Pieces of a Man*.

161

I had actually heard about the Hopkins fellowship program during my first year at Lincoln. My roommate during the second semester that year was Steve Wilson, and he had a friend, a drinking buddy, who had been his counselor at a summer program Lincoln ran to prepare high schoolers for college. This counselor, a Baltimore guy, had graduated from Lincoln and gone on to the Hopkins writing program. His reputation on campus said that he was a great writer with a tremendous catalog of things he had written. I was impressed because Steve was impressed—and Steve wasn't easy to impress.

Steve and I had gone down to Hopkins once that second term of freshman year to see "B. More" Franklin. Steve wanted to go because he would rather go anywhere than go to class, and because I had stolen a bottle of Jack Daniels Black on our most recent trip to the Conowingo Liquor Warehouse. Actually, I had stolen a fifth of Bell's scotch, a bottle of Ballantine's scotch, *and* a fifth of Jack, but that had been Friday and it was Wednesday when Steve and I decided we should share that last bottle with another writer.

Steve had already painted a picture for me of B. More, told me a few things about their adventures and what he thought about Hopkins and Baltimore and everything else. I was a little intimidated and a whole lot of curious about this guy that Steve would drive fifty-odd miles to drink something with that he could otherwise drink alone. I was also curious because this guy must have been good. He was in the Hopkins graduate school and Steve had endorsed him. But when I thought about that I paused. B. More could be good, but not because of any of the information

I was working with. I wanted to read something of his because it was possible that the brother got into Hopkins the way I had gotten into Fieldston. It could have been that Hopkins needed a Black guy, or, better yet, a local-Black-makes-good type. Good community relations. In my case, at Fieldston I had covered a bunch of minorities: I was the Black student, the ghetto student, a single-parent-Southern-Black-ghetto student all rolled into one. A utility scholarship recipient, like a baseball player who can play any position. Not an All Star anywhere, but being an All Star at any of those things wouldn't have been good because it would have necessitated my specializing in one.

As it was, I had been All Mediocrity at Fieldston, which was All Right for both of us. In retrospect, instead of me beating them out of $2,200 a year for three years by being a mediocre student who only wanted to be left alone while he wrote stories, they owed me three more scholarships for three years each for covering so many categories.

Anyway, according to Steve, B. More was even more memorable for either his agility or his disregard for his own life. The two of them had left campus one night during the summer program on Steve's motorbike, headed for the liquor store three miles away in Oxford. They had squeezed in just under the 9 p.m. closing wire, and purchased a gallon of some brand of wine they should have been paid to remove from the premises. On the way back, B. More was on the back of the bike toting the jug. Suddenly, going too fast down a hill, they hit a pothole that sent them airborne. Not only were they disengaged from the seat and each other, but B. More "dropped" the wine.

163

Dropped is in quotation marks because it is questionable whether something has been dropped if it goes up instead of down. And if it never touches the ground. Because there, going thirty miles per hour with oncoming traffic, B. More let go of Steve, caught the wine in one hand, and, miraculously, regained his balance back on the motorbike seat. Steve described this with all the enthusiasm of Russ Hodges screaming, "The Giants win the pennant! The Giants win the pennant!"

Everything had been fine on that freshman year trip at first. B. More had taken the Jack I offered him lovingly, caressing it and rocking it like a baby, going through a dozen do-you-know-how-longs. He was really funny.

Steve was pleased. I never was much of a drinker at all. A little wine if I was showing off, acting suave, but no bourbon or scotch. I just stole it because the Maryland liquor warehouses were easy. And we kept the money we were paid for picking up bottles for other students. That is, unless we wanted more than I could steal. Steve often did; he was an alcoholic.

B. More might have been an alcoholic, too. Although he claimed he was broke and had been for a while—and as a result hadn't had a drink since the last time he'd had some money. But drinking, he added, was not the reason he was broke. He said he didn't drink "that much." Maybe not. But he liked to talk about how much he didn't drink. And then he and Steve got into a deep discussion about how much "that much" consisted of. Then they changed the subject. To wine. They talked about new wines and old wines. Then it was red wines and white wines. Then Italian

164

wines and French wines. They were all labels I'd never heard of; I knew Scuppernong.

I went around a corner to a luncheonette full of Hopkins people with armloads of books and serious looks on their faces. Two were talking about the school, saying there were one thousand undergraduates and eight thousand graduate students.

I got two grilled-cheese sandwiches, French fries, and two Dr Peppers. All they wanted were clean glasses and ice. They had that and were laughing when I left.

When I returned to B. More's room, the subject had turned to writing and half the Black Jack had blackjacked them. They were discussing the merits of Ron Wellburn's serious scholarship as opposed to Everett Hoagland's erotica. Too deep for me.

As I finished my lunch, B. More said to Steve, "Wellburn wrote me about this scrawny, Afro-wearin' chump," pointing at me with the bottle.

Steve giggled and his braces showed. "What'd he say?"

"That Spiderman is a better writer than he is or than Hoagland is. That he's better than you are, too."

Steve was nonplussed. He hoisted his glass.

"He is," Steve said. "He practices all the time."

"None a that bothered me," said B. More. "But he said Spiderman was better than I am."

For some reason I felt the conversation had turned a corner that was leading down a dead-end street.

"Tell me something," he said, still not looking my way. "Is he better'n me? A fucking prep?"

Steve turned his glass up and drained it.

"Yep," he said, reaching for the bottle of Jack and pouring himself another couple ounces. "He's better'n all of us because he don't drink. But that means he ain't a real writer yet. When he starts to drink . . ."

B. More got up, picked up the whisky bottle that was about two-thirds gone, and, holding it by the neck, walked into his bedroom and closed the door behind him. I didn't see him again for three years.

I knew another Lincoln student who was at Hopkins at the time I decided to drop off my application. Edward "Rocky" Collins was a year ahead of me when I arrived, class of 1970. He went to Hopkins a year ahead of me, too. But though Brian Jackson and I both knew him, neither of us knew his address in Baltimore. So I went straight to the building that housed the writing seminars.

I arrived in the department office about 1 p.m. and found an almost vacant reception area, manned only by a woman who was obviously busy. Her chair was in a front hall that led to a series of doors facing a desk and a cluster of phone connections. She was clearly the do-it-all who controlled the hall and access to all the professors. I stopped and gave her my kindest smile.

"Excuse me, ma'am," I said with my smile on full force, "my name is Gil Scott-Heron and I'm here to file an application for the fall seminars."

"Well, I'm just so sorry," she said, deflecting the brute force of my grin. "But unfortunately all of our positions in the group are taken."

I don't know what I expected her to say after "I'm so sorry," except maybe, "You're in the wrong department."

There was no way there were no more positions, no how. I knew she hadn't said "no." And if she had, I couldn't possibly know why.

No positions?

I didn't say that out loud. I just dimmed the enamel glare a little bit. What I was thinking was that back in my room I had a calendar on my wall that was all fucked up; I had a calendar that was at least a month behind the rest of the world, because I had a brochure that I was sure said to get applications in by March 1. *No positions? Right!*

"I know what you're thinking," the lady said, and then she went on to prove it. "Ordinarily we accept those applications until March 1, but this year we just had so many applications that we have no more positions. I'm sorry."

"Me, too," I said, sitting down opposite her.

She looked at me sympathetically. I sat down like I was sitting in an electric chair. It was a situation that just didn't sit well. What I wanted to do was scream at myself: *Hey! Don't just do something, sit there!* So I did. There is actually an ology called sitology, which I would like to have applied to the situation at hand, but I couldn't. It should at least have been an excuse for what I was doing, but it wasn't. I knew I was going to have to say something to this little lady shortly. I was wishing I had something scientific to say, but I had already eliminated sitology.

"Sir . . ."

She didn't really want to dog someone who had just received bad news.

"Sir . . ."

"Yes, ma'am," I said softly. "I heard you, ma'am. I was just thinking it was a shame to have come all this way and not even have a word with the great man himself. D'you think I could?"

I took a furtive glance down the hall.

"Ohhhh," she said like someone who bought three of the same vowels from that blonde on *Wheel of Fortune*. I could see that we agreed on something. I was still nearly knocked out over the way she had said "we" have no more positions. But we agreed on something now. The "Great Man." Now there was a genuine look of sympathy instead of that other one.

"He's at lunch now," she said, "and . . ."

And he probably had been, more than likely. Except that just at that moment he wheeled around a corner and into the reception area. There was no doubt. Going about no miles per hour was the poet Elliott Coleman.

I wasn't really joking or exaggerating when I had called Elliott Coleman a great man, because for people who knew poetry and knew him, he was a great man, a great poet in terms of his honors and awards, and an extremely nice man as I learned. Here's a rub that relates to appreciation, particularly my appreciation of artists and people. There doesn't seem to be a lot of room available sometimes for me to express appreciation or friendship or an especial fondness for people who are not Black. No, that's not exactly true. The person doesn't have to be Black, he or she just can't be white. My occasional reference to a Mark

Twain or a Harper Lee or an Elliott Coleman or a Robert De Niro or who the fuck ever, if they're not Black it seems at times that I'm not supposed to enjoy them or appreciate their art. I'm sorry. Get over it! 'Scuse me if I'm wrong, but isn't that part of what we were fighting against for years: the fact that no matter how good a brother or sister was, white people would not appreciate them. Wasn't it bass-ackwards (a Black reverse) when we were so thoroughly annoyed by the number of white people who would line up to see Miles Davis or any number of Black artists that we didn't support and didn't seem to claim until it was mentioned that a lot of white people went to their shows? Well, which is it? Or which was it? Yes? No? Maybe? Answer me this: if you're in an accident, God forbid, and you need a blood transfusion, and they bring in five pints of type whatever-you-are, do you seriously give a fuck who gave up the blood or what color the contributor was as long as it is the right color blood? Do you seriously care whether it was a Black man, a white woman, or a purple midget? Type O was what you needed and what you got. Elliott Coleman was not my favorite poet. But Elliott Coleman was a poet emeritus with a long list of awards and honors that people did not give him because there was nobody else available. If you think there's no point to this, take off the George Wallace mask you're wearing; or is that really you pretending to be all the kinds of expressions we claimed we were trying to get rid of or away from? That's carrying nostalgia too far, buddy. Otherwise keep up the good work.

I picked up my little bag of things with my life in it and walked slowly into Dr. Coleman's office as he was crouching into the seat behind his desk. He had obviously heard me coming, so I did not surprise him. The fact that it was me, someone he did not know, might have surprised him. At about six-foot-two plus three inches of Afro, I could have surprised him.

He assumed I was supposed to be there, standing in front of him, because I had gotten past the part of the royal "we" sitting between him and "not we." The fact that he did not know me, that we had not met, scampered across his expression with the speed of an adverb on amphetamines.

He said, "Mister, uh . . ."

"I'm Gil Scott-Heron, sir," I said, extending my hand. "And it's really nice to meet you."

He was either too polite or too tired to follow his first word with another one, so he asked me with his eyes: *And what do you want?*

"Sir, I've been told by your lady out there that you have handed out all of your fellowships, but I need a minute of your time."

I put my two books and an LP in front of him without saying anything right away. He reached for the books first, slowly rubbing a pale, bony finger across the laminated cover of the book on top. He stopped, sat back in the chair a bit, and then pulled a pair of reading half-glasses from his jacket's breast pocket and slowly put them on. He did everything slowly, but was obviously used to it that way, with no irritation or frustration. His fingers looked arthritic, a couple on the right hand permanently bent at the knuckle. He picked up the poetry book, obviously attracted to its unusual shape. He picked up the album briefly and then sat back and looked up at me again speculatively.

"Sir," I said, keeping the respect there in my voice and in my eyes, "I heard the fellowships are gone. All twenty-seven. But I'd like to make a proposal: if any of the twenty-seven you've awarded has done as much work as I have, maybe I don't deserve one like I think I do."

He looked over the glasses at me and reached for the phone, still not giving me a long look or a lot of words.

"This is the first time we've had so many applications," he was saying as he dialed. "The program has become really popular . . . Hello, Stevie? Elliott. I've got a little problem with my numbers. Yes, I do need one I can assure. Well, yes, I'm looking at an extraordinary situation I will explain later. Yes. Yes. Thank you. Thank you, Steve."

And he nodded. Like Uncle Buddy.

22

After Spring semester, 1971, I got a place in Chester, Pennsylvania, until I started at Hopkins in the fall. I finished my second novel, *The Nigger Factory*, there. I got a real kick out of dealing with the New York white folks about the title. It was a goof to hear these oh-so-modern people, who were so articulate, have marbles in their mouths when there was no way to avoid saying the title.

When *Pieces of a Man* came out that summer, FM stations once again got behind our music. The number-one station in Philadelphia, WDAS-FM, had a guy named Dan Henderson working prime time. The station had switched formats early in 1971, and the programming and the style was like a whole new radio thing. Dan used long, interconnecting segues that made his shows like sets. It became the industry standard, but at the time it was brand new to me, and it was perfect for my kind of music. I got a big boost from that station.

Howard University began broadcasting around the same time, and they adopted the same kind of format on their station, but without commercials. It was beautiful: Howard's WHUR-FM was on in every house in D.C. and WDAS was on throughout the Delaware Valley.

That summer, 1971, word reached me that Dan Henderson wanted to speak to me. It was arranged that I would go to the station and do an interview and all. A friend of Dan's picked me up, and he had some herb he called "The One." And it was the One. I smoked a joint and when I sat down on the couch in the lobby at the radio station, I could not get up again. I was not asleep or comatose, I was smoked.

> I was petrified and ossified
> I felt good, but lay out on the couch like a piece of wood
> Engaged in several detailed conversations,
> I could do anything except change my location.
> Answered some questions
> Heard some damn good suggestions

I simply could not move for about two hours. I think it must have been hash oil. When we smoked it we were laughing and having a great time, but I should have never laid down on the One.

Dan passed on some phone numbers because he knew some people who wanted to get in touch with me about gigs; I immediately thought he was a good guy at that first meeting. Not long afterward, he became our manager.

Bob Thiele at Flying Dutchman was anxious to follow up *Pieces of a Man* because it had been another success. For *Free Will*, the next album, we did the songs that we had left and the poems that we hadn't had room for on *Small Talk*. We knew that we were leaving the label; that was the end of my contract. I had signed a three record deal and that's all I had planned to do.

By that time I had a pretty good idea of Bob's focus and what kind of a man he was. Despite our age difference and different lifestyles, we had one major thing in common that made it cool to hang out with him: we both really loved music. He was probably the biggest jazz fan on the planet; he was out there in the middle of things almost every night, doing a session, out at a club catching a set. Still, the single most impressive thing about Bob was how he was able to be comfortable as a celebrity. I don't know how valuable that sounds, but to be honest it was an incredibly important thing to learn, because it became "how to be a celebrity and still be yourself." It was an area of the world I knew little about and looked at with most trepidation. Bob did not allow what people believed his fame deserved. Somehow he stayed within an orbit where he could continue to be himself: a calm, comfortable person who enjoyed himself and enjoyed music. His vibrations defied disruption. I never saw his ego lead him around or elbow his family or friends out of the way.

After Esther Phillips's cover of "Home Is Where the Hatred Is" made the charts, other artists covered more of our songs: Penny Goodwin did "Lady Day and John Coltrane," the Intruders did "Save the Children," LaBelle did "The Revolution Will Not Be Televised." Brian wanted to be a recording artist, make a career of it. But I still wanted to be a novelist. Until the stuff got produced, it hadn't even been important to define myself as this or that. I had a job washing dishes once, but nobody asked me if I was a dishwasher-poet. Until the lyrics were published as songs, nobody ever asked me anything about it. It was just something I liked to do. That hadn't changed. I wanted to continue to write songs, but I didn't see myself as a recording artist.

By the time I received my masters from Hopkins in 1972, my plans as far as where I would go with that MA were sketchy. I knew I wanted to teach, and on the college level. I didn't see myself as a successful or happy person teaching at a lesser level; I had neither the patience nor the disciplinary training to work in classrooms full of high school or junior high students. And I had enjoyed the composition course I ran for undergraduates at Hopkins.

Then one morning I got onto a crowded Amtrak train in Baltimore, bound for New York City to have a conference with Grace Shaw, the lovely woman I had worked with at World Publications on *The Vulture* and at Dial Press on *The Nigger Factory*. I appreciated Grace a great deal as an editor. She had scolded me about the original way I attempted to resolve things in the second novel and I went back to what I had projected as the conclusion in the first place.

It was a midmorning express, and it was too full, oversold with standing room only. I found a spot next to a neatly dressed, well-groomed brother whose face looked familiar. His profile was distinct and, though it took me a second or three, I realized I knew it from the cover of a book called *The Rise and Fall of a Proper Negro: An Autobiography*, that had been published the year before. I was standing next to Leslie Lacy.

He had gotten on in D.C., and was going to New York to visit his publisher. Leslie was Assistant Professor Lacy at Washington's Federal City College. What he described to me as we rode on was close to an ideal situation. Federal City College had been

175

started in 1968 and was still building toward accreditation. There was a clear need in the English department for instructors and particularly instructors with letters, papers, and books that had been published. He was confident that I would be approved for the FCC English department. I agreed to submit a job application.

Once I got the position at Federal City College, Brian and I got a house together in northern Virginia. Leslie and I became good friends and working associates at "the shoe box," the building shaped just that way at E Street and Second Avenue, Northwest. Over the next three years, Brian and I were regular guests at Leslie's apartment on Sixteenth Street. Leslie ended up moving to the Bay Area around the same time I requested a leave of absence from FCC to pursue music full time, which happened when Brian and I were signed by Arista Records.

I was recognized in certain music scenes in D.C., like at Blues Alley or the Cellar Door in Georgetown. But I was more comfortable and more frequently seen near the Georgia Avenue offices of Charisma, the company that became our booking agents. Brian and I became fast friends with Ed Murphy, a great name among the nightlife folks in the District, who owned a supper club between Howard University and the Charisma office.

Ed Murphy was known affectionately among the hustlers as "Eight Ball," and his club was well-serviced and clean. Its location, next to a junkyard, was compensated for by the sheer attraction of the owner to the late-night club folks. In time, Ed began to feature entertainment on the weekends and did a lot of business with Charisma. Freddie Cole, Hugh Masekela, Roy

Ayers, Terry Callier, and Norman Connors played either at the supper club or, later, across the street at the Harambee House. Ed's club was also one of the few venues where piano genius and soulful vocalist Donny Hathaway seemed comfortable and projected the power and sensitivity of his talent.

The people who knew me, either from D.C. performances or as an FCC professor, were familiar faces at Ed's. I could generally count on seeing someone from the English department there, and I could blend in with the folks at the back bar without fanfare.

I think I was a better songwriter when I was teaching writing. When you work on songs, you have to tell stories in a limited number of words, just a few lines. You have to be economical. And when most people talk about good writing, they talk about economy.

Songs began taking shape in D.C. The lyrics to the song "The Bottle" were inspired by a group of alcoholics who gathered each morning outside a liquor store behind the house where Brian and I lived just outside D.C. I went out and met those folks. I found out that none of them had hoped to become alcoholics when they grew up. Things had arrived along the way and turned them in that direction. I discovered one of them was an ex-physician who'd been busted for performing abortions on young girls. There was a military air-traffic controller who'd sent two jets crashing into a mountain one day. He left work that day and never went back. In the song I was saying, *Look, here's a drunk and this is why he is an alcoholic*, instead of just glossing over the problem. I generally used an individual or an individual circumstance as an example of a larger thing.

Alcoholism and drug addiction were both illnesses, but people really only saw the condition and not the illness, so that's why I wrote the lyric from a stark point of reality. I always liked to give a very personal and constructive viewpoint to whatever it was I was writing about.

Dan Henderson, who was still our manager, and his wife, Wilma, eventually moved into the house with me and Brian, too, and in the fall of 1973 we went into D&B Sound in Silver Spring, Maryland, and began recording the album *Winter in America*. D&B was small, but it had a comfortable feeling—and it had Jose Williams as the engineer. The main room was so small that when Brian and I did tunes together, one of us had to go out in the hallway where the water cooler was located. I did vocals for "Song for Bobby Smith" and "A Very Precious Time" from there, and Brian played flute on "The Bottle" and "Your Daddy Loves You" right next to that cooler. A lot of people wanted to know who it was playing flute on "The Bottle," because it wasn't specifically credited on the *Winter in America* album. It was Brian. He also played flute on "Back Home." Those are all his arrangements. By the time we did *Winter in America*, Brian had become a very good flute player. He also played Fender Rhodes on the album. We'd first encountered the instrument five years earlier on Miles Davis's *Miles in the Sky*, but when Brian and I first started we couldn't afford a Fender Rhodes. We'd had a Farfisa, a Wurlitzer, we just put together whatever we could. Now, though, he was hooked on it.

The other people who appeared on the album showed up on the last day. Bob Adams played drums and Danny Bowens bass, and they added one more thing, too. Bob said he was disappointed that the poem I had been doing as an opening monologue in concerts, "The H2Ogate Blues," wasn't on the album. The song was my way of explaining to people outside the Beltway what Watergate was really about. I got a lot of political insight from being in Washington. But the reason I'd left it off the record, I told him, was because nobody outside D.C. seemed to know what the hell I was talking about. He replied that even if people didn't understand the politics, it was still funny as hell. So we set up to do one take, a "live ad-lib" to a blues backing. My description of the colors, the three thousand shades, was off the top of my head, and the poem was done with a few index cards with notes to be sure I got the references straight without stumbling. I still stumbled. After we got through it, we listened to it play back with an open studio mike and became the audience. There were some great comments in the back, particularly during the intro. The poem worked well; it felt like what the album had been missing. Not just the political aspect, but, as Bob had said, for the laughs. The Watergate incident itself was not funny, and neither were its broader implications. But as a release, a relief of tension on *Winter in America*, it provided a perfect landing.

23

Winter in America came out in 1974 and the single, "The Bottle," became a hit for us. The impression people seemed to get of me from my songs was of some wild-haired, wild-eyed motherfucker. Once again, I felt people who wrote about me and Brian should have looked at all that we did. It was pretty obvious that there was an entire Black experience and that it didn't relate only to protest. We dealt with all the streets that went through the Black community, and not all of those streets were protesting.

By the mid-1970s, the middle-class people who were just in the movement for the adventure of the moment had gone on to do whatever it was that middle-class people did. There were still a whole lot of programs in the community that could be effective, but a lot of the people who were aiming their heads toward that when they were in college weren't there anymore. They'd been kidnapped by Exxon. Surviving became the ideal after a while. A whole lot of people got killed, betrayed, or put in jail for talking about helping the community.

Most of the times when people pulled me off to the side at concerts, the songs they wanted to discuss didn't have anything to do with politics—even though those songs were the ones that were most explicit. People wanted to say something about "Your Daddy Loves You," because it seemed to them that we'd written it about them. The songs that people wanted to talk about were the ones that were more personal than political, more private than public, more of an emotion than an issue.

Still, there shouldn't have been any confusion in people's minds about whether or not they were in a fight—all they had to do was to look in their pocketbooks. Somebody done took their motherfucking money. When we got into things that related to politics, a lot of the time people would say, "Man, I'm just interested in cash." And I had to hip people to the fact that if they were interested in money, that was the best reason to get into politics. There was a war going on in this country and you tried to find your best weapon.

I've always looked at myself as a piano player from Tennessee; I play some piano and write some songs. The fact that I've had some political influence is all well and good, but I never considered myself a politician. I never joined any of the political organizations because once you joined one, it made you enemies in another. Various groups argued back and forth and wasted energy that could have been used to try to do something for the community. Which is why I stayed out of most organizations. I wanted to be available to all of them. I played for Shirley Chisholm. I played for Ken Gibson. I played the Nation of Islam's Saviours' Day celebration. I played for anybody who was trying to do something positive for Black people. Just count me in and I'd be there.

One special performance at Ed Murphy's supper club came up in February 1975. For half a year, WHUR, Howard

181

University's radio station, had been broadcasting updates about the case of Joan Little, a sister who in August 1974 had stabbed a prison guard who had tried to rape her in a North Carolina jail. Practically the whole Black population of D.C. was tuned in to WHUR, and its news department kept its finger on the pulse of the community. The Little case was a focus of national attention in Black papers and magazines.

One night I happened to be sitting at a friend's place with Chris Williams, who had closed his club, the Coral Reef, and was looking for a better location for a new one, and Petey Green, one of the true legends of the Washington street, and who had been released from jail and was telling it like it was with his own radio talk show. An update on the Little case came over the radio and Chris said that if he still had his club, he would throw a party and donate the money for the sister's defense fund. Petey agreed. The idea hit us to talk to Ed, and I said I'd have my group play the date if Ed got involved.

Sure enough, things quickly got organized. Ed agreed to donate the venue and we got in contact with WHUR to spread the word. But late January and early February is when Washington gets its harshest weather. The night before the benefit, a snowstorm hit the District and continued through the next morning, forcing us to delay the show until the next night. I had to hastily reorganize things for various members of the Midnight Band whose flights in from New York and Boston had been cancelled.

The next night the crowd came tiptoeing carefully through lanes cleared through the accumulated snow plowed to the sides of Georgia Avenue. The supper club was not a huge place, but

182

some of my favorite places to play were smaller, more intimate venues, like Ed's or Blues Alley in D.C., Al Williams's Birdland West in Long Beach, S.O.B.'s on Varick Street in New York, and First Avenue, the Minneapolis club Prince later made famous. We played two sets, and at the end of a successful evening we stood in small clusters of five and six while Ed and the hosts shuffled through the cash, deducting the expenses for the service staff and cleanup crew. They finally emerged reporting a clear profit of $2,300 for the defense of Miss Little.

Something real good happened then. Two hustlers, street brothers who will remain nameless, though they were recognized and answered to fairly descriptive nicknames, came out of their huddle briefly. Each of them had a hundred dollar bill in his hand.

"Make it a straight up twenty-five hundred," one of them growled as though raising the bet at a poker table.

Ed took the bills they offered and called for the bartender to pour them another as they put their heads together again in their corner.

There were a lot of things that a lot of diverse people had in common in those days. Russell Means, who was head of the American Indian movement, had a lot in common with Joan Little, who had a lot in common with Inez Garcia, who had a lot in common with the San Quentin Six; all of them were symbols of how America needed to change but had not.

The reality, of course, was that the people were not helpless or defenseless or without the means to effect change. It was just that nobody was going do everything; we were trying to say to brothers and sisters, *Let's pool our energies and talents and try to get all of this here, instead of the little bit you might be able to get on the corner.*

I was trying to get people who listened to me to realize that they were not alone and that certain things were possible.

24

I had continued teaching through the end of 1974. But Brian and I had started working on a new album to follow up *Winter in America*. And we played a lot of live shows.

Dan Henderson invited Clive Davis to come to a show at the Beacon Theater in New York City. We'd heard that Clive was starting a new company called Arista. What we didn't know was that Clive was already scouting us for the label—turned out he really dug "The Bottle." I had never met the man until he walked into the Beacon.

Dan was just salivating—and nervous. He was like a long-tailed cat in a room full of rocking chairs, and the guys in the band were all talking about it before Clive's arrival. You had to know Dan to know how unusual it was for him to be excited or nervous—anything except extremely fucking cool.

Clive showed up at the Beacon and saw what we did and how we did it. Physically, he was not imposing. But there was definitely a power there, a magnetic shimmer. He was an Aries, and maybe it was nothing more than an extra luster to the aura of the fire at his core. In reality, I don't know what it was; maybe he only seemed to have that something to me because his history preceded him and caused the curious—like me—to look for it. But it was there when he mixed with other people and the world.

He looked different from Bob Thiele, whose wardrobe was casual without looking hippie or bohemian—jacket but no tie, cords not jeans. Clive Davis was always dressed and pressed: tailor made, expensive materials, understated but obvious at the same time, and even after hours he dressed nine-to-five. Also, unlike Bob Thiele, whom everyone called Bob, Clive was always Mr. Davis.

I think Clive had already made up his mind, because talks progressed quickly after the show. The music trade papers made a big deal of the fact that we were the first act signed to Arista, because they were all waiting to see what Clive would do when he got back into the business. But I don't think it was too significant. We were available and we had been working on new material.

Graduating from Flying Dutchman to Arista meant an elevation to another level of visibility. I went to a couple of concerts with Clive during the next few months. Very early on in our relationship he took me to see Elton John at Madison Square Garden. I think he was trying to show me what he saw me doing without making that speech.

The first time I went to his office, it was still down at 1776 Broadway and posters of Tony Orlando and Al Wilson— remaining traces of his previous label—were still on the wall. He had his feet up on the desk, talking freely about the future of his new company. By the next time I visited him, he was up at 6 West 57th Street, a street as closely associated with the music business as Madison Avenue was with advertising. Clive's new offices occupied an entire building as far as I could tell, and they were also fully staffed, with all the clamor of a big city newsroom, bright as daylight with fluorescent tubes running the length of the pathways between cubicles. Clive was still at ease.

I was the de facto leader of the Midnight Band, but that was a longer way than anyone seemed to understand from 57th Street. The band members felt I had talked my way into publishing houses with my manuscript; I had talked my way into Flying Dutchman and a record deal and I had talked on my first record; I had talked my way into Johns Hopkins and a masters degree. As far as they were concerned, all I needed was someone's attention for a few minutes and I would talk them into anything. While I appreciated their confidence, I felt it was misplaced. My most outstanding liability was that I was naïve. In my life, I was appreciated for my honesty. However, in the record business I was finding that honesty was a missing component.

On 57th Street, which was supposed to be the new launching pad for my career and for the Midnight Band, I came to see how most artists were viewed: expendable, easily replaced by others. At the Arista office I could hear and feel that I was around music people; they liked music and gave you a feeling about what their homes and lives were like. At other places, like the Copyright Services Bureau, an office full of entertainment lawyers Clive approved of, the atmosphere was totally different, with the *click-clack* of typewriters and the hum of copier machines. All those lawyers and managers and accountants were as thoroughly plugged into the music business as the aorta is to the heart, but with a cynicism and disdain that made me think at times that they didn't care for either singers or music.

On 57th Street, they could see money coming. See it the way a trainer can see a colt's time for one and a quarter miles when it first puts its weight on legs as wobbly as wet straws. Smell it the way farmers can smell rain that's still two days in the distance. Feel it the way a grandma can feel that same rain from an equal distance in the marrow of her bones. And even taste it the way standing outside a bakery makes your mouth water. If you were part of a record company on 57th Street, you were on the money, part of the bedrock of the biz. Or at least you were eligible. This was the inside of the inside.

I didn't feel like a part of a profession—not one that mattered to the busy folks with briefcases banging their knees and thighs as they half-walked, half-trotted everywhere they went. It wasn't just that I was Black, though that was never far from my consciousness; I felt like an undercover man who had shown up without his cover. Even anesthetized by good Colombian weed, I felt tense and out of place, and it was because I really was. I wasn't unfamiliar with New York—just this part of New York, midtown. I had a house in Virginia, roughly three hundred miles south of 57th Street. In Virginia I could think. I could sit in the yard with a glass of tea and a book in the afternoon. In Virginia I could continue to write the songs and poems that people enjoyed and made me happy.

But whether I liked it or not, I began to have to spend more time on West 57th Street. More than a certainty that I had the business expertise to direct our group, the band members figured I was the only one who really had the time. After all was said and done, I was the one who essentially had no life. The New York guys, Adenola, Bilal Sunni-Ali, and "Cosmic" Charlie, all had families and other vocations. There had never been any commitment on their part to full-time pursuit of positions in the record business. They all loved to play music. They made as many concessions as they could to band rehearsals, making the gigs, and teaching us all what the rhythms meant and how they could be used to help us say things. Victor Brown lived and worked in Boston. Brian, Doc, Danny, and Bob Adams lived and maintained their lives in and around D.C. They were all intelligent, with degrees and other professional expertise where college degrees would not benefit you, but none of them had either the interest, the expertise, or the independent image separate from their contribution to the group to be recognized as a spokesperson for all of us. Especially to speak for me.

Arista started releasing records on January 1, 1975, and brought out our album *The First Minute of a New Day* on January 15, 1975, making it the first minute of a new day for Clive Davis, too.

I had to take a leave of absence from Federal City College, which eventually became permanent. What I had once dreamed about—contributing to the Midnight Band when I could free myself from my teaching and writing—was impossible. I had mixed feelings about leaving the place just as it was combining with D.C. Teachers and the Washington School of Technology to become the University of D.C., but the problem was success. *The First Minute of a New Day* hit the charts and remained on them for weeks and months.

189

While our new lawyers at the Copyright Services Bureau negotiated a deal for me to do a movie score not long after the release of the album, I was back in New York, staying at the Salisbury Hotel. After a day of trying to satisfy the brilliant choreographer George Faison with rhythm for a proposed dance number, I stumbled back to the hotel and almost had a heart attack.

I had already turned the key to let myself into the room when I realized several things: (1) Someone had been in my room, (2) Someone had been smoking marijuana and (3) They were still there. I felt like a cheap, condensed version of "The Three Bears," some production that could only afford one bear.

I wasn't in much of a mood for figuring shit out but I figured that if they were Spirits I could negotiate with them because they smoked reefer. (It did cross my mind that I had left some excellent reefer in a shoe box under my bed. But no matter.)

> These had to be some damn bold thieves
> To come in my room and just roll up their sleeves
> And probably some of my Colombian weed
> And not even have the decency to leave.

I decided it was either Manny Lopes or Norris Little, the head of Charisma, because whoever it was had to have heard me turn the key in the lock and heard me come in and there hadn't been any response. So I turned the corner into the main part of my living quarters where four dread brothers were busy with a great quantity of reefer on a newspaper in the middle of the floor. They barely noticed me come in. One of them, the one I recognized, was Bob Marley.

The dread brothers were fairly cordial. Truth was, they didn't know whose room it was. Or that it was the room of one particular person. Nor did they particularly care. They had been out in Central Park playing soccer until their package arrived and were offered the key to this hotel room until their rooms were ready. I had the impression that I could join them if I wanted to, and would be welcome to share a little herb; but that was all. I never got the impression that they gave a damn that it was *my* room. And they probably shouldn't have. After all, wouldn't I have said, "Make yourselves at home"? And hadn't they? Was there a rule that said they had to ask first? Did it matter which order the making-yourself-at-home thing had to follow? Evidently not.

I did notice a nasty looking gash on Bob's toe, however, and spoke on it. "Seems like you need to do something about that toe, my man."

I just kind of threw that out there as the first wave of making-yourself-at-home crept into my attitude.

"The doctor give him somethin'."

One of the brothers offered around a joint as thick as a sausage.

"But him ol' head too hard to use 'im what it got."

Bob was sprawled across the floor, propped on one elbow. He waved his man off.

"Jah heal," he assured me. "Jah put t'ing for healin'."

"Jah might've put that doctor here for healing," I offered. "Jah's gotta be mighty busy."

"Jah heal," was Bob's last comment on the subject.

And for whatever reason my mind works the way it does because I found myself looking at their soccer ball and thinking, *He takes a licking and keeps on kicking*. And then my mind moved on.

25

Less than a year after Clive had decided to start the label, Arista was the fifth biggest music company in the world. So in September 1975, the Midnight Band played two shows at Madison Square Garden as part of a celebration of the label's successful first year of operations. It was as if Clive had decided to let New York celebrate his anniversary. To cover the whole day he planned one show in the afternoon and one at night.

I used to minimize the importance of playing at Madison Square Garden and swear that it was no big deal. It was a big deal. I was forced to face that long before I stepped into the place as a piano-playing band leader. The first time had been as a basketball player in my last year at Fieldston. What I most remembered about that season was that we should have been conference champions. But we weren't.

I had never been sure who arranged for Fieldston to play against Collegiate, one of our conference rivals, in the earliest of three games that started at about five o'clock. There was an NBA doubleheader afterward, with Detroit against somebody in the first game and the New York Knickerbockers playing against somebody else in the second game. I would be there late.

I think we lost the game. I know I had one of my worst games, fumbling and juggling my way up and down in near arctic cold; trying to dribble around a few dozen dead spots hiding among the loose floorboards like spiders in the corners of an old house. The cold seemed to wrap around my legs and ankles like a frozen blanket, compliments of the ice beneath the boards that the New York Rangers skated across during hockey games. That experience raised my level of respect for professional basketball players. And hockey players, since I figured the skating surface was probably in no better shape than the basketball court.

Madison Square Garden was not a great concert venue, either. I used to say as part of my evaluation of the Garden that when you played there you sounded like the Knicks. That wisecrack ignored the fact that New York had some of the best sound technicians and concert producers in the world. And not only were they the most proficient, they were almost always that way in a New York minute, because that's how long it took them to change sets between acts and get your sound in house order. A New York minute.

For some reason that Clive Davis kept to himself, I was back with the jazz artists and put on during the afternoon slate of the Arista celebration. To tell the truth, since Clive had come to see us after hearing "The Bottle" and shown interest in "Ain't No Such Thing as Superman," I had not known where we would play. But I had anticipated it would be whenever Clive expected people who had danced to "The Bottle" would be in attendance. That was the song we'd been asked to play on a TV special a few months before, which had also been a celebration of Arista artists. But Brian and I had also played with Ron Carter and Hubert Laws at Flying Dutchman, and, in spite of split airplay, that made us jazz in certain industry circles. So we were lined up to play on the program with Anthony Braxton and Oliver Lake and other innovative Arista artists. No problem.

There had been no real question that I was being presented for my literary background when *Small Talk at 125th and Lenox* was released. The fact that I was back in classes at Lincoln and had written a novel and a book of poetry was emphasized. The *Small Talk* liner notes were taken from a conversation I had with Nat Hentoff, a sensitive man with both literary and music credentials. And the first media appearances I made were with Father O'Connor, the "jazz priest" on WRVR-FM and on a radio show hosted by Mr. Ossie Davis and Miss Ruby Dee, featuring a conversation about writing novels with John A. Williams and John Oliver Killens.

The small success of the poetry album and the larger audience of the album of songs, *Pieces of a Man*, brought critics and largely critical journalists back to me with "who are you?" type questions: "How do you see yourself?" for instance, or "Are you jazz or poet or singer or . . . ?"

I had started looking for them to ask, "Vegetable or mineral?"

Every answer that I tried to supply inspired more questions. My problem was that I had thought when I finished the album it would be their job to say what it was and, if necessary, what I was.

As I started doing more press as a result of working with Arista, it became obvious that I hadn't taken a long view of how

I would handle these types of questions. They started coming with an attitude: "Who do you think you are?"

And they weren't going for, "Just a piano player from Tennessee." But I admired Langston Hughes, a man who set no limits on himself. And I didn't want to get stuck doing one thing, either. One of the things that was evident to me way back when I'd gotten into John Coltrane's music was that you had to keep reaching. I think when you stop reaching, you die. It's like Earl Weaver, the longtime manager of the Baltimore Orioles, once said: "It's what you learn after you know it all that really counts." After you think you have accomplished something, there's a tendency to relax. There's always a need for you to feel there's something else you need to do, something else you need to grasp.

The night of the Arista celebration at the Garden we played again, this time with the more pop program. I could claim that Clive thought the Midnight Band was like New York, New York, so nice he had to let us play twice. But that wouldn't be quite accurate. After the first show, with the jazz artists, Clive's right-hand man caught up with us in front of the venue and told us that Eric Carmen's truck had turned over on the New Jersey Turnpike and that Clive needed us to play again.

When we walked back in later that night, this time without a stage diagram or a sound check, the union sound man pulled me over and said, "Hey, Gil, have we got the same stage set up?"

When I nodded, he walked away. And when we came out to play after one of those ten-minute set changes, the lights were correct, the equipment was on spot, and the house sound and monitors were in sync from the first note. A New York piece of business.

26

I have never been very fond of doing interviews. I suppose that has been apparent to some of the people who have interviewed me. The only reason I'm using qualifying words like "very" is because there were some interviews that were actually fun to do and I did enjoy them. I have always enjoyed talking to Brother Imhotep, aka Gary Byrd, no matter what radio station or TV show he was working for. Why? Because it was always live and not fake. What do I mean by fake? Easy. Sheets of paper and notebooks full of questions that always make me feel like this person isn't really familiar with my music, doesn't put my records on the box, doesn't read my books, and couldn't pick me out of a lineup without a cheat photo they looked at before they looked through the one-way mirror. I was not comfortable when the questions were prepared. If the questions were coming from a list and there was nothing live going on, the interviewer might as well mail me the list of questions and let me mail it back.

When the interviewer had a tape recorder I felt like I needed to have one, too. Just because there had been so many little things that I read back in magazines that were just flat-out wrong. I hadn't gotten any ugly vibes from the guy or the woman during the interview; a lot of the time what I said just got "lost in transcription." It was not enough for the transcribers to have ears like an eagle. They needed ears like a Heron, and a sense of humor like a Heron, too, because that's where most of the distortions and missed portions took place. Not only do I have a voice with a low end that rumbles along like a subway car with a flat wheel, the way I combine English with American with street and slang and all them whatevers disoriented transcribers and I guess they were tilted so often they just settled for what it sounded like.

It's not like I was deliberately throwing the transcribers off track. Hell, I wasn't talking to them. I didn't know them. I didn't even know they were listening. The only person I was talking to, or thought I was talking to, were the people doing the interviews. If they didn't say "What?" or "What did you say?" I had to believe I'd been understood. For somebody in the recording business, I had very little faith in some of those little cute-ass tape recorders sitting on a table. I'll tell you something else. Here's a word to remember, especially about cassettes: calibration. I had another show at the Beacon Theater with Grover Washington and my regular bass player couldn't make it. But he was rooming with a friend of his in D.C. who also played bass. That friend told me he knew my songs, said he'd been listening to my stuff for two weeks, practicing. So I said okay, great. He meets us in New York and every tune is a fucking disaster. Every tune! He was playing everything about a note and a half higher than we were. It was because of calibration. Cassettes played higher. In fact, they played even faster when plugged into the wall than when played with batteries.

The truth about interviews? Unless they're done live, it's just damn hard to trust them. Plus, when you were on the radio with Imhotep you got to talk to people who called in with questions. That was always fun. I swear, that's how it was with me; I started to want my records to be live, too. I had some good things from the studio, but looking back I love things like *It's Your World*, recorded in Boston on July 4, 1976, and *Tales of the Amnesia Express*, recorded live in Europe.

I did interviews live on foreign TV shows, too. The first was a French show. It was like roller skating through a minefield with a blindfold on. I wore a hearing aid and took my seat at a table with the other guests after we played our song. The host asked me a question in French. The interpreter told me the question in English through the hearing aid. I answered the question in English and a French translation of the answer was broadcast to the studio audience. It was a strange experience.

Shows were very different in different countries. The shows we did in England were on the BBC without commercials. I performed in front of a studio audience in a room that felt like a warehouse or an airplane hangar. In Germany we performed on a show called *Ohne Filter*, which means "without a filter," live. All the groups that were going to be on the show set up in this large studio on separate stages, four or five groups, and the cameras and crew went around from band to band.

There was a live TV show in Barcelona, Spain, that was really wild. It was a combination of talk and performances, and it was broadcast live. We had a dress rehearsal during the day and I was damn sure the show wasn't going to work. The whole thing was like a dyslexic fire drill. We went through all three of the tunes we were going to play, and I saw cameras swinging past on cranes and other cameramen with handhelds walk through, never stopping, and leave. When we finished the rehearsal, the director said, "Thank you, Gil, that was great."

I said, "*De nada, amigo.*" To myself I was thinking, *This is crazy.*

But they weren't crazy and I hadn't seen nothing yet. They were professionals who did the show every week and knew exactly what they were doing. They also knew something about this evening's show that I didn't know. They were presenting another group on that night's slate, a dance group whose leading dancer and spokesperson was a transsexual. The group came on right before us and we watched her numbers from a balcony box. Their most interesting piece was a choreographed number where each verse ended with a double bump and the leader's breasts hopped out of her outfit on the last beat. Every time. And the studio audience roared. Every time. Obviously there was nothing we could do to compete with that.

At Arista, the company's publicity was supplemented by a Black firm from Los Angeles. A good brother named Bob Brock, who I really came to appreciate, took every opportunity I gave him to put me somewhere that Black folks would see my picture and connect it to my records. It was Brock who set up a tour of the new Johnson Publishing building in downtown Chicago in 1976. He promised a lot of painless publicity. He probably would have been right if my touring partner had not had a big hit called "Love to Love You, Baby," as redundant a lyric to hit the public since "Amen."

A woman led us through the corridors to the small squares cut out of the walls where we would shake hands with mystified employees. She was not impressed. She dutifully tried on a smile that stretched as tight as a drum skin across the bottom of her face. By the fifth or sixth cubicle, she had organized our introductions into a kind of rhythmic mantra she could recite on automatic pilot: "Donna-Summer-love-to-love-you-baby-Gil-Scott-Heron-Johannesburg." I didn't think she was going to make it. I didn't think I would.

What I got was a whirlwind of revolving doors with thin brown arms attached to dozens of weak handshakes. Sometimes there was a glimpsed almost-a-smile on someone's face but by noon everybody's handshakes were limp and loose and every smile was mechanical. Occasionally, once or twice on each floor, one of the two photographers on duty would eel his way through a cluster of rubbernecking assistants and jam folks together like flowers in a bouquet and request—or demand—a "smile!" then blind us and disappear.

This would eventually provide the payoff as a "photo of the month" in *Jet* magazine a couple of pages after some secretary in a swimsuit. It also paid off in another story in another Johnson publication about the "Miracle on Michigan Avenue," the Johnson Building itself, which I must admit was a beautiful, solid piece of architecture that upgraded the downtown area and provided many jobs for young Black media aspirants.

The building tour was over at half past noon, and I got off the elevator on the floor that was marked cafeteria and walked into a thoroughly different aspect of Johnson Publishing.

It would be too simple to say it was "different from upstairs." I expected the lighter, brighter atmosphere and a hum of conversation between diners. What I could never have anticipated were the two ladies in charge. They ran the line of diners along the rails with personal, down-home good humor and an efficiency that would have stood them in good stead with Chrysler or Boeing. They knew who I was and what I'd just been through and added their own "special" iced tea for "loosenin' up jaws that been smilin' too much." I found a small table for one between the main section of tables and the food line, feeling better and more comfortable by the second. Those ladies had no idea that they had just saved Bob Brock a tremendous cussin' out.

That was when I saw one of my real heroes. The owner and publisher and one-time sole representative of soul magazines, Mr. John Johnson. Here, for me, was a real Chicago celebrity.

As a child, when I'd visited my mother on Sixty-eighth Street between Wabash and Michigan, the neighborhood had been changing into a magnet for the upwardly mobile and quite a few celebrities and famous faces; I met Cubs pitcher "Sad" Sam Jones and Olympic hero Jesse Owens, whose feats in Berlin over those two weeks in 1936 were tremendous, winning four gold medals in the House of Racism in front of a hundred thousand fanatic followers of a religion of hate who believed him less than human. Haters. That was pressure. And I applaud every reference to his courage and dedication to athletic excellence.

But my admiration for Mr. John Johnson was special and personal. Not just because I got to see a few lines I might have said paraphrased as "the quote of the week" from time to time. What I really appreciated was that when Mr. Johnson was probably still working for enough profit to reclaim his mother's furniture, he wrote about my father.

Looking at John Johnson, I had that autograph impulse again. The first time I was on both radio and television I'd had it, too. On Ossie and Ruby's radio show with John Killens and John Williams I'd wanted autographs. On Joe Franklin's *Memory Lane* I'd had a seat next to Elvin Jones and I'd wanted to say "sign this, sir" instead of "nice to meet you." In the meantime, I'd met Quincy Jones, Miles Davis, Roland Kirk, Chico Hamilton, Gato Barbieri. Man, I'm telling you, I could have had a great collection. But I had tried to get over it.

Mr. Johnson strode full of energy through the cafeteria in his own business, tossing small waves and hellos as he passed. He included me in the waves and when I stood he took a second look and we stepped toward each other.

"How are you, son? Scott-Heron isn't it?"

"Yes, sir."

"I heard you were having a look around."

"Yes, sir, it's very impressive. I just came through to see if I could get a write-up in *Ebony* like the one you did for my father."

That comment brought the publisher's eyes up sharply as he took a closer look at me.

"Your father?"

"Yes, sir," I cut in trying to joke. "Named after me and featured in a nice article you wrote in '47 or '48."

"Scott-Heron," he said, trying to place the name.

"No, sir, his name was Gil Heron, not Scott-Heron. He played soccer for a team here and you wrote him up."

"We should go and take a look," he said, looking at my tray.

"Oh, I'm finished. I couldn't eat another bite."

It was a good time to move along. I could sense other folks feeling as though they might approach and I understood why he was setting such a brisk pace across the cafeteria. At the same pace we moved along toward what Mr. Johnson called "the morgue."

It wasn't quite that bad. That's one of those publishing words they used to refer to where the history of the publication was kept. In a subbasement of the building were two huge rooms. One was stacked with file cabinets full of microfilm and the second was even cooler, with actual copies of the magazine lying across rollers in perfect condition.

It didn't take him long to find the right light switch and come up with index information that led us to the right aisle and the right roll, and I saw a cover I recognized too late to say anything except, "Yep, that's it."

Whatever strategy might have been used to minimize my curiosity about Gil during my childhood, it had been effective. Any question I asked about him was answered immediately, honestly, and without negative connotations, but only that. There was nothing further. As a result I knew little beyond that old three-page story in *Ebony*. Otherwise, I saw only the same half-dozen photos in the family album. There was no real incentive to maintain concern about him, no more than my curiosity about my grandfather or my grandmother's parents. He just wasn't important.

So imagine my surprise when I arrived at a place where he was important. It was the beginning of a European tour that would take in seven countries over a three-week span. The dates began and ended in England, but in between the opening shows in northern England and the closing five days in London's Jazz Café, we had three days in Scotland and then shows in Belgium, Austria, West Germany, Switzerland, and Paris. For the most part we played medium-sized clubs or midsized concert halls.

We arrived in England on a Tuesday and were picked up and taken to the hotel. While the band and crew got organized for sound check, I checked my phone messages and ran up an exorbitant phone bill. (Hotels in the United States charged by the sentence back then; in Europe it was by the word. Sometimes I made calls over there and was totally speechless. At other times I should have been.) Two of the messages were from a guy who was promoting the shows in Glasgow, Edinburgh, and Aberdeen, Scotland. His calling me, twice, wasn't real good news. I called him.

"I need some help," he said. "Edinburgh's okay, but the other two are weak. I need you to do some radio and press. I need you to do two phone interviews tomorrow for weekend editions, and do you have any objection to live TV? I've got to let them know today."

"Any time after noon would be good for the phoners," I said. "As for the live TV I can do it, but if they want a song before dark I'll play and *you* can sing—my voice is on a vampire schedule, no appearances during the day."

"No, no singing, but it's a good show for promotion. And we'll probably need a lot of things during the day Friday, okay?"

I made a train reservation for an early whistle out of Manchester for Glasgow on Friday morning. The band could hold on for the minibus while I got up with the sun and did the rails north.

When I arrived in Glasgow, the promoter met me smiling and styling, looking good in a sports jacket and feeling good for a reason.

"All three shows are sold out. All the press is done. You just need to be there today for *Glasgow at Five*. And be ready to talk about football."

He meant soccer, the world's football. But why the hell would I need to talk about it? What would I say? Do Cole Porter: "I get no kick . . ."

He handed me a newspaper. On a page he had marked was a full-page story on me, my music, and my albums. And there was a picture of a young man in uniform kicking a soccer ball. "The Black Arrow," said the caption. It was a picture of my father.

The most intriguing question on *Glasgow at Five* on the evening of my appearance could have been "how could the son of the Black Arrow not know what a bull's-eye is?" But because the promoter had told me to be prepared to talk about football, I was prepared. A little bit. I knew Pelé wasn't spelled P-A-Y-L-A-Y.

Still, the more detailed the questions on football they asked me, the more likely it would be that their television audience would call in for a DNA test. Huge questions would be raised about my right to be an Arrowhead.

It was too bad I wasn't a big star who could tell these folks what questions to ask. Too bad this wasn't the old days of television when the phony quiz shows "prepared" their contestants by giving them the answers in advance. I would have been willing to pause dramatically while some "thinking" music played. And then, just when it looked as though I was stumped, I would bring on my big hundred-watt "aha!" before I gave the right answer.

The promoter had told me the combination of elements on this show would be a Scottish orgasm: there would be talk about soccer, nostalgia about soccer, and living evidence that they had never allowed their racism to interfere with soccer. It was just like they'd been telling all the other Europeans: "You can carry that racism thing too far, you know." Too far would be if it interfered with soccer, particularly anything that delayed or brought any controversy to how the Scots maintained their interest in the most intense rivalry in sports, Celtic (Glasgow's Catholic team) versus Rangers (the team favored by the city's Protestants).

I listened in from backstage to the charming and amusing recollections of the team captain of Celtic during my father's tenure. He had been invited in for the show. I don't mean to give you the impression that I was nervous. Because I wasn't. And to prove to all of Scotland that they couldn't unnerve me, on my way to the TV station I had stopped by a sporting goods store. You don't have to be prepared to understand the rivalry between Celtic and Rangers, but maybe you have to be a little something to come onstage wearing a Celtic scarf and a Rangers hat. I'd bought them at the sporting goods store. I pretended not to notice the director and cameraman collapsing with laughter.

27

I met Lurma Rackley at a club in Georgetown, Washington, D.C., when a friend introduced us. I was enchanted, impressed, captivated, fascinated, all within the first fifteen minutes. She was kind, beautiful, warm, intelligent, had a lovely smile and a pleasant sense of humor, and she gave you her total attention when she spoke to you. And she got all of my corny jokes.

When we'd met I was still teaching at Federal City College and living in northern Virginia; she was a journalist living on Georgia Avenue. We'd begun to see each other regularly. My music career was doing quite well, and I was traveling a lot with the Midnight Band, but by 1976 Lurma and I were a recognized pair.

We both believed she could not have children, even though I knew she loved children and had wanted a family. But she must have discovered she was pregnant in late August or early September of 1976—without ever telling me—and suddenly I could not get in touch with her and didn't know why. I was confused at first, and then upset and a little angry. She could have told me if she had someone else. I decided she would have to get in touch with me.

Washington was a major city, but really a small town with a thick grapevine. In mid-1977 I heard that Lurma had given birth to a son. At first I dismissed the idea as absurd. Then, on accepting it, I concluded that she indeed must have found someone else. And I gave up waiting for a call or explanation or reprieve.

I met Brenda Sykes in November of 1977. She came to a show of ours at the Roxy, with her former UCLA classmate Kareem Abdul-Jabbar. Kareem and I went all the way back to his days at the Dyckman Houses, where I worked as a summer gardener. We had also seen each other around various basketball courts in the summer when folks were calling me "Little Lou." I'd had a decent game as a two guard, but two years playing forward at Fieldston, at six-foot-three, did my ballhandling and jump shot no good. Kareem had told Brenda we were friends, and she had asked to go with him to a show next time we played in L.A.

We were doing a run of shows at the Roxy, and had two that Thursday night. Kareem brought Brenda backstage between them. Naturally I recognized her. Aside from having seen her in a couple of movies, her picture regularly appeared in Black magazines. She honestly looked better in person. She had beautiful eyes and a lovely smile, and seemed sincere when she said she had enjoyed the show.

They had to leave because Kareem was in training, but I made a point of inviting Brenda back when she could see both shows. Later in the week, she did come back.

In December 1978 we decided to get married, and when we were planning the wedding we had to call Kareem up about the date, to be sure he was free. It had to be a day when he had no game, he was in town, and he had time, because I wanted him to be my best man.

Not long after Brenda and I were married, we decided to have a child, and Gia, our daughter, was a couple of months old when Lurma came by my house on Martha's Road in Alexandria with Rumal. I had never seen the boy, but I didn't need DNA confirmation to know he was my son. He looked exactly like pictures I'd seen of myself on the front porch in Jackson at his age.

Lurma had a request.

"I came to ask you not to tell anyone that he's your son," she said, and the expression on her face was so serious that I never hesitated to give my word.

I was so stunned at the sight of this pint-sized me running around on stubby little legs in front of my house that I don't really remember if anything else was said.

And then they were gone, turning left and around the circle that was Martha's Road. The whole event might have lasted three or four minutes, but I stood out front there for a long time reviewing what I had seen, what she had said, and what I had promised.

Over the following years I fell into a pattern, even after I left Brenda and Gia on Martha's Road and moved into my own studio apartment. When I was approached and the subject of a son in Virginia was broached, I laughed it off as though the question was a joke, nothing serious, nothing real, nothing I ever gave a legitimate response to.

I never mentioned Rumal to anyone. I never talked about him with Brenda. My mother remained a close spirit despite living in New York while I bounced around D.C. and Virginia and eventually headed west, but I never even got close to a discussion with her about her grandson.

I rarely went a long time without wondering how Lurma was doing and how my mini-me was coming along, but it would be many years before I found out.

28

One thing Clive Davis pounded into my head from our first meeting at Arista was that any act that wanted to get out of nickel-and-dime clubs and into major concert halls needed to have an AM radio hit, a single, a top-ten single that made the music directors and radio disc jockeys throw your vinyl on the turntable every two hours or so. A song like "The Bottle" or "The Revolution Will Not Be Televised."

In 1978 we got that kind of play with "Angel Dust." And because of that tune we found ourselves featured as the second act on a three-act R&B get-together with Lakeside and Rose Royce at the Centroplex in Baton Rouge, Louisiana.

The Centroplex was located near the campus of Louisiana State University. The huge, sprawling institution was the size of a small city and practically guaranteed a sellout for major concert acts.

At about 4 p.m. that afternoon we sauntered into the near-empty auditorium and made our way to the dressing rooms. That is, all except Keg Leg, whom we left with the house "bumpers," the guys who were there to lift equipment onto the twelve-foot-high stage on a hydraulic lift.

I never had officially determined the exact spelling for the name I'd given the head of my road crew. I suppose it was two words—Keg Leg—rather than Kegleg. It might have become moot after everyone, including his mother and his wife, cut it down to Keg. Whatever the spelling, he was my man.

One of my unofficial titles with the Midnight Band might have been Dispenser of Nicknames. It was a labor of love, something I did automatically at times, primarily for the humor. It was a habit I'd picked up at Lincoln, where almost everyone was known by a nickname, so much so that when the person's real name was needed a lot of folks drew a blank. As a freshman, when I'd run for class president and the names of those elected were posted, several upperclassmen wondered what happened to Spiderman when they read that Gil Heron had been elected. On my floor in the dormitory I had a Hawk, a Taboo, a Butterball, and a Bird, and I had established a number of handles for members of the Midnight Band as well. Barnett Williams was the Doctor, Charlie Saunders was Cosmic Charlie, and Brian Jackson was Stickman; along with Keg Leg those were my most successful as they extended beyond their associations with the group.

At the Centroplex that afternoon, I forget what occupied my thoughts for that first hour or so, but I do remember looking up and seeing Keg making his way toward me.

"Boss," he whispered in his own hoarse way, "how bad do we need this gig?"

It was so direct and off the wall that I didn't speak right away.

214

I am not easy to surprise. I admit that I am no Uncle Buddy with a nod and a polite "thank you" with a bee stinger in my eye, but I am not one to give you a frozen-faced grimace and silent scream if the unexpected shows up either. I had seen one of our percussionists come out of a darkened bathroom after starting to brush his teeth with Preparation H. I had seen the expression on a D.C. executive's face after he mistook a solid piece of Colombian cocaine for a throat lozenge and popped it into his mouth. In fact, speaking of cocaine, I had been in a living room in Southeast D.C. when a brother in too much of a hurry tried to pour a half ounce of powder through a wet strainer.

Keg Leg, with his barrel-shape body set solidly on legs that were as sturdy looking as rolling logs, constantly left me with a smile or a head shaking with disbelief. He was one of the most definite Aries I had ever met, but I am positive that the spontaneous way he responded to circumstances had never been predetermined by the proclivities of his astrological placement. The things he said and the moves he made automatically prepared me, but I was not ready for "How bad do we need this gig?"

"Well, uh, we need 'em all," I managed quietly. "But not if it's a situation we can't handle," I continued vaguely.

"Thank you, boss."

Whatever response he was looking for must have been hidden in what I had answered. Because without further syllables he turned his hat around backward and headed back out the door with all of us trailing in a ragged line behind him.

His destination was definite and direct. Striding with as much speed as his short legs would manage, he left the dressing room and headed straight down the center aisle toward the stage. Standing in the center of the stage, directing the four-man Rose Royce road crew, was one of the largest brothers I had ever seen outside of a wrestling ring. He was a good half a foot over six feet, and had left three hundred and fifty pounds far behind.

Keg Leg was headed straight for him. He started up with what for him was a scream.

"Listen you big . . ." I didn't catch the last word.

"First I'm kickin' your ass and the rest a y'all get on line!"

He couldn't have brought much more shock to that stage if he had started speaking the Gettysburg Address. With the conclusion of the announcement, Keg stepped directly to the giant road boss, placed his huge head into the center of the man's chest, and started to back him across the stage.

"Yo, yo!" the big brother called out, taking another quick step back. "What the hell . . ."

Keg was adamant.

"I told you when them humpers started packin' they stuff! I told you when you made them put my stuff back down on the floor! That's what the hell they in here for. I had everything onstage and you made 'em take it down. Screw you! I ain't liftin' that shit back up here. I'm kickin' yo' ass, you sumbitch, and then everybody who don't like it!"

"Wait up. Hold it!"

It was all the big man could do to look around Keg at the rest of his men.

"A.J.," he called to one. "I want you guys to put their stuff back up here. Just put us in the corner there and then put their things up here for him."

Keg looked back at the rest of the crew. Without enthusiasm, they were nodding and looking over the edge of the rear of the stage where all of our drums and keyboards and cables sat in a pile where they'd been set after Big Man made the humpers take them down.

Keg was still fuming as he stepped away, but his anger had melted away. It was like watching air let out of a scaled down brown bulldozer. His anger had filled his chest and made him seem larger and fiercer.

Soon, as we all stood and watched the Rose Royce crew working our stuff over the edge and up the stairs to the work space, Keg was himself again, joking and speculating on what had happened to Lakeside. The Dayton, Ohio, group had been scheduled to open the show and word had it we might have to play first because they were running well late.

"Them snakes and gators out there in the swamp got 'em," Keg told us. "They know when it's city folks an' don't know where the hell they going. They put up detour signs and lead 'em right down to their dinner table."

I don't remember anybody ever speaking again about Keg's challenge to that man-and-a-half at the Centroplex. Hell, in Starkville, Mississippi, he reached out of the bus window with a pipe in his hand and smacked hell out of a gas station attendant who insisted on filling our bus with a cigarette in his mouth. Keg was the type of Aries they write about in the astrology books, the kind who will come across a problem and start working on it. Rams rarely came down from the mountain tops just to start trouble. But there's nothing in the neighborhood up there among those impossible footholds, so if you're up there they'll ram the hell out of you.

I'd realized that about Keg since the day I met him. There were a dozen of us waiting in front of the Charisma office on Georgia Avenue in Northwest Washington. I had purchased a new Cary Van for our equipment and my road manager, Tom Abney, sent Keg Leg to pick it up. At nearly closing time, we stood out front waiting to see the truck with its sun roof and burglar-discouraging metal grille across the back.

It didn't take long before we spotted it rolling toward us. The driver, still in shadows, pulled past us and put himself in position to parallel park. Not so fast, Brother Man. Before he could back into the spot a nearly new Mercedes-Benz turned out of traffic and pulled into the parking space head-on. We could all see the triumphant driver, a hurrying African dressed for business in a white shirt, striped tie, and suit jacket. The Benz driver opened his door a crack and began fumbling with his keys and an attaché case in the shotgun seat. Then the door slammed shut again on the driver side of the Benz, the street side.

That was when I got my first look at my new road man, Dennis Little, the nephew of the Charisma boss, Norris Little, who had asked me to hire him. It struck me immediately. The brother, about five-foot-seven, looked like nothing so much as a huge barrel set solidly on plow-pulling thighs. He now planted himself against the Benz driver's door.

"I am here first," the driver responded, rolling down his window to protest. "I have this space, man. I have this space. I am here first."

"Yeah, you got that space," said Dennis casually, "but you can't get out of the car."

I don't know what I expected to hear the brother say, but whatever it was that wasn't it. If I had been reviewing a list of possible lines with only that line on it, I would've had trouble picking it. Of course, it was perfect. But the African hadn't picked it, either. He rolled the window up with the quickness. He looked at the imposing bulk that blocked his exit to the left and then stared out at us through the passenger window. We all stood there motionless, speechless.

He rolled the window down again. "I am here first."

Then he realized that this was ground that had been covered. With a shrug of dejection, he put his key back into the ignition and started to back up. Dennis, without a further word, backed off and let the Mercedes pull out. With that he backed the van in perfectly, hopped out, pushed the door closed, and flipped the keys to me as he passed the sidewalk cluster.

"Nice ride, boss. I really like the sun roof."

And from that day on he had been Keg Leg.

29

The next time I played Madison Square Garden was in September 1979, four years after the Arista celebration. I was working with a quintet of Carl Cornwell, Ed Brady, Rob Gordon, and Tony Green. There was a weeklong series of concerts being held by "M.U.S.E.," the Musicians United for Safe Energy, a group formed by Jackson Browne, Bonnie Raitt, James Taylor, Jesse Colin Young, and some others after the accident at the Three Mile Island nuclear plant in March of that year. I hadn't had a lot of time to get myself together for that one because we had only been invited about two weeks in advance of the event.

The shows started at 7:30 each night because there were a bunch of different artists playing. We were scheduled to play second, behind Peter Tosh. Not. Because when "hit time" arrived, Peter refused to go on and somebody from the group of musicians who were running things was standing halfway down the twisting ramp under the arena waving frantically at our limo driver as we pulled up. If the first act wouldn't or couldn't go on, everybody moved up. The organizer asked whether we could go on first. Hell, we could play at four in the afternoon.

A documentary film about the event called *No Nukes* came out later, and we appeared in it doing something from our set. If we looked a little disheveled (and I managed to do that pretty often), that time it was because we went from the limo to the stage. No problem. Well, there was one problem. The night before, when Chaka Khan came out to play, the youngsters from New Jersey were hollering for their man: "Broooooooose!" They started the call every time the house lights went down. But Ms. Khan didn't know about that traditional call. She thought they were booing and left the stage.

I was introduced to the house by Browne, and before I could remark to myself on his being another Jackson, I was hearing the same calls for Bruce that had sent my Chicago sister back behind the curtains. Those yells came rolling down over me from the darkness of the upper section of the stands like giant waves as the five of us, not Springsteen, emerged from the shadows behind a truckload of instruments and equipment. At the time I wasn't aware of what had happened the night before, but I heard what they were saying and I knew who was backstage. So I gave them a "good evening," and told them that Bruce would be with them later and that I'd appreciate it if they'd let me do my little bit since I was already out there and had a band with me.

No problem. They either figured "what the hell" or were too drunk to know I wasn't Bruce, because they calmed down and let me do my three songs. We opened with "South Carolina," slowed it down a touch with "We Almost Lost Detroit," and closed with "The Bottle." I guess I noticed all of the film and recording equipment all over the apron, but I honestly hadn't given much thought about making the cut that would give me space on the vinyl or in the film. That was a bonus.

I was working at T.O.N.T.O. studio in those days, Malcolm Cecil's Santa Monica facility near the beach, and when I got a call from California about being mixed for the release M.U.S.E. was producing, I told them to go to Malcolm. I was in New York at my mother's house when I got another call, this time saying Jackson Browne was catching a Friday night red-eye flight from L.A. and would need my signature on a paper when he landed. I gave him my mother's address—she was up on 106th Street at that point—and said I'd see him there.

It was raining and gray in Manhattan that Saturday morning. My mother was standing near the window cleaning up some breakfast dishes when she spotted a limousine cruising to a stop in front of her building. Odds were it was Jackson, based on how many limos we used to see at Franklin Plaza. I joined her at the window and sure enough, a tall, thin dude with dark hair hopped out of the back seat and trotted through the sprinkles to our front door and we buzzed him in.

He looked like he had been forced to stand up all the way from L.A., but he'd landed in a New York frame of mind: one step behind the world. Didn't matter. My mother wouldn't let him leave.

You start to feel New York on the pilot's approach to your runway, when the plane straightens out after that final wide turn and you plunge through the clouds and find yourself eye level with the skyscrapers across the river. There's an immediate jolt of adrenaline that brings your body up to city time. With apologies to San Francisco and the beautiful skyline that causes folks from there to call their town "the city," I have never felt my arms and legs energized and my pulse rate rise in the Bay Area the way it does when I'm in NYC.

And people always remind themselves not to be "city slicked" by fast-talking New Yorkers who give you five minutes worth of information in thirty seconds and charge you for an hour every fifteen minutes. It is so much of a lifestyle that it has broken down to life without style. Even well-meaning folks can be misunderstood by visitors stunned and mystified by a life speed the locals clearly consider "the usual." Sometimes the visitors are determined not to let New York interfere with their visit, to let nothing deter them from their business.

Jackson Browne came into my mother's apartment locked on leaving, on getting to where he was going. But my mother was as firm as she was friendly. And I had to listen to the tape before I could approve it anyway. While I looked around for the cassette player, she was guiding him to the table.

"Come and sit down, you poor thing. It will only take a minute and you've got to have something to eat."

Jackson reluctantly sat down and relaxed, maybe for the first time in hours.

I listened to the tape. It was an abridged version of "Detroit," smoothly shortened to fit the producers' request that it not exceed three and a half minutes. I was okay with whatever, recognizing the recognition of my participation that would come with being included on the album and film. Hearing the song, I was reminded of how that whole evening had gone and how much I had enjoyed seeing folks from the music community working together and trying to do something positive.

30

I saw Stevie Wonder with Barbara Walters on *20/20* one August night in 1980. Seeing Stevie on that show made me realize he was braver than I would ever be again without the TV equivalent of a prenuptial agreement—I'd been double-crossed too many times. So there I was, watching Stevie go one-on-one with the queen bee of beating people up.

I didn't doubt Stevie's ability to represent himself, but TV ratings are not based on making subjects look good. They don't even have to make you look like you. They have to make an audience look. But it's hard to make Stevie look bad. He is as clever with his vocabulary as he is versatile with his keyboards. He was adept at saying what he thought about your line of questioning if it was out of order, always maintaining that same smile of his. I nodded at the screen as he played a few chords of "Happy Birthday" on the piano, with a smile.

The news was that Stevie was going on tour in October with Bob Marley and would be promoting his new LP, *Hotter than July*. He was also planning a rally in Washington, D.C., in January 1981, to bring attention to the question of a national holiday honoring Dr. King. Happy Birthday.

I watched Barbara Walters because Stevie couldn't. With the half-glasses sitting on her nose like an acrobat on a seesaw, reading glasses that she used to read Stevie while she scanned her notebook.

I knew the announcement of the tour meant that Stevie would be coming to D.C. and I knew when they got there I would have a ticket.

It didn't work out that way. What I mean is, I got to the Washington concert but I didn't have to pay. And that was also something that I could not have predicted. I didn't find out I'd get in through the stage door until November.

A few days after I saw Stevie's interview with Barbara Walters and told myself that I wanted to see his show, I got a call from an old New York friend named Clive Wasson. I didn't know what kind of work Clive was doing, but I could almost hear the L.A. in his voice.

It was a pleasant conversation. We had some people that we both knew and spent a few minutes going over their current situations before Clive got down to business. He was working for the folks who were promoting Stevie's tour with Bob Marley. The problem was that Bob was on tour with the Commodores and was playing in the next few weeks in the same cities Stevie would do in early November. And just where would the Midnight Band be in early November?

I had spent the better part of five years getting people familiar with the Midnight Band onstage and on three albums. But now that the name had indeed established some recognition even among promoters, there was no Midnight Band. We had

225

reformed and added women to our songs on *Secrets* in 1978, and then took those women vocalists on the road. After less than a year we'd cut back to a quintet we'd called A Mere Façade, but the West Coast representative of our record label came to me in Denver one night and said, "Who are these Arab dudes you're playing with—who's Emir Fasad?" After I got up off the floor from laughing, I needed another name change because the potential for phonic distortion was obviously more extensive than I could overcome. People continued to refer to whoever I brought with me as the Midnight Band, but Brian's departure, in March 1980, had erased the last trace of "Midnight" from my music. At that point I had reconnected with Carl Cornwell, the play-anything wizard I had known since my days at college, and we reconfigured the rhythm section and added horns. The band we organized had a totally new sound, and I called it the Amnesia Express. From mid-April through early July, I had been on tour with the new group and then recorded an album scheduled for release in late November.

All I had in my calendar for November was a gig in Atlanta and a solo show at Kent State University. I figured I'd play a few gigs before Christmas so the guys could all play Santa Claus, but what Clive was proposing wouldn't interfere with any of that.

"I'd be glad to be employed for a couple of weeks," I told Clive.

I gave Clive the number for my agent in New York to discuss the dates Stevie had on tap for his first two weeks. As far as I was concerned, I was looking at found money. It was looking like our folks would have a Happy Thanksgiving and we could work on a Merry Christmas later.

Things were looking up.

31

Show business is just like any other business in certain respects. Of course, people in show business have a visibility that paints a "larger than life" aura around them. Their work in music, movies, or some facet of entertainment makes them a part of people's lives. They are so well known in the corners of everywhere that it feels as though they've lived more than one lifetime. The fact that certain aspects of the arts endure beyond the span of normal expectations makes them a part of generations born after their contributions were completed.

The exploits and exploitation of the arts make individuals with no more talent than a turnip famous for ages. The stories their lives inspire give them reputations that inspire continued repetition. There are heroes and zeroes. There are people of sincere and genuine talent and others who couldn't do wrong right. Just like, I imagine, every other walk of life.

You meet some people that you wish like hell you never had, and others who make such an impression on you that you feel convinced you made the right career choice. You meet some people you are proud to call your friends, and others who are so crooked that when they die you're sure they'll be screwed into the ground. The influence these people have on your life depends on when you meet them. I will always believe that you need to meet good people, talented and generous people, in order to later withstand the bitter disappointments that destroy the careers of so many talented people.

I started at the top when it came to wonderful, talented, and generous people. During my first week of publicity for *The Vulture* and my book of poetry I was a guest on a New York radio program hosted by Mr. Ossie Davis and Miss Ruby Dee. And in all honesty, I don't remember a word I said if I said anything, because they also had John Killens and John Williams on, the two brothers who were both great Black novelists, and I think I just sat there in the studio with my mouth hanging open.

I doubted if Ossie and Ruby remembered me from that. Apparently, though, they had kept up with me; prior to our first gig on the *Hotter than July* tour, which kicked off in Houston the last week of October 1980, they invited me to do a TV show they now had on Houston's PBS channel.

The Ossie and Ruby show was action-packed and we could thank PBS for that. Before there was cable TV and umpteen hundred channels, PBS stations were primarily broadcast on VHF and their programs were on one of the four or five lines in your daily TV guide in the paper. That way, even though their prime time programs were sometimes buried under an avalanche of promotion that the networks gave their shows, there was more of a possibility to notice what they were offering. One of the shows I religiously tried to catch was *Ossie and Ruby!* because there would be certain sections of the show featuring the cohosts doing a reading or comic skit that showed real versatility and talent.

The day before we taped the show, I checked into our hotel about midday and arrived at the studio in plenty of time for the round table production meeting where I found out what we were doing. I knew the band would enjoy it. There were songs we played on most shows, like "Winter in America" and "Storm Music," along with a couple of songs we had never performed on a show: most notably "Jose Campos Torres" and Vernon James' composition "Morning Thoughts." I felt as though the staff had done a great job because they had packed twenty-eight minutes of our songs and poems to put into a thirty minute show. I didn't raise one objection or have anything to add. I sat through the meeting nodding at them like a bobble-head doll.

The biggest rush was that I felt as if I was sitting with royalty. It was like the feeling I had when I met Quincy Jones or Sidney Poitier. I knew there would be excerpts from the show that people would see, but I wished folks could see me just sitting there, having a meeting with Ossie Davis and Ruby Dee like I belonged there. It was terrific.

Everybody appreciates movie stars and music icons, even people who share their profession. We are all fans, marveling at their mastery over their medium and fascinated by their fame. By the time I went to Houston, I had met Clive Davis, Miles Davis, and Ossie Davis, and was knocked out for a minute by each one.

By the time I got back to the hotel, I felt ready for half of a Texas meal. I understood that a whole Texas meal was an entire steer and that I would probably have to cook it myself;

while I didn't see a sign in the room that said "no hot plates or bonfires allowed," I had no one in mind who might want to eat the other half of a steer, so I started considering alternatives. Besides, there's always somebody in those hotels assigned to "watch the band" and I just knew someone would rat me out when I tried to drag my steer up to the fourth floor. I called room service.

The lady who answered when I called the room service number on the phone had either just started working there minutes before I called, or had perfected a "deniability" telephone process that even a recording of our conversation could not challenge. By the time I hung up, I had no idea if or when anything was coming and was overwhelmed by a feeling of gratitude for having been allowed to thank her. I had been reading specific orders from the menu, but may as well have been reading the Yellow Pages backward in Latin. The one thing I remembered her saying quite often was, "Y'all shore tawk funny, huh?"

She offered to read my order back to me, but I told her I was in my thirties and didn't think I had that long to live.

There was a slight possibility that the band had arrived while I'd been at the TV studio, but I doubted it. My brother Denis, who was road manager by that time, had been a passenger in one of the two vehicles that were rented that morning to transport the band while I flew down. There had been a four-door Chevy and a station wagon, eight musicians, and a road manager leaving Jefferson City, Missouri, for six or seven hours with a meal and under the speed limit.

I had a room list from the desk clerk and dialed my brother's room but didn't get him. I put a ball game on my hotel room TV set.

Room service arrived. I have no way of confirming or denying if it was either what I ordered or what I wanted, but by the time it got there I was hungry enough to eat the tray the brother brought it in on. I do remember giving the brother a lot of money, possibly all I had in my pocket, thanking him for bringing whatever it was and saw that it was a plate from Wal-Mart and a plastic knife and fork.

People in Texas seem to have tremendous egos, no matter what part of the state they're in or what part they play in it. Their partisan perspective toward their state was probably appropriate when they were what they hadn't yet been told they were not anymore. The thing I enjoyed more than anything else about Texans was their absolute certainty about how glad everyone should be to be there, where one could be treated to a grand tour of the myths and misinformation all Texans have at their fingertips and recite without provocation like children reciting the Pledge of Allegiance.

I remember a brother in a bar asking me where I was from, and when I answered New York he told me that Texas had become New York because that was where the biggest and the most of everything was—in Texas. It had been in New York before Texas "got 'holt of it." The "it" Texas had "got 'holt of" was the part of the conversation I had missed. Fortunately this almost-a-conversation was taking place after a show, back when I was still drinking, and I wasn't unhappy about someone else using me to talk to himself.

"It" mighta been the Astrodome. I seemed to have remembered that when they opened the stadium it was called the eighth wonder of the world. Probably by a Texan, I decided. But, hell, it coulda been oil, which they had mostly run out of, or DFW, the Dallas airport, where every airline had its own terminal. Or space, as in land, which it had more of than anywhere in the States except Alaska, but who the hell wanted to run around shouting, "We're number two!"

The brother who'd begun this attack of the similes was continuing unabated, not making any progress toward the point, so I'd waved for another drink and continued in my own meticulous way to think of things his point might be, feeling that when I thought of it I would know it and have no more need of his confirmation than he seemed to need of me to listen. And then it hit me: the question must have been "how do you pronounce H-O-U-S-T-O-N?" That was the only New York/Houston conflict there's been since the Houston Astros and New York Mets were added to the National League together. The Mets won in '69. And New Yorkers still called it "House-ton." The way it was spelled.

In my hotel room, the ball game on TV was over. I had not been involved enough to know who had won or even who played. I vaguely remembered taking the tray and what I'd been given for dishes outside my door as though someone might want them back. I should've put them in the middle of the hall with a sign that said, "Beware! Toxic Waste!" I could just imagine some brother zipped up in a foam rubber space suit and a ten gallon hat moonwalking that bullshit down the back stairs, holding it out front of him with some Texas-sized prongs.

232

I called my brother's room again. No reply.

Usually I could imagine, but now I was drawing a blank. I hadn't actually seen them leave Jefferson City, but I'd seen everybody that morning, which meant that no one had fallen in love and couldn't be located. No one was from Texas or Missouri, so no one had been stricken with homesickness within driving distance. In fact, everybody had been kind of anxious to get to Houston because of the TV show and all the good things I had said about Mr. Davis and Miss Dee without having to make anything up. Hell, even if they'd all quit they would have called so they could laugh in my ear. And my brother would have needed a new face and an assignment from the Witness Protection Program. And they knew me. Hell, I'd do the fucking TV show anyway. I'd just have to tell the producers I'd been a-band-doned.

There was a western on TV now. I couldn't believe it. It would be sort of like seeing a bunch of Chinese people coming out of a Chinese restaurant in Harlem with doggie bags and getting back on the tour bus. What else was I waiting for? Must have been a western in Houston.

It actually might have been good. I didn't see enough of it to even complain about it. I suppose it played through or played out like the ball game I couldn't recall. I can't recall the movie for an entirely different reason. During the game I had been thinking about nothing. During the movie I couldn't seem to find the nothing channel I'd been thinking about all through the game.

I got stuck with a short loop that played over and over, then over and under, then over passed under, like Malcolm's loop of

233

the vocals on the last three minutes of "B Movie." Something new was added but the way back to the beginning was still there. It was never over.

The band members are congregating near the ticket counter. My brother is road managing, passing out tickets that will get us to Missouri. There is foolishness between the usual suspects about the usual subjects: their women or girls, their wives and girlfriends, their Mrs. and Miseries, and the Misses they missed. Then there's your all of the above. Brady and Gordon. Sheffield and Larry Mac. Vernon James wears a brief smile and says nothing. Bags and suitcases are sliding through to a lady who is about half the size of some of the luggage. Someone slides through to help. Probably "Astro," flirting.

And the harshest part of the loop, the over that washes over me and runs over me, the part that takes its time and then takes my time and gets closer as the images get closer, changing to a sharp, like shards of glass, stark, like a scene I can't get passed, that won't pass, even when I close my eyes.

It's Kenny Powell, the young drummer with his reluctant, almost a smile. Neat, clean, without hurry. And a couple. Adults. With him. No doubt that it's his folks. His parents. Cordial. Comfortable. Ready to acknowledge the usuals, the guys they know, who know them: Brady and Gordon. Astro. Then turning to me. They know me. I sort of hear Kenny's soft voice just above the clamor.

"Gil, these are my folks."

And I hear them clearer each time.

"Yes, how are you. We've just come to see Ken off and to ask you to please take care of our son . . ."

And it ran again. And I saw . . . that the movie was over. The western was over. The airport scene in my mind started over. And I opened my eyes to look around the hotel room, where . . . the phone was ringing.

It was my brother. And the details of his explanation were not lost, but were just words to me. There had been a blowout. Kenny was driving. They had spun across the median and across the highway between spurts of traffic headed in the opposite direction. They came to rest, to a stop past the shoulder on the other side, through a break in the restraints that ran thigh-high to a point only a few feet from a drop down into a ravine. They had gotten out of the car, undamaged but immobile, leaning like a drunk on the wheel where the tire was ripped. They sat there until Sheffield arrived on the scene. They got in, cramped and happy to be cramped. And came to Houston.

235

32

I had played in Houston at a place called Rockefeller's, where the guys who ran the club walked around with sidearms, sho' nuff, forty-fives in holsters. Like Matt Dillon from *Gunsmoke*. On first glance, I thought having the folks who hired me provide their own armed security seemed a mite melodramatic; a little bit too Texas and Wild West for me. But knowing about an after show robbery at the Beacon Theater on Broadway, where a producer was actually shot for the gate, gave me cause to reconsider and say to myself, *Hell, maybe I should be wearing a gun up in this camp, too*. At the very least, I couldn't say what these folks should *not* do.

On October 31, 1980, back in Houston to start the *Hotter than July* tour, I was tired already, sweaty and exhausted from a five-minute trudge uphill, learning as I trudged why this block-sized enclosure was called "the Summit." A place called the Summit would be at the top of a fucking hill, right?

I had just found a stage entrance for a venue I had never played. The places I had played in Texas on prior trips could fit into this sprawling hothouse about ten times and still leave room for the Rockets to play their games without me getting in their way.

Finally, holding a four-letter filled conversation with myself about the hundred-degree temperature in this desert in fucking November, I pushed through the door marked PERFORMER'S ENTRANCE and found myself being eyed suspiciously by a six-gun-packing guard before I heard a buzzer and was waved on through. An inner glass door with a cardboard placard taped on it saying TO PERFORMER'S DRESSING ROOM provided further direction. I had made it. I was inside the Summit.

I wasn't interested in a dressing room right then. At an ill-lit fork in the hallway, another handwritten message said, TO THE MAIN STAGE, so I made my way vaguely on through the maze of dimly lit corridors. I dragged on cautiously, following signs that indicated I was headed toward the arena floor. Suddenly, after feeling that I might have been better off calling AAA for a suggested route, I turned into the lights of the vast arena, as busy as a small town. Men and women in work clothes were pulling metal folding chairs off of racks that might have once carried station wagons cross-country. The men had developed a style of flipping the seats open from their rigid straight backed status to a position where behinds built with uniquely flexible angles could survive for three or four hours.

I had on my rose-colored prescription lenses and was scanning all the rows of fabric-covered fold-ups bolted to the floor in ascending stages that merged in a design of discomfort. I put my personal attaché case down for a minute.

It was an impressive sight. Choreographed chaos on a Roman scale. But suddenly somebody called my name. Well, not exactly my name, but somebody's name for me, the name he always used, my astrological sign. So I knew who it was. It was somebody who shouldn't have seen me come in. Howzat?

The call for me rang out again, echoing around in the cavernous hall: "Air-rees!"

I scanned the upper reaches of the place, looking for Stevie Wonder.

And there he was, in a seat near the top row in the bowl-shaped theater. He was leaning forward in my direction from the sound booth. Alone. There was no mistaking him. His corn rows were surrounded with a soft suede cover. Large, dark sunglasses hid most of the top half of his face, and a huge, joker's grin furnished the lower half. He had a wireless mike in his hand and, again with the grin, was saying, "Come on up here, Air-rees!"

I started for the stairs, still scanning. Now I could see there was an engineer-type person in the booth, but his back was turned to Stevie and I didn't believe I knew the man anyway. Or that he had identified me.

He hadn't. But since I hadn't figured it out yet and Stevie was having such a good time messing with my head . . .

"How you been, man," I said as I climbed. "If you saw me get outta that cab from the airport, you shoulda helped me pay for it."

"We felt your vibes, Air-rees," Stevie said, and he laughed out loud, shook his head, and held his hundred-watt smile.

I was close enough now to see that the headset Stevie was wearing was not yesterday's setup. This one had an almost invisible wire around his head with a tiny mic attached to the ear phones. It was supposed to be for communication with other sound and light stations around the bowl, but this one was modified and made Stevie look like a switchboard operator from outer space. No matter what Stevie said, I knew his brother Calvin was in here somewhere with the same type of headset. If there was anybody as likely as Stevie to joke around in a billion-dollar arena with a million dollars' worth of sound equipment, it was Calvin. Wherever Calvin was, a good time and a lot of laughs were always near.

I sat in the same row with Stevie, a couple of seats away, and watched the workmen and women constructing the stage set and aligning the floor seats on the canvas that covered the basketball court. They were roping off the first five rows, which would probably be reserved for the VIP guests and press. There were also men in blue coveralls stacking speakers three-deep in front of the stage, tying up the massive maroon curtain, bolting it to fasteners on the apron constructed for just that purpose.

A complete sound team was now onstage, clearing space for the drum risers, Stevie's band members were appearing here and there. The work area was filling up: electricians, light technicians, security personnel, supplementary sound amplifiers, monitors, speakers and cables, side fills, multicolored gels directed at points along the stage floor where band members would stand and sit during their performances were being placed according to stage diagrams on clipboards.

I saw Malcolm Cecil wander in from backstage, opening sound crates and jotting down the contents on a thick pad. Malcolm would be handling the audience sound for me on the first few nights while my regular engineer, Dave McLean, handled my onstage monitors for the band.

I was thinking that most audience members would be glad they hadn't seen any of this preparation. It was too much like the work they wanted to leave behind when they bought tickets for a night of relaxation.

Several of the sound crew wore jumpsuits with Britannia Row stenciled on the back. There had been a rumor that Stevie had hired the UK's biggest road production company to handle this tour. They had just completed the Pink Floyd tour for that group's hit album *The Wall*, which meant that not only could they supervise and coordinate sound and light support for this show, the crew could also construct a wall between the onstage performers and their audience over the course of a two-and-a-half-hour show. Great. If I found out I needed a wall.

"How you been, Aries?" Stevie asked.

He and I had an astrologer in common, a D.C. lady named Amali, who sent me a monthly lunar return reading when I was not in the city. She had told me about Stevie's interest in the stars and his own production company was called Black Bull. I was used to him hailing me with Air-rees, though I did not call him "Tau-russss!"

About five years before, Amali had ignited my interest in astrology. She had been doing a reading for Norris Little, also known as Brute, and I had wandered to the threshold of a back room they had commandeered at a party. All I'd wanted to know was whether or not Brute still needed a ride home before I made my exit. Without even looking up or really acknowledging my presence, Amali had said, "You don't know anything about this, do you Aries?"

I had to admit I didn't know Sydney Omarr from Sydney, Australia.

"Well, you just wait right there until I finish this, and I'll get to you," she said.

She went on with her talk to Brute. I was still trying to figure out how she knew I was an Aries and how she'd known I was standing in the carpeted doorway without turning around. I was still looking for the mirror on the opposite wall that had given me away when she got up from her seat, leaving a befuddled Brute contemplating his life.

When she turned and walked over to me, I was more impressed and even less inclined to think zodiac. She was short and petite, light caramel with huge liquid eyes. There was a hint of mischief lurking just behind her attempt to be all business. She picked up a little notebook and pen.

"My name is G . . ."

"I know what your name is," she said. "What I need to know is your place of birth, day of birth, and time of birth."

"I can give you all that," I agreed slowly. "But I'm not tryin' . . ."

"Look," she indicated impatiently, "I ordinarily charge fifty dollars apiece for these work-ups, but what I'll do for you is a birth chart and a lunar return chart and it will mention specific days and events. If none of these things come about, you owe me nothing."

I hate it when people call me out like that, when you're put in such a position that you really look like a jackass if you don't go along with it. How can you refuse a hundred dollars' worth of service for free? Hell! You don't believe it, right? Okay, fine.

You're in a win-win situation. If you're right, you win. If she's right, you win because you learn something.

I told her: born in Chicago, April 1, 1949, at 11:20 a.m. No matter, there was no way she resembled a shriveled gypsy with a crystal ball.

"How long does it take to be an expert in this?" I asked without sarcasm.

"I don't know," she said. "I've been at it for eight years and I'm a novice."

I had more confidence in her immediately.

"Who's that old geezer?"

I was jerked back to the Summit on a string.

The Britannia Row booth engineer had come out of the sound cage and was standing behind our row, between me and Stevie. He was pointing accusingly at the stage floor and a gentle white-haired soul with slightly bent posture, dressed in jeans, and opening and closing crates of equipment, jotting and scribbling what he saw on a wrinkled note pad.

"That's Malcolm Cecil," I said, leaning back to look the engineer guy over. He was short, muscular in the way equipment men will be, wore glasses, was pale from his constant time indoors, and wore a sour expression on his face. "I got Cecil to do sound for me a couple of nights," I said to Stevie. "You don't mind, do you, man?"

Stevie didn't mind. I knew that he had worked with Malcolm in L.A. on the more or less solo LPs they had done half a dozen years ago, and that they then parted company under circumstances I did not understand.

To the engineer I said, "He's just taking stock."

I was surprised with the energy of his displeasure.

"I'll take his stock," the Brit said with vehemence.

I laughed. "I wouldn't do that if I were you," I said. "In fact, I wouldn't do that if you were me."

He said something that sounded like a negative assessment of Taureans. "Bullshit," he snorted, walking away. "That old geezer."

Calvin had joined us in the back row. Sure enough he had a copy of the communication hookup Stevie had been wearing and a smirk on his face.

"That was good," I told him. "That was all I needed to hear. As if I didn't have a problem already, now I gotta worry about Calvin playing detective and telling on me."

I gestured toward the sound man.

"Somebody better tell him to forget about messin' with Malcolm."

It was easy to underestimate Malcolm. His shock of white hair and bent physique from years of tilting forward over soundboards could grant you the right to feel that the man lived a turtle's life and never peeked out of darkened studios and had all of the physical potential of a stick of furniture. That would be another one of those conclusions I mentioned. It went with, "Yeah, we got a pool," hearing the running approach and crash and adding, "but there ain't no water in it."

"Who's this big dude coming," I asked Calvin.

"That's Grayer," Calvin said.

We were joined by a suitably casual but exceedingly large

243

brother in a pea coat, a sports shirt open at the throat, and well-worn jeans. He had a light brown complexion, round face, a big head with a lot of hair, and an expression when he looked at me that said he had seen one of my species before under a microscope. He had a little square over his breast pocket that said STAGE MANAGER. That meant he was the man responsible for the clock and keeping shows on schedule, not so much when you got onstage as when you got off.

I agreed to be on by 8:05 p.m. each night and to hit my last note no later than 9:05. That would give the humpers and stage muscle twenty-five to thirty minutes to change the sets for "Wonderlove" and Stevie. Stevie's set would run the clock out, but at 11:30 or so he would call for backup to do his last two numbers: "Master Blaster," the reggae-flavored tune that included the line that was the title of his new LP, and "Happy Birthday," his tribute to Dr. King.

Grayer must have been six-foot-six and he looked as though his sense of humor had been baked off him somewhere outside. I could picture him striding around the backstage area most nights with a cinematic scowl on his face. That was for show. Grayer turned out to have a sense of humor that was approximately his size, but he was also willing to go a round or two with the next person holding a conflicting opinion if their opinion meant something.

Big Jim, as I learned to call him, was from Boulder, Colorado, and a fan of mine. It turned out that Grayer was wearing such a hard-assed attitude when we met because he had heard that the Midnight Band of mine had a reputation as "somewhat unpredictable with regard to the clock." That had worried the people producing the shows, worrying about us starting and stopping on time. I thought that was funny as hell, knowing that Bob Marley and the Wailers were coming in after two weeks.

"Them brothers don't start rolling their show joints until they're ten minutes late," I told Grayer. "I'll be around an hour in advance."

I meant that. It lasted for about twenty-four hours.

That first night Stevie was a clown onstage, a ham, a performer—not old but old school. Maybe schooled by Smokey Robinson himself on how to work a crowd, how to pace a show, how to stretch a song out and get the audience into a call and response sing-along. He also had a fondness for life on the edge—literally. Especially the edge of the stage. He scared the shit out of me the first time we were out there onstage together for "Master Blaster" and "Happy Birthday."

I went over and joined Stevie behind his bank of assorted keyboards at center stage. Stevie sang the verses and I tried to harmonize on the choruses, more or less singing along in neutral, trying to do no harm. After the verses were done, the two of us went on patrol. He placed one hand on my shoulder and we walked the perimeter of the stage, giving fans on the side and behind the stage a chance to say "I love you, Stevie."

It was fun, singing about a good time and having one, slowly strolling around, waving to hundreds of smiling faces while thousands more clapped in rhythm. All of that was cool. It wasn't the takeoff that got me nervous, it was the landing, when we got back to home base by the keyboards.

The vibes were positive and love was truly in the air, and it seemed to embolden Stevie out there. He started creeping forward, moving back out toward the edge of the stage. I tried to hold his arm, but we were clearly not on the same page. Finally, still smiling, Stevie started moving back away from the edge, and I felt like dialing 911 because I'd just about had a heart attack.

33

At 7:15 I still feel groggy
And the day ahead looks gray and foggy
I'm suffering from a bad case of day-old jet lag
I start to try and slow-motion drag
Myself into a nice wake-up shower
Where I would like to spend an hour
But the clock is ticking so as I get in it
I'm thinking more about ten good minutes
But just as the water decides to get hot
Someone at my door gives a loud double knock
And I'm thinking the last thing that I need right then
Is to give up this shower to let room service in
So one-handing a towel around my waist
And gathering what's left of my own stork-like grace
I head for the door while I'm still soaking wet
And focusing on how the coffee I'll get
Will hit the right spot and somehow make it clear
What the hell's going on? *What am I doing here?*

Here was the hell of this business: for stretches at a time, your schedule could be as bare as a dressing-room refrigerator ten minutes after Keg Leg decided it was time to load up and hat up—at which point he transferred all extra beer, juice, and sodas to a cooler on the bus or the back of the truck. Then, quicker than you could say *what the fuck is going on,* your life was an avalanche of things you didn't have time to do and it wasn't your life anymore. And it made no difference how long you had known the tour would be starting on a particular date and how much time you had to prepare so that you wouldn't be rushed, you didn't get everything done and you were rushed.

Naturally it wasn't all your fault. To be brutally dishonest and childishly unwilling to accept responsibility for personal oversights and overwork: none of it was your fault! After all, between your office and the record company and the booking agent and promoter's office and your band rehearsals, your time was eaten up like goldfish in a bowl with Jaws.

There is a certain element of going on a concert tour that must be similar to giving birth. In a creative-writing course I'd taught at Federal City College, I had asked that my students write about an experience they had gone through that they could recall vividly and in detail.

One young woman chose to describe the ten hours she had spent in labor when her first child was born. After hearing her read, one of the first questions from the class was, "How many children do you have?"

She said, "Four."

The following question was, "If the first experience was as disagreeable as you wrote, why would you have more children?"

And she said, "Somehow you forget how bad it was."

For me, going on tour was like that. Every time I had a 7 a.m. wake-up call after a collapse at any time past two and was looking bleary-eyed at seven hours or so on the highway, there's a tendency to wonder, "What the hell am I doing here?" Like the woman in "Labor Day," you know that the end of the road is not the end of the day. When you arrive at wherever, that's when you have to go to work. So, considering the discomfort and inconvenience even when everything goes according to schedule, why would you go out? You forget.

On Saturday morning, November 1, at the Houston Texas Holiday Inn, when I got my seven o'clock wake-up call, I remembered.

The beauty of those "flashups," since they couldn't be called "flashbacks," was that the whole gauntlet of grief was self-inflicted. I signed on for the shows. I saw where I had to be and when. I came in after 1 a.m., called the desk after 2 a.m., asked for a wakeup call at 7 a.m., and got over my amnesia at about 7:05.

If anything can make you unhappier than inconveniences on the road, it's probably inconveniences and *not getting* on the road. Like if there's anything worse than choking down only a couple bites of a really nice-looking cheese omelet because you're going to Baton Rouge, Louisiana, it's leaving that omelet and a cinnamon roll and the rest of a pot of coffee and not going to Baton Rouge. Well, that's a little stretch. Because we were going to Baton Rouge, but I hadn't needed to leave 75 percent of my breakfast after only 25 percent of my shower and getting down to the lobby half-dressed. Understand?

I was not incredibly happy. I had sharpened my sarcasm on that first weekend's routing with Stevie, making sure he knew there was no shortcut to Dallas from Houston by way of Louisiana. He took the needles with his customary smile.

"Who put this weekend together, Marty Feldman?" I said to him as though it hadn't already been explained.

We were going from Houston to Baton Rouge to Dallas. The ride to Louisiana was obviously a few hundred miles out of the way. It was simple. The Dallas arena was booked for Saturday, November 1, and available Sunday, November 2. Tours never wanted to miss a Saturday night, and the Baton Rouge Centroplex was the closest venue of the size Stevie was looking for. Plus, with Louisiana State University located there in the state capital, there was a sellout down the street. Gotta go there.

The question we had asked ourselves when we saw that rather unusual zag that should have been a zig on the tour map was, "How do we go?" Because clearly we had to get back the next day. So two cars were reserved at Houston's inner-city airport, Hobby. If the cars had been put on hold at Houston International we'd have been halfway to Baton Rouge when we picked them up. At least they would have been there. At Hobby, they were not. At least both of them were not. The car that was available when we arrived at just past 8:30 was quickly filled with five band members to pick up Route 10 east just outside the airport. Which left five folks for the second car that wasn't ready until nearly 10 a.m. By that time, Malcolm Cecil, the house engineer on these gigs, was about to start pulling out some of his rather substantial head of hair. What had been a schedule with a good hour and a half of room in reserve got tight when the car wasn't ready.

When Malcolm finally pulled up in the vehicle, I climbed into the shotgun seat and immediately fell asleep. I was surprised to wake up twenty or so minutes later still parked in the terminal lot.

Malcolm had lost his usual smile. Or thrown it away. The car was ready. Four of the remaining five of us were there. But what Malcolm wanted to know was where the hell was Ed Brady? I knew where. And after weaving my way back through the terminal building, sure enough, I found him. Bent over what was then a fairly new form of video game called Space Invaders. Brady could kill a couple of hours in front of the ever-advancing electronic invaders without pause.

Shortly thereafter we were off to "Looz anna," but by now Malcolm's hour and a half window had been slammed on our fingers by Avis and Space Invaders.

We fretted and slept and slept and fretted. Up front, Malcolm and I were constantly recalculating our distance and possibilities. It was kind of ironic because in Houston the only exchange between me and Grayer, Stevie's stage manager, had been about my group playing on time. At the speed Malcolm was driving, nearly seventy-five miles per hour when space opened up, we were figuring a razor-thin margin, like out of the car and onto the stage. But while Malcolm could do seventy-five in wide-open Texas, we weren't in Louisiana long before the flashing lights were right in our trunk. As he pulled over onto the shoulder, Malcolm told us very seriously, "Don't say a word, guys."

251

While feigning sleep, I caught a glimpse of a Louisiana state trooper's Rod Steiger profile as he sauntered up on us with his notebook in his hands. Malcolm's hands were full, too, and when he rolled down his window he threw the whole thing, both hands full, into the air.

Right after that he was giving an Oscar-winning performance.

I didn't catch the whole speech because I was biting my lip and burying my face in my hat. The queen had less of a British accent. Before collecting the credentials he had deliberately dumped, Malcolm had adapted a tone and attitude that he added to thorough frustration and criticism of American treatment of its visitors. How in the hell was he supposed to cope with delays from the car rentals, time wasting directions, et cetera, when all he was trying to do was get "the African boxing team" he was in charge of to the Centroplex on time?

Rod Steiger might have had it written into his contract that he be supplied with a dictionary or an interpreter. *Our* Rod Steiger had neither. And holding Malcolm's driver's license limply in his hand, he wobbled back to his cruiser. He returned with a bit more confidence.

"I'm sorry 'bout all y'all's problems," he said respectfully to Malcolm. "If y'all can jus' pull in behind me we'll get you to the Centroplex."

With lights flashing and sirens wailing we made it on time.

Later that night we found out that Bob Marley wasn't just resting up from his roadwork with the Commodores. He was sick and had entered the Sloan-Kettering clinic. I knew what that meant. Cancer. Bob Marley had cancer. Or, to be honest, cancer had Bob Marley.

I talked about it with Stevie; he was worried and upset. I was told to keep the news a secret. But naturally there were too many people on the inside of the circle, and the rumor mill was going full blast. The promotion was being handled by Dick Griffey Productions, and they had to have some information about who they were supposed to be producing. That, plus there was pressure being applied by Stevie's record company, Motown. If Bob wasn't going to do the tour, what about one of their new rock and rollers? They would give the tour more support. Buy more spots for radio and more space in newspapers.

I had been totally honest when I spoke with Stevie on the question of doing the whole tour. Yes, I was interested. No, I didn't think I would have much trouble rearranging my dates. And yes, my new album, *Real Eyes*, was due out around Thanksgiving. But no, my label could not be counted on to do a lot of advertising before it was released. If Stevie was worried about the promotion money that would have been contributed to pump up Bob and the Wailers, well, maybe he'd better go with the rockers.

Stevie disagreed.

He confirmed in Dallas on November 2, 1980, that we would continue for the duration of *Hotter than July*, through the rally in D.C. and on into February 1981. And now my staff were busy in New York and D.C. trying to rearrange the appearances I was canceling in order to do Stevie's entire tour.

253

34

There were a couple of places that were cool to play because they were hotels and your room was next door or upstairs. On Peachtree Street in Atlanta I was right upstairs, but by the time I got there after two shows at the Agora—previously scheduled, without Stevie—on November 4, 1980, Ronald Reagan was the president.

It was not supposed to raise an eyebrow. Living in the D.C. area, I'd read the papers and listened to radio and TV quoting polls that all predicted his victory. But the reality of it was still something of a shock, like a brief contact with an open circuit.

It was an occasion to stay up a little when, after being hoisted to my room by a creaking elevator, I found myself watching the president of the United States of America playing second banana to a monkey. Ted Turner's Atlanta superstation was doing all-night monkey shines, playing one of Reagan's movies with the monkey, Bonzo. *Bonzo Goes to College*, I think it was. Anyway, one of the flicks where the monkey had all the best lines and all the laughs. There was something unsettling about watching the president of the United States holding hands with and talking to a monkey.

It was nearly 1 a.m., but I called Virginia and spoke to my wife. Baby Gia was asleep, gaining pounds and inches daily. Brenda was sleepy and on her way to bed. Everything was good there. We would see each other in two days and they were going with me to Montreal on Saturday. We decided to discuss the details when we were both awake.

But before she hung up, she read my mind and said, "Oh yeah, isn't it a scream? He really won."

It was a scream all right. Some people were screaming now and the rest would probably have to take a number because we'd all be screaming sooner or later. I was rolling a joint and being relieved that he had not won by one vote because I had made no arrangements for an absentee ballot.

It was Iran, of course, more than anything else that I felt defeated Jimmy Carter. The fact that Americans had basically been taken prisoner, held as hostages in the embassy in Tehran for months, and President Carter had been unable to get them out either by negotiation or helicopter invasion. Evidently, when Carter had vainly ordered military helicopters across the desert, he forgot to tell the siroccos and other sandmen to lay down on their jobs and the furious winds caused a collision between the American air vehicles, which canceled the raid.

The whole fucking situation had been bizarre, starting with Carter's campaign promises to stop the supply of military support to certain world leaders, including the Shah of Iran, but he found out after the election that the deal was set in concrete and couldn't be stopped, at least until the Iranians insisted on the departure of the Shah and the arrival of the venerable Ayatollah from France. The pictures from Iran of his arrival, with what looked like a million people marching and whipping themselves, was something I'd not likely soon forget.

The Shah had been accepted in Egypt and aside from his bank accounts, he was carrying a clear message from the new leader of his country: "Do not go to the United States." Some twenty-five years past, in 1954, the Shah's father had been chased out of Iran and went to the United States. Eight months later there had been a countercoup that put the elder Pahlavi back in the castle. The Ayatollah had not forgotten 1954, and when his directions were ignored and the Shah arrived in the States, allegedly for cancer treatment, the U.S. embassy was surrounded and the fifty people inside became virtual prisoners, to be held there until the new government was stabilized. Later that same week, the Blacks inside the embassy were released and told they were free to come home. All except one, the radio operator, accepted the offer. So I imagined four dozen people sitting around in there listening to the radio.

The seizure of the embassy started a slide in Jimmy Carter's popularity, forcing a man who would rather not be threatening to okay the plan hatched by the people whose job it was to hatch crazy shit.

Another movie with Ronnie and the monkey came on. Americans had a thing about animals relating to people on a human level. There was a talking mule, *Mr. Ed,* and a TV show with a dog who was smarter than its owners. There was less than hidden meaning in the choice of Reagan movies being shown. "Message" movies. An idea whose time had just shown up.

What I was thinking was that America had just voted to make Stevie's job harder than a long shot.

Most presidents were good for two terms. Unless some disaster took place during their first term. What happened at the embassy in Iran was essentially not Jimmy Carter's fault. And as far as one could see there was nothing that Reagan could do about it. The failed rescue attempt was not Carter's fault, either, but was seen as his failure. His only hope had been for the workers there to be released before the election. Otherwise he could have been running against a man with one leg and he would still have looked like a jackass in the Kentucky Derby. So the voters elected another jackass instead. Great.

I had to take the Republican victory as another obstacle for Stevie. And since I was now signing up for the remainder of the tour, forty-odd dates that would last another four months, I was set back, too.

I would have liked to be down the hall with the band talking about the show. We had sounded pretty good in the club that night. I always felt better in smaller venues where we were closer to the crowd. But I was going out first thing in the morning, so I couldn't afford any monkey business. You dig?

I was scheduled for a solo performance of poetry and music on the campus of Kent State University on November 5. I was in rare form, telling a mixed audience of students, faculty members, administrators, and noncampus residents of the town that Ronald Reagan had been a political cast member since the 1960s. (In fact there had been several Californians from places like Santa Rita who had wanted him cast aside.)

It was unbelievable to me that the country as a whole had a hole in its head. Even with a good director, Reagan had never been anything other than nondescript. Nothing he had done in Hollywood recommended him for a position that at times called for the best actor in the world.

I could claim my objection to Reagan was out of concern for the man's personal well-being. Aside from his age, I thought the man might be suffering from an inner-ear problem. There was often a connection between the cochlea and one's balance. And Reagan seemed to be tilting to the right.

It was apparently a problem that started in the 1950s, when Reagan had been a Democrat and considered something of a liberal during the McCarthy era. As the president of the Screen Actors Guild, he was called on to defend fellow artists like David Susskind and Dalton Trumbo from the mail-monitoring senator from Wisconsin and his crony, Roy Cohn. As the years passed, the governor started tilting.

First he changed parties and became a Republican. Then his ideas brought him a reputation as a conservative. Finally, by the time students were locked up in a compound overnight in Santa Rita, he was labeled an ultraconservative. That might have been an illness he contracted because of his state's proximity to Arizona, where the old guard Barry Goldwater was guarding the conservative doctrine. Turning conservative might have been considered a regional revamping of political posture or just a role adjustment. Whatever. By the 1970s there was very little difference between himself and Attila the Hun. The problem now, as I saw it, was how far was too far to the right.

And as unfamiliar as East Coast voters were with the specifics of a West Coast governor's political positions, there should have been enough ex-hippies in America to render Ron's run null and void. But it was not his Hollywood that fanned my flames. It was that as president he would choose justices for the Supreme Court.

The audience at Kent State that November night was the kind I enjoyed: folks who were aware of current events, were quick to pick up on my use of the California state-guard language, my facility for phrasing, my dissection of diction, even my most outrageous puns were taken in fun. Politics was not my favorite topic on poetry stops—or in life. As a rule, heaping helpings of political opinions were a quick way to either bore people to death or become their least favorite poet.

But if you were alive on the planet earth and Black, particularly a Black American, in the most awkward and uncomfortable position imaginable, that of a certified, tax-paying citizen, with roots in the land around you that went back three hundred years, you still got the short end of every stick except the nightstick, and there was damn near no way you could not have political pressure on you and therefore have political opinions.

You were the odd man out.

I told my laughing group that I felt another poem coming on, and skewered the political past of the ex-head of the Screen Actors Guild, the ex-ambassador, ex-governor, et cetera, claiming that the man had more Xs than a Black Muslim mosque.

Somehow I had developed an extra sense, "social forethought." And so many of the people, places, and things I

259

mentioned, even my throwaway lines, became significant later. Ronald Reagan was a good example. Back in 1974, in "H2Ogate Blues," I'd identified Reagan, then an ex-governor of California, as part of America's new wave of leaders.

I told the Kent State audience I was "half and half" about the Republican victory. Personally, as a citizen, I was sorry as hell. But as far as my career was concerned, it was great. I didn't want to constantly be caught trying to make a fool out of the president. I wanted a man who could do that for himself. A man like Nixon. A man like Gerald Ford, whom I'd dubbed "oatmeal man" in 1975 in "We Beg Your Pardon," off *The First Minute of a New Day*. ("Anybody who could spend twenty-five years in Congress and nobody ever heard of him has got to be oatmeal man.") Of course, I'd heard of Ford. And had not thought the career congressman from Michigan would provide any good material. The man had never given anyone a clue that he might even have a personality.

But he did have a knack for inadvertent physical comedy. There were pictures of him as a college football player in the era of leather helmets. He once tripped and tumbled all the way down the stairs of the presidential plane, Air Force One. That inspired the song called "Don't Just Do Something, Stand There." And he was good for the occasional malapropism. Like when he was asked during an interview with a sports announcer at the baseball all-star game whether he stayed current with the game, and he replied, "Oh, I manage to see a few games on the radio."

And now I had Reagan. Write on!

By the end of February 1981, I had completed 80 percent of "B Movie," my most seriously hilarious political tirade.

Leaving Kent State that night, though, I had to admit that my full attention hadn't been on the crowd. I was doing a concert on the very spot where the peace movement had been shifted into overdrive by the shooting of four demonstrators by the National Guard. What a bitch of a year that had been. And now I was off to rejoin my band to continue to support Stevie on the *Hotter than July* tour.

35

I had no choice aside from moving quick
An ex-country hick whose image was city slick
The last one they would've ever picked
When I was in school doing my weekend stick
Compared to my classmates I couldn't sing a lick
And through record store windows when they saw my flick
On the cover of an LP they wished for a brick
Because it wasn't just out there it was actually a hit
And what they were wondering was what made me tick
It was that in spite of themselves they could all feel it

In reality I was heading for work
In the back of a cab I was changing my shirt.
My Mickey Mouse was saying it was five to eight
So theoretically I was already late.
Next to me on the backseat were my daughter and my wife
And I'd probably say never been happier in my life.
Light rain was falling on the Montreal streets
And I slipped on my shoes and leaned back in the seat
As we pulled up to the Forum where the Canadiens played.

Tonight: "Stevie Wonder" the marquee proudly displayed
But not a word about me or my "Amnesia Express"
But I was feeling too good to start getting depressed

It was only four days since I had found out for sure
That Stevie wanted me opening the rest of the tour.
News of Bob Marley's illness was a helluva blow
I thought. And the eight o'clock news came on the radio
It looked like a sellout though the weather was damp
And fortunately no cars blocked the underground ramp.
As the cab took the curves beneath the old hockey rink
I was lighting a Viceroy and still trying to think
Of how Hartford had sounded and the tunes we should play;
Made mental notes of the order and felt it was okay

Keg Leg, my man, stood near the security line
'Cause I never had I.D. and couldn't get in sometimes
I was carrying Gia as we moved down the hall
And I nodded and smiled as I heard my name called.
Things were getting familiar and I was finding my niche
But I didn't want to give producers any reason to bitch.
I told my brother to get the band ready at eight o'clock
And it was damn near ten after when I moved into my spot
James Grayer gave me a smile and tapped his Mickey Mouse
The lights went down and the crowd perked up
Because I was finally in the house.

I was a late-afternoon arrival in Boston, having gone with the wife
and daughter back to Virginia between dates. Which was why
I didn't know anything at all about the conflict, confrontation,
and, finally, conflagration at the hotel the night before.

263

It was just as well, because I must admit my first thought when I was asked whether I'd heard about it was, *No, but I damn well should have!* I had naturally thought of Keg Leg and my brother Denis. (That was a helluva thing, wasn't it? Keg Leg having been named Dennis at birth made him even more pleased about finding that nickname when he was working with Denis Heron.)

"It was a bitch!" I was told, but I moved on to my dressing room to check my Rhodes. And then I saw Grayer. Big Jim had two black eyes.

Not having been there, I could not say what took place. And not having spoken to Grayer personally about the incident, I could not say what an eye witness reported. And though I heard in detail what at times seemed to exceed what an eye witness could have eye witnessed with only two eyes, I could only say there seemed to have been a difference of opinions over the two days, and it appeared that one of those differing points of view had been defended by James Grayer, the manager of stage, time on stage, and, based on the veracity of his tenacity against a quoted number of simultaneous opponents, kicking ass.

The opposing points of view were said to have been held by an erratically shifting number of hotel security guards and a gentleman whose evening was looking like it might be written up as if his job had been to escort a young lady to the bar for Mr. Grayer.

Whatever the ultimate number of participants holding the perspective counter to Grayer's, Stevie Wonder was unhappy. And he made his dissatisfaction about Boston's image as a cultural phenomenon, a legend in its own mind, a leading battle-ground against busing, a place of prejudice and bigotry only Jim Rice of the Red Sox could truly describe day by frustrating day.

In the middle of his two hours, when he was left on the stage alone to do "Lately" and "Ribbon in the Sky," Stevie started talking. And if there was ever any doubt about how perceptive he was, about how well a man could piece together his feelings from pictures drawn for him, how completely he was able to read the tenor of a time, the climate of an area, the tension-soaked atmosphere of a city, those doubts would have been erased in six or seven heart-stopping, pin-dropping minutes when the Boston Garden was like the sound of fifteen thousand people who had just inhaled: there wasn't even the sound of anyone breathing as the brother spoke. You would remember not the words, but how Boston felt. Like it had been read from stones dotted with Braille.

36

By 1980, I was an old hand at playing Madison Square Garden. If I had still been living in New York, I could have gone through a yawn or two on my second night there with Stevie. New Yorkers had a shield of cool oblivion and paid little attention to the Garden, the Empire State Building, and even the Statue of Liberty.

Indeed there were millions of New Yorkers who had never visited any of those landmarks and knew only that the Garden was down near Times Square and that you played ball there.

Only the most literate music fans would mention that Madison Square Garden was also a concert venue. And even they would have to say *also* a concert venue, indicating that was not its primary function. Sort of like why there were so few hockey games at Carnegie Hall.

I might have been losing my arenaphobic attitude by that point. I had now done seven shows without an "airplane hangar effect," echoes that never died. I was deciding that arenas that weren't auditoriums could be modified like cafeterias that weren't gymnasiums that I played basketball in while at Fieldston. I had already decided that my prejudice against arenas was selective, that I didn't necessarily dislike playing in front of

266

a lot of people. In fact, the more the merrier. I was starting to compare the experience to playing on television, which I had initially hated. The idea of having my songs and my band all squeezed through a midrange mono speaker the size of an ash tray had depressed me as much as the thought of doing a lip-sync on *American Bandstand* or *Soul Train*. It had almost broken my heart to see the Temptations stumbling their way through "Ain't Too Proud to Beg."

There was one thing undeniably advantageous about playing in a venue like Madison Square Garden. There would be, on certain occasions, an energy generated that turned a concert into an event, that gave an indoor performance an air of a festival, an aura of celebration. That was the special buzz, an inaudible hum of excitement and energy that vibrated through everyone in the place. It was running all through the Garden; in the darkened tunnels that led to the dressing rooms and the storage spaces crammed with sports equipment and other event paraphernalia. Hell, everyone from Jumbo to Tom Thumb or whoever P.T. Barnum had promoted had plodded or pranced through these shadowy passages. I felt it.

Beneath bright Broadway and traffic-choked avenues, there were other worlds that existed; worlds of magic and music and miracles. And tonight this was to be the world of Michael Jackson.

Another Jackson. Just what I needed.

Thousands of fans who fantasized about being like Mike, or simply liked Mike, would get a special spectacle this evening because the Prince of Pop was already in the house and rumored to be loosening up his nearly liquid limbs in some private pocket along the passageways by the time I finished my set. He was to be a very special delivery and join me and Stevie when we closed the evening. I got to see different performers join us onstage from Houston to Hollywood. You couldn't predict the next surprise Stevie would spring on his audience as we crossed the U.S.A. and Canada. It had become so routine for rockers and high rollers to finagle their faces into the finale that there was hardly a double take from the regulars or roadies, but the Michael Jackson rumor sent some shivers through both the rulers and the riffraff.

I was pleased that everyone else was pleased. From the road representatives of Dick Griffey's Concerts West to certain venue venerables of the Madison Square Garden hierarchy, there was a noticeable neurosis and noise in the arena that evening.

I had met Michael and a couple of his brothers before, but I couldn't say that I knew him or that he would have remembered me. I admired him, of course, since there was no way not to appreciate an artist who had sold as many records as McDonald's had sold burgers. I had been a guest of Greg Phillinganes on one sunshine-splashed afternoon at a studio in L.A. where the Jacksons were regrouping to do an album. Michael was one of the few phenoms remaining when I arrived and Greg organized a brief introduction to folks. I was cool with that, even pleased to meet them in person. It had not been as electric as meeting Quincy Jones or Miles Davis, but I wouldn't forget that it had happened. But what did I know? Only that this youngster, with the hair falling over one eye and a voice so soft and quiet that your ears had to reach for it, was record royalty.

Maybe all performers are schizophrenic, with a broader distance between their jobs and their homes and with more space between their fame and their families. The bigger their marquee, the greater the gap.

But I had never noticed that as a certainty. There was a separation, to be sure, between personalities in public and when they were relaxing offstage. Kareem Abdul-Jabbar was always recognized and greeted everywhere he went. He was obviously outsized and outstanding, even while seated. In public the brother was always serious. But there was a private person, cringing and covering up with the rest of us when the alien burst from some astronaut's chest or collapsing and holding his sides while watching an Amos 'n' Andy video.

Thanks to my access to folks who were no strangers to success, I had met a thousand names more recognizable than those who owned them. I had met Muhammad Ali on several occasions, always a bit awed by his size and agility, but relaxed by his natural warmth and humor. He kept a smile at the ready, at the corners of his mouth and in his eyes as they searched out his surroundings.

But these casual encounters with artists off duty gave me no warning about how the electricity would elevate, how the excitement level would rise in the arena when Michael Jackson joined us onstage as the band went into the reggae rhythm of "Master Blaster." He would raise the voltage.

I often try to tell people how special Michael Jackson was, as though they don't know. Because I myself didn't know. I thought I did—until he came out for "Master Blaster" at Madison Square Garden.

Stevie called for the monitor man to pull the rhythm track up and with a wide grin beckoned for his "special guest," someone who needed no introduction. I looked behind me as he took three steps, paused a beat, and stood straighter and taller, turning solid then as from mist to man. I don't see that well. Sometimes.

He didn't just walk onto the stage. He turned solid as he came. A trick of the light. He glided past me into the spotlight. There was a surge of energy from the crowd that lifted the sound in the arena from stereo to quadraphonic and even the temperature seemed to rise when he touched the perimeter of the spotlight. And as the crowd's suspicions were confirmed by recognition, the buzz turned into an active roar. The monitor volume was overcome and Stevie's smile got wider and he clapped his hands close to his chest and waited for the turn, caught the opening when it swung around again and the house roar slid down to thunder again.

When the hook arrived it was like a huge transport landing on foam: "Didn't know you would be jammin' until the break of dawn . . ." Michael and I began on the beat and on the same harmony note, but as smoothly as he had floated from the shadows to my side, his voice climbed to the next harmony note where he seemed to cancel our collision and make himself at home again, two notes further up the scale.

After another chorus with me holding the mike for Mike I realized how prepared he was to do this and how unprepared I was to do it with him.

He knew the song. All of it. The lyrics, the changes, and all of the harmony parts. Hell, I hadn't got my part right until we got to Hartford. Tonight I felt like a six-foot mannequin clutching the base of the wireless like a giant gray ice-cream cone, frozen into a position of extending my arm between us, trying to collect both of our voices. It felt like reaching for water with a butterfly net. I was committed to remaining stationary and holding the sound stick steady. Michael might have been, but even while standing still he seemed to flow in every direction. Without a further thought I handed him the microphone and strolled to the shadows on our side of the stage.

In essence I got to watch two wonders at once. Up close: a smiling Stevie at center stage behind his keyboard bank with his head slightly tilted in what had been my direction; and sliding in and out of the circle of soft light that usually told me where to stand I saw this youngster, bending with impossible balance, twisting the tempo around him like a thread that spins a top. And then he reversed it, twirling like a boneless ice skater. The symmetry was perfect because he was as still as a statue when the foundation of the verse appeared and Stevie came in again. I was looking ahead and saying I had thirty more shows to try that, to get it like Mike. Probably not.

37

I suppose that as long as we live, Stevie Wonder will call me Air-reez. But only when it's appropriate. Like at night, after a show, at a group gathering in somebody's hotel space.

There was a game the members of Wonderlove seemed to set up with Stevie. The door to a back room was closed. Stevie would have a seat beyond the room's double beds and the group members would sit along the walls and on the beds. Quietly. Holding conversations with the people near them. Waiting. To near silence I opened the door, an unsuspecting party seeker, and threw a freezing rope that fell on the shoulders of the occupants. I saw Stevie in a straight-backed chair leaning toward me with a half smile. There was an empty second in a room full of expectation and then Stevie pulled himself erect and shouted, "Air-reez!" and everybody laughed and clapped and looked at me like a pickpocket with his hand caught in a mousetrap.

I never knew how he did that, and I never asked him because I always thought I would figure it out. And it wasn't as though I gave up there, threw my hands up in disgust and vowed to change my aftershave. I was not born on April 1st thirty years before this get-together for the future amusement of Wonder-love. I got caught because somebody whispered my name and I knew Stevie could hear a fly pissing on a piece of cotton down the block. *Just wait until next time*, I thought.

The next time was less than two weeks later. A similar situation. It was after a concert and all the band and crew rooms were in the one hotel. I wasn't sure that things were arranged until I was directed toward the back of a suite by a grinning Calvin. I nodded my understanding and, taking no chances at all, I tiptoed with rubber soles on carpet up to a door that I inspected with suspicion. I had a plan.

With a quick wrist flick I twisted my way in and put a finger against my lips to the group as I shut the door behind me. My expression said, "Nobody breathe!"

Stevie was stunned. He'd been quicked and he knew it. He was sitting up straight and his head was rotating slowly like a gyroscope. I was watching for breathers, but then with his face to the ceiling, he grinned my way and shouted, "Air-reez!"

I don't know what to tell you about that. It was probably the time I should have asked him how he knew it was me. After a while, however, I started to feel like a guy waiting backstage for a magician to ask him about his performance. They were not telling and I shouldn't be asking.

I took a glass of punch somebody offered and a seat on the bed next to Stevie, clapping him on the shoulder. The room had resumed a party's volume. Music. Teasing. Guys and girls who had become close friends on the road or maintained relationships over the hundreds of highways were telling each other

273

secrets. Stevie was humming something and tapping the table in front of him like a keyboard.

Malcolm Cecil always had stories about incidents that took place when he was recording Stevie. Like a game they used to play in the hallways at the Record Plant in L.A. The hallway was about ten-feet-wide, and Stevie would stand in the middle of the floor with about four feet of space on either side. The object of the game was to get by Stevie on one side or the other without him catching you. According to Malcolm it couldn't be done. I would have suspected that Malcolm, practitioner of Tai Chi, would certainly have perfected a silent step among the pirouettes and paces I'd seen him go through, but no matter. Evidently Stevie was a master of a superior art. Ears like an eagle.

When you spent time with Stevie, the extraordinary became commonplace, the unusual was unremarkable and the previously overwhelming could be overlooked. The things that made him seem extraordinary to me were not confined to the stage. In fact, they had nothing to do with this stage presence. But I'd also been going out more and more to catch earlier parts of his show, well before he called out for me to join him.

I liked the opening. I liked the strength of it, the sudden flashes of light and color and movement. I'm sure I got as big a kick as anyone else when he was captured by the spotlight rocking like a pendulum with dreads from side to side and cranking "Wonderlove" into "Sir Duke." I was also pulled from the reverie of my dressing room to catch the transition that took place in the middle of the set, when the band members seemed to evaporate like mist and Stevie was left alone at the keyboards.

274

There was something unbelievably poignant about the isolation. The darkness of the giant arena was filled with silent memories and "Lately" became a magic carpet he rolled out for us to ride.

I still wanted to believe I was a better lyricist but there was mounting evidence to the contrary on an album of surgical sensitivity called *Hotter than July*. I left my dressing room during the solo section of Stevie's set to listen to lyrics that were more than something to say while playing piano. If you happened to notice a man leaning at an awkward angle in the shadows of the tunnel connecting us to privacy, it was only me eavesdropping on the chill and lonely certainty of "Lately."

38

Different dates on the tour were memorable for different reasons. Some days I took notes, though most of those notes seem to have been done as a joke, some kind of acrobatic way of pulling my own leg. There were either a few lines written before the show along with whatever expenses I needed to note, or, after the concert, in the early a.m., there was a separate page or two that described something that happened or that I felt during the day or evening. There was rarely both, rarely an occasion when I wrote something before and after a show. December 8, 1980 in Oakland was a before-and-after day. I still remember the after feelings now.

I rarely missed things Stevie said to me. But when I saw him at the bottom of the backstage stairs at the arena in Oakland, I thought I must have misheard him. Maybe it was the shock at what he had said. Maybe I hadn't missed what he said and just thought I did. It was something I didn't want to hear.

But no, I must have mistaken Stevie for sure.

"What did you say?" I asked him, trying to get above the noise.

"I said some psycho, some crazy person, shot John Lennon!" Stevie said. "And I'm wondering how to handle it."

I am not so silly or naive as to suspect that there is an ultimate evil. But the death of a good man, so rare as to be nearly extinct, is a thorough tragedy. And what do you say about it to seventeen thousand people who have come out to see you and enjoy themselves?

I got that same feeling I'd felt when I heard that Dr. King or someone else was killed; that sense of a certain part of you being drained away, a loss of self. There were certain events in your life that had such historical significance that you were supposed to remember the circumstances under which you received the news for the rest of your life. That was probably what some section of humanity used to illustrate man's superiority over other animals: "memories of miseries that memorialize."

Having those memories was like turning down the corner of a page in your life's book. But maybe animals turned down corners of pages, too. They might not choose the date of the death of John Lennon to see as a date of loss and mourning, they would be more likely to remember the date the Ringling Brothers died or the day the woman from *Born Free* was born.

I was sure they talked about important things. I didn't have the dialogue down pat, but I could picture a conversation between two lions on a late-night walk across the savannah.

"Yeah, that's where it was, man," one of them says. "Right over there by the watering hole. A big mean-looking thing with sharp teeth and the strongest grip you ever heard of. The gorilla called it an animal trap. Man, that thing grabbed Freddy Leopard and held him for hours. The gorilla got Freddy loose but his leg was all fucked up and he's still walking with a limp."

Just exactly what did those recollections, those dog-eared pages, prove? That you were connected to the human race? It couldn't be. Because if so, people born since then, who weren't around then, couldn't be connected. That's why there were history books and parents and other folks to tell you what happened before you got here.

And why did you need to remember those things? Most of them were about someone being killed or assassinated. You could almost feel as though you needed an alibi: "Where were you the day that such-and-such a person was murdered?" They were pages in history books, however. I didn't know why. I didn't know what it proved. That you were connected to the human race? They were usually the least human things you could imagine. Unnatural disasters.

I always knew where I'd been. I was in last period history class at DeWitt Clinton High School when the principal announced from the bottom of an empty barrel: "Ladies and gentlemen, I regret to inform you that your president is dead." He was talking about John Kennedy, shot to death by someone in Dallas.

I was in the little theatre at Lincoln when a guy everyone called "the Beast" had thrown open a rear door and shouted, "The Reverend Dr. Martin Luther King has been shot and killed in Memphis, Tennessee."

I was in my bedroom on West 17th Street when man first reached the moon and I had written a poem called "Whitey on the Moon" that very night (for which my mother had come up with the punch line: "We're gonnna send these doctor bills air mail special to Whitey on the moon").

I was drawn back to a conversation with my grandmother as she reenacted the national shock that shook America when the news came down that Franklin Delano Roosevelt was dead: "It was just incredible," she said with her eyes getting wide. "Nobody seemed to think that he would ever really die."

And now I would always remember the night John Lennon died. Yeah, because of who told me and where, but also because of the effect the news had on the crowd. It proved we had been right, Stevie and I, when we hastily decided that it would serve no purpose to make that announcement before he played.

"No, just wait until the end, before we play them songs," I told him. "Hell, ain't nothin' they can do about it."

And that had been soon enough. The effect of Stevie's somber announcement on the crowd was like a punch in the diaphragm, causing them to let out a spontaneous "Whaaaa!" Then there was a second of silence, a missing sound, as if someone had covered their mouths with plastic, so tight not even their breathing could be detected. I was standing at the back of the stage outside of the cylinder of light that surrounded Stevie, next to Carlos Santana and Rodney Franklin, who were joining us for the closing tunes.

Stevie had more to say than just the mere announcement that John Lennon had been shot and killed. For the next five minutes he spoke spontaneously about his friendship with John Lennon: how they'd met, when and where, what they had enjoyed together, and what kind of a man he'd felt Lennon was. That last one was the key, because it drew a line between what had happened in New York that day and what had happened on that motel balcony in Memphis, Tennessee, a dozen years before. And it drew a circle around the kind of men who stood up for both peace and change. That circle looked suspiciously like a fucking bull's-eye to me. It underlined the risks that such men took because of what all too often happened to them.

Stevie said it made the rally five weeks in the future just that much more significant. All I was thinking about was that it made security more significant. That was for damn sure.

But it was another stunning moment in an evening of already notable cold-water slaps, a raw reminder of how the world occasionally reached inside the cocoon that tours and studios and offices on West 57th Street provide. It stopped your heart for a beat and froze your lungs for a gasp; showing you how fragile your grip on life was and how many enemies you didn't know you had.

It also gave Stevie Wonder's tour and his quest for a national holiday for a man of peace more substance, more fundamental legitimacy. Not just to me. Everyone seemed to understand a little better where Stevie was coming from and what this campaign was all about:

It went from somewhere back down memory lane
To hey motherfuckers out there! There are still folks who are insane
In 1968 this crowd was eight to twelve years old
And they weren't Beatle maniacs but they did know rock and roll.
The politics of right and wrong make everything complicated
To a generation who's never had a leader assassinated
But suddenly it feels like '68 and as far back as it seems
One man says "Imagine" and the other says "I have a dream."

Stevie took his heart with him onstage some nights. Both parts of his heart. The warm part and the part that sat in fear. It showed his feelings. In the whole arena that night in Oakland there could not have been a legitimate doubt about his sincerity. His respect for Dr. King and his friendship for John Lennon took shape and gained dimension as he left the campaign trail and gave seventeen thousand that could have been seventeen million or just seventeen a look at what most men will deny they have: an inside where all the insanity and madness of this world really hurt and enraged you.

I had felt a little of that from Stevie before. It was simmering there on *20/20* when he was creating a song for Barbara Walters. It was in his voice in Boston, Massachusetts, when he stopped a show to review that city's record of racism. It was a grasp of an essence of things about life that far exceeded whether Stevie could hold a note or play a scale or write his name, much less a tune. This was a man whose humanity and compassion was real, as visible and as certain as the tears that seeped from beneath his dark glasses and flowed freely down his face onto his clothes. Tears he never bothered to wipe away.

Stevie's talking was like a jazz solo, spontaneous and immediate, an expression so honest as to be almost embarrassing. I was trying to find things to look for around my shoes as tears took a front-row seat in my eyes.

Later, I could not remember us playing those last two songs, though I was sure we had. I could only bring back three solid images of that night, two of Stevie: the first one was of the brother standing there waiting for me at the bottom of those stairs. The

281

second was of him standing alone in that spotlight, crying. And the third was of me standing there next to Santana with our eyes sweeping the floor as though there was really something to look for.

I carried one other memory out of Oakland with me. It was about an article in the paper the next morning, a review of the show that slammed both me and Stevie to the floor, starting with the first paragraph: How dare I be called the Minister of Information, it said, and how dare Stevie be called the Ambassador of Love to the world, when neither of us had the decency to mention that a friend or a fraternal brother had been killed.

The implication of this was racist in its nature. It implied that because I was Black and Stevie was Black and John Lennon was white and therefore not a "Soul Brother," that there had been no mention from the stage about the murder.

Keg Leg was outraged: "What the hell he talkin' 'bout, boss? Stevie standing up there all that time talking!"

"It's about the deadline, Keg," I tried to explain. "In order to get that article in the paper this morning the reporter had to leave by 11:00. And Stevie didn't start talking until 11:30."

What that meant was that seventeen thousand people knew what happened, but three hundred thousand read in the paper the next morning that both Stevie and I were far less than we ever intended to be.

39

January 15, 1981

What's amazing about people who are supposed to "think of everything" is how many things have *never crossed their minds*. It's obvious that what that expression is meant to indicate focuses on a specific subject, like whatever is going on in your life or what you're involved with at the time. By the middle of January 1981, I should have known a whole lot more than I did about what I was involved in and what was going on in my life.

That was never more clear to me than when I saw how things looked from the back of the outdoor stage set up on the Washington D.C. monument grounds as Stevie's rally for Dr. King got under way. I can't even explain to you how little I knew, but I will try to explain it to you the way it occurred to me.

I would never claim to be the smartest son of a gun on the planet. If I had claimed that, all of you readers would know by now that I was lying. But by the same token, by then I had been in this business for ten years and had to feel as though I knew more than when I started. And also, by then, I had been working on the *Hotter than July* tour for ten weeks, and had some new information crossing my mind as I climbed the back stairs onto the temporary stage and looked out at perhaps fifty thousand people standing shoulder-to-shoulder across the expanse of the Mall chanting, "Martin Luther King Day, we took a holiday!"

As of January 15, I could look back ten weeks to Halloween since I'd been working on the *Hotter than July* tour. It was a project that, when taken as a whole, was set up to cover sixteen weeks, or four months, a third of a year. The endeavor was cut into two six-week halves with a break, a rest period, that lasted a month. Since the tour had gone on break from the West Coast in mid-December, my life had not been free of upset and disruption, but businesswise and musicwise things were on schedule. My new album, called *Real Eyes*, had been released around the first of December; some support for our performances over the next two months or so could be expected. That meant everyone would get paid and some of the music I was writing and arranging for our virtually new configuration with the horn section was starting to fit. That was good.

In essence, this rally was the halftime show before the second six-week half. But if you've ever seen the Florida A&M marching band, just how long do you think it takes to perfect those steps, formations, baton tosses, improvisations, and instrument playing?

So nobody that I could see up there seemed likely to jump up and start majoretting up and down Constitution Avenue, but I was pleased to see how many people thought Stevie was worth supporting.

One thing that knocked me out looking at this halftime show was how much I had not thought about. Like how much work was involved in organizing a fucking rally. That was what Stevie had done and what had to have taken up so much of his offstage time when we were playing and what must have consumed what I was calling a "rest period," the month off between December 15 and today, Dr. King's birthday. This had to have dominated a great deal of his time and probably much more of his thoughts. The rally. Ways to publicize it, ways to dramatize it, ways to legitimize it.

Some of it was obvious. You had to have permits, like a license to have a parade. That seemed bizarre, but it took a necessary number of police to close certain streets or divert traffic or just stand around looking like police. And on the monument grounds there were wooden saw horses and security and crowd restraints and a stage and sound equipment and technicians to set it all up and run it. And I was enjoying another piece of equipment I felt was necessary: a heat-blowing machine to warm my chilly backside.

I had no idea what this was costing, what the total expenses were. Nor did I ever ask about it and have the expenses incurred by Stevie neurotically concealed from me. I didn't have any way to justify saying, "Hey, just what the hell is this gonna cost?"

I considered that this information was probably something that was being distributed on a need to know basis, and apparently I did not have that. I didn't worry about why.

My respect for Stevie Wonder expanded in every direction that day. I was following his lead like a member of his band, because seeing as he had envisioned was a new level of believing. It was something that seeped in softly, and when you were personally touched by someone's effort and genuine sincerity, your brain said you didn't yet understand but your soul said you should trust.

We had been to Mayor Marion Barry's office earlier in the day. There I was introduced to the winner of a citywide essay contest that had run in the D.C. school system. The theme of the essay was why Dr. King's birthday should be a national holiday, and the contest was open to middle and high school students. A seventh grader won, and I thought the fact that he was in the seventh grade was the headline out of that. After they introduced us, I took a few minutes to read his essay so I would know what to be listening for—my cue when he came to the end, because now, at the rally, I would present him to the crowd.

It was a gray winter day, the type of gray that looked permanent, not bothered with clouds or memories of blue. Gray, sullen, not threatening but sporting an attitude. Somebody was organizing things, checking out how many speakers were on hand who wanted to say a few words.

When we got to the part of the program where the kid was to read his essay, I introduced him and walked back offstage. I kept one ear on the loudspeakers because I had to be on it when he was through. That would be no more than five minutes, max.

At some stage, I heard the kid having trouble reading his own essay. I thought he might have been nervous with the big crowd and the TV audience, it must have felt like everybody in the world was watching him. I could hear the crowd getting restless and a couple of folks started giving the kid a hard time. Suddenly, mid-sentence, or maybe in the middle of a word, the kid stopped. He turned around and went back to his seat. It was a seat of honor, right behind the podium in the middle of the stage.

It was quiet now, just a sprinkle of sympathetic applause. I found my list of speakers and introduced the next one, but I realized something had gone wrong. As the next speaker approached the podium, I went over to the kid and said, "Let me see that essay there, brotherman."

And sure enough, he had stopped at the top of his second page, a good five or six paragraphs from the end. He had been reading from a mimeographed copy of his essay, and the ink was faded—I would have needed night goggles or some shit to see what was on that paper.

I waited until that next speaker was through, then went up there and explained to the audience that I was going to introduce the kid again, and that he was going to read his essay to the end, and that they were going to listen. Yeah, I knew it was cold, I said, but it was cold for this kid, too, and he was reading from a faded copy, and I didn't want to hear nothing from the crowd but applause, period. "Have some patience with the young brother, please."

After I introduced him, I walked backstage again. He started to read again, and I heard him coming to the point where he had faltered, the part on the page that was damn near invisible. He started to falter again, and I listened for some wiseass to say something. But then it started to go smoothly, and I looked over and there was Diana Ross standing next to him with her arm around his shoulder. Without being in the way, without making it her essay, she helped him over those rough spots. My man's confidence got a lift and the crowd started to appreciate what he had written. I stood there thinking, *There must be thirty or forty adults up here on this stage, and she's the only one of us who thought to go up there and help the brother!*

Jesse Jackson spoke, too. His attitude was about changing the laws and about people needing to know more about Thurgood Marshall and needing to know more about what happened, because the way to change America was through the law. You see, if you don't change the law, you don't change anything. You could burn your community down and somebody else would build it up; all you were doing was burning down some houses. But if you changed the law, then you had done a whole lot to change the foundation of society.

To be sure, I looked at the appearances there and then as a tribute for respect for Dr. King. But they were also an indication of respect for a brother for taking a step to bring a positive idea forward, to remind some of us that we could hardly criticize congressmen and other representatives for inaction if their attempts to push ideas important to us out in the open received no visible interest from those it purportedly would benefit most.

Yeah, this piece of legislation to make Dr. King's birthday into a national holiday looked like a long shot, especially being raised just after America had elected Ronald Reagan, who would be inaugurated at the other end of the Mall in five days. But if our community was to make valuable contributions, then those who made them had to be recognized as offering something of value. Why would the next one of us feel that he or she should make the effort, marshal the strength, and somehow fortify him or herself against the opposition that always seemed stronger, longer, with more bonified, bona fide other side, if even a man who won the Nobel Peace Prize was ignored where those efforts for peace had done the most good?

Something was wrong with ignoring a man here that the world had acknowledged everywhere. To bring about a change inside the minds of people is difficult. That's why there are books and teachers and laws. A change in people's hearts is even more difficult to gauge. There has to be some sign from those who represent them in a society where folks live together without touching. There has to be some assurance that we have learned that those who showed the world did not present offerings that only people outside our country needed. Certainly recognition of a Desmond Tutu or a Martin Luther King by panels of objective individuals pointed out the value of those they honored beyond the constrictions of geography; that the work they did, in essence, came from this or that community but was of value to all mankind. How could this country purport to lead mankind and ignore what mankind needed and respected? Any American, raised in an atmosphere of abuse and violence, who suggested that centuries of deliberate discrimination could be overcome without responding to the oppressors in kind was not just valuable, but invaluable.

This was what Dr. King signified and this was what Stevie Wonder was calling on America to honor. All holidays should not be set aside for generals. To have the country honor men for doing what they did at a time when difficult personal decisions made their actions worthwhile for the overall good meant the same thing for all citizens.

That had been both the point and the ultimate disappointment of what had once been called "the Civil Rights movement." What was special about the 1960s was that there was only one thing happening, one movement. And that was the Civil Rights movement. There were different organizations coming from different angles because of geography, but in essence everybody had the same objective. It came so suddenly from so many different angles, things happening in so many different towns and cities at once, that the "powers that be" were caught off guard.

The powers had taken control when Eisenhower was elected. He held office while they secured a grip around our throats. He even spoke about it before he left office. But there was a fuckup. An oversight. They overlooked the same folks that they always overlooked. See, this was not long after Ralph Ellison had summed us up in *Invisible Man*. We were the last item on the last page of the last program. But that didn't last. Because the last thing they had counted on was active dissent. Until the 1960s "the movement" had been the exclusive property of middle aged and old people. Then it became a young people thing, and as the 1960s opened up, the key word became "activism," with Stokely Carmichael and the SNCC, "Freedom Rides," and sit-ins. There was a new feeling of power in Black communities. And once it got started, it was on the powers like paint.

But at some point a difference was created between "equality," "freedom," and "civil rights." Those differences were played up because something had to be done about the sudden unity among Black folks all over the country. Folks got more media attention whenever they accentuated the differences. There were media-created splinters. Otherwise the Civil Rights movement would have been enough, and would have been more successful. Accomplishing the aims of the movement would have made "gay rights" and "women's rights" and "lefts and rights" extraneous. But divide and conquer was the aim of programs like COINTELPRO. And even though it ended up working damn near backward, it worked.

They separated the fingers on the hand and gave each group a different demand; we lost our way. Separated, none of us seemed to know to watch out for COINTELPRO. J. Edgar Hoover was dead, but in D.C. they honored what he had said: Fuck every one-a-them.

There I was at the halftime show, looking up and down the field, and *I could see* for the first time. I could see what this brother had seen long before, what really needed to be done.

We all took the stage.

The crowd continued to chant, "Martin Luther King Day, we took a holiday!"

Stevie stepped up to the mic and addressed them:

"It's fitting," he said, "that we should gather here, for it was here that Martin Luther King inspired the entire nation and the world with his stirring words, his great vision both challenging and inspiring us with his great dream. People have asked, 'Why Stevie Wonder, as an artist?' Why should I be involved in this great cause? I'm Stevie Wonder the artist, yes, but I'm Steveland Morris, a man, a citizen of this country, and a human being. As an artist, my purpose is to communicate the message that can better improve the lives of all of us. I'd like to ask all of you just for one moment, if you will, to be silent and just to think and hear in your mind the voice of our Dr. Martin Luther King . . ."

40

In the summer of 1985, my daughter Gia, who was five at the time, was visiting my mother for a few weeks in New York City. As can happen with diabetics, grandma ran too hard one day, ran down, and then ran out. It was up to her granddaughter to run over to the phone, hit the 911 buttons, and tell the operator where to go—like where she was calling from.

That was the part that most impressed me and everyone else upon hearing about the save Gia made, that a five-year-old, just visiting New York, knew what street she was on (East 106th) and what apartment number they were in (19A). Not only did that take a good memory, it took a good set of nerves not to panic—at five or fifty-five. Since they had the right angle on what and where, the EMTs were able to beam in with the glucose and said it was "too close" to black out and urged mama to sack out for the rest of the evening before the next session of 911 roulette.

The incident proved how smart the daughter Brenda and I had produced was. She was intelligent, and turning out to be a nice person. The parents could not dictate or direct the intellect; they couldn't make a lick of difference in terms of whether their offspring had one of their IQ scores or the other's, one minus the other's, or both of their IQ scores added together. But they did have a lot to do with what kind of person or how kind a person their child became.

Sociology and every other inexact approximate science of odds and oddly negative prognostication be damned. Those sciences of vague, uneven basis and potential seemed to have been discovered to generalize and generally discourage humankind from being the kind of humans they could really be. That reminded me of that old Brook Benton tune about "the odds against goin' to heaven, six to one." Well, you had to figure that was absolute bullshit! I knew that odds-maker Danny Sheridan covered a bunch of subjects out there in Vegas, and that the British had odds on damn near everything, but I still doubted if numbers had or would ever be posted on heaven or hell, aside from the sure bet that you'd eventually have to get the hell out of here.

A few years later, I called my mother from London on her birthday, June 6. We had a few laughs before she reminded me that it was a real long distance call; we agreed we'd pick it up again when I got back to the USA. I told her I'd try to call her from Newark airport in New Jersey, where I was heading next before getting a late shuttle from there back to Washington.

Providing it took the usual amount of time to locate my bags, roll them through customs, and find my next boarding area, I'd have a tiny window to make a quick call—if everything worked.

It didn't. My big Continental jet from Heathrow landed an hour and a half late because of a storm. The last flight to D.C. was in thirty minutes, and was overbooked by too many seats for me to dream of catching, even if I stood on the wing. What do do?

I decided to go to Newark's Union Station and try to catch the last southbound Amtrak train of the night. While waiting for a cab, I called my mother. I couldn't reach her because the line was busy. I shrugged it off and got a taxi ride from a hassled and harassed brother complaining about the weather.

I missed the last train south by ten minutes, arriving at Newark station shortly before ten o'clock. The next train wasn't until three in the morning, a red-eye that arrived in Washington at six or seven in the morning. I could wait for that, the ticket agent informed me.

I looked unhappily around the dismal accommodations provided by Amtrak for Newark train riders. Obviously this station was for catching trains, not waiting for them. There wasn't even a newsstand or a soft-drink machine. Nothing to make you feel like you'd be waiting for anything but a robbery.

I made another call to my mother, to cry on her shoulder. But the line was still busy.

There was a 9:55 to New York's Penn Station.

I went back to the ticket agent, who was closing up for the evening, putting away his money and tickets.

"I'm going north," I said.

Suddenly I could almost locate my lopsided grin. I brightened considerably. Hell, in New York I could eat and get a magazine. There were people and signs of life. It would beat the hell out of waiting for God only knew what in the gloom of Newark's near morgue.

I heard the whistle of the arriving train and had just enough time to grab my bags and struggle down a flight of stairs before it *shushed* to a stop.

Two phrases came to mind right away when I arrived in New York City. It never failed. The first one was from Stevie's song "Just Enough for the City," when during the opening you hear his brother Calvin saying almost reverently, "New York! Just like I pictured it!" That was the perfect phrase with perfectly paced awe at the wonder of it all. The second phrase was, "New York, New York—so nice they named it twice." This was doubtless a contribution from a self-employed New York poet whose artistry was unrewarded by the city jaycees, whose perspective ran more to Frank Sinatra than to a frank description. Which also meant there might not have been many kudos available for the person who coined the term "the Big Apple," which was rotting to the core just then.

There was another saying that fit New York like a pimp fit in Times Square: 24/7. That was street folks' description of something open twenty-four hours a day, seven days a week. New York was that, and several institutions of legitimacy were counted on for day and night service, 365 days a year. No down times, just shift changes.

Penn Station was one of them. With trains bound for somewhere, everywhere, anywhere, and nowhere, there was an ongoing chaos that could remind you of the world's steady spin regardless of terrestrial complications, or involve you in how the madness of thousands of destinations could be coordinated in the brain of a human being.

At that moment, I was being impressed by the system of coordination that got the cheeseburger I was eating from wherever the hell it had been just in time to save me from starvation. I took a minute before I decided on dessert and called my mother again. It was a little late, but hell, she was the one doing the yakking on the line. It was busy again, so at slightly past eleven I ordered a milkshake to help me contemplate.

I didn't like what my contemplating was indicating.

Maybe you had to know my mother or know the Scotts in general, as she was a good representative of them. They were not loud, talkative, gregarious, flamboyant folks. They were not great users of telephones. The three hours I'd been unable to get past a busy signal would have been three months' worth of her talking. There might have been a talk once in a while with Mrs. Cox, her good buddy from Jackson. And there were one or two other ladies and a male friend who called. But I could hardly remember a phone conversation of hers that lasted more than fifteen minutes. And a conversation this late? I wouldn't call her after ten o'clock without a life or death situation.

At midnight I tried again. Busy. I just knew the line wasn't "engaged." And there was no reported trouble on the line. When the line had been busy at 8:30 and 9, it was unusual enough, but now it was into the realm of unbelievable. My name would not be the first name to come to mind if the question was bravery, but I was not one to panic. And I wasn't going to panic now.

Still, I made up my mind quickly. I thanked the phone operator, found a locker for my luggage, and hailed a cab in front of Penn Station. I headed for 106th Street.

Soon I was banging—no, make that BANGING—beating with both fists on the door of apartment 19A in the presence of a startled woman from the Housing Authority Police who was determined not to show she was startled. Beating in flurries of five that rang out like cannon shots without room to echo in the closet-sized hallway. Until even the barricaded, blasé, mind-your-own-business New Yorkers were disrupted. Until the lady in her neatly pressed uniform touched my arm lightly to say . . .

"Who is it?" came a squeak of a shaking voice from behind the door.

And then again, "Who is it?"

I was shouting, "It's your son! Open the door!"

"My son doesn't live here anymore," I heard.

Then the door opened as far as the chain restraint would allow, revealing my mother—or at least as much as I needed to see.

There was a gash across her cheek, with dried blood and drying blood like a halo around it as it turned shades of blue. Recognizing me, she let us in; her son and the lady in uniform who was now speaking into her radio.

I helped my mother back to the kitchen and safety while we waited for the ambulance.

41

In late February 1989, I was playing a weekend at Blues Alley in D.C. and noticed Lurma—the mother of my son Rumal—in the audience. It had been a long time since I'd seen her, though I had never stopped wondering why she had forbidden me to say anything about Rumal and therefore forbidden me from saying anything to him. I wondered who he thought his father was. Maybe the man rumor had connected to Lurma from time to time. I remained mystified until that night.

I went over and sat down, spoke to her, even took a picture with her. She told me she needed to talk with me, so I invited her to my hotel after the show.

I literally had no idea what we would talk about, but I knew it must have something to do with the boy. That was obvious.

Starting very slowly, she said, "I think it's time you had a talk with your son. He's beginning to ask me questions I can't answer."

"Birds and bees questions?" I asked with a crooked smile. "And does that mean it's all right for me to tell people he's my son?"

I wish I could describe all of the expressions I saw flash, focus, and fade from her face. About three seconds stretched out between us as we looked into each other's eyes. Both of us were looking for things we were surprised not to find. I was looking for the honesty I could always count on from her the quick reply or retort that she would lay in front of your shallowness or bounce off your arrogance. She was looking first for an indication of snide, then fake, a pretense of misdirection, then an attempted stab at some joke in poor taste. And finally, her judgment collapsed on shock and recognition.

"You've never mentioned him, I mean Rumal," she started, stopped, started.

It was my turn to be assertive.

"Never," I said. "To anyone. You told me not to tell anyone he was my son, and I haven't. Not even my mother."

"Your mother," she repeated.

"You didn't point out any exceptions," I told her, looking away. "So I couldn't make any. I haven't told my brother or sister or, hell, anyone. Does this visit mean I can tell them?"

As we talked further, she took me back as far as her visit to my house. She was trying to buy a house for her and Rumal in Alexandria. She felt as though she needed to have a fiancé with her when she showed up to see the house. That it was better to take a colleague from the *Washington Post* with her who could help represent stability and didn't want word circulating through the negotiations that her child was actually the son of a married man on Martha's Road.

She got the house. It was a three-story brick row house on Pine Lake Court. And as soon as the deal was complete and the papers signed, the brief charade with her coworker was abandoned. But no one had ever told me anything.

It had been obvious that some of Lurma's buddies at the *Post* and the *Washington Star* had not been sworn to secrecy. Unless they could only fuck with me about what they knew. And if they reported back to Lurma about my vague, evasive, and vacuous responses when they asked about my son, what had she thought? And what had she expected me to say? *Yes, quite right, I'm a thorough shithead. Of course I know about the boy. Lurma brought him over to my house. Matter of fact, when she calls I hang up. When she writes I throw the letters away. So now that she's resorted to messing with me by messenger I'm mortified.*

None of the above. She was standing in the middle of my hotel room while I sat down opposite her. She was talking to herself more than to me, about people knowing things.

"Yeah," I agreed, telling her the names of some of the people who had asked me questions over the years. "But they all came up slidin' and hidin', like they were back in junior high, like 'psst! Hey, Gil!'"

"And you said . . ."

"Nothing real! Or nothing at all. I gave them all of the information I could: None."

I ran out of words around then. Because I had run out and run down. And sort of felt run over.

I knew what I was being told within all she was not saying. But there was nothing I could do.

Lurma came out of it first and sat down. I asked if she wanted something to drink, some juice or something.

"How is he doing? Hell, how are you doing?" I tried to laugh.

"I'm fine," she said. "He's doing well."

301

She was a little brighter as we moved on to her favorite subject. Our son.

A month later I had been in a cab on my way to JFK Airport to catch a plane to Brussels when I suddenly directed the driver to go to Laguardia Airport instead, to the terminal where the shuttle to D.C. flew.

An hour and a half later I was knocking on the door on Pine Lake Court. And then Lurma was at the door with a little smile.

It was good to see her. I was at the right place.

I became very fond of Rumal Rackley, and I've been amazed at the similarities in our lives despite the distance we started with between us. He has the disadvantage of looking a great deal like me, with the same wide smile that he flashes on occasion and the same offbeat sense of humor. He was also a fairly good student, and our lives ran parallel all the way to graduate school. We both had beautiful mothers from Southern states who were college graduates. We both went to private high schools—in his case Sidwell Friends in Washington. We both went to Black colleges—he graduated from Hampton University. And he went on to grad school—at Tuskegee's medical school.

My third child, a girl named Ché, was born in England. She is a real trip, thoroughly full of near atomic energy, and allegedly possessing an IQ that equals her mother and father's combined.

She's a curious, furious, hurricane of movement with more questions than *Jeopardy*. Her specialty is hotel rooms. She finds them fascinating, with altogether too many things to explore.

How I became a father again at nearly fifty years old is a story I will save for another time.

42

On a typically warm Los Angeles evening in 1990, we were scheduled for two shows at Club Lingerie on Sunset Boulevard. The producers, the folks who ran the club, had to return some money when the second show was cancelled. I take 100 percent of the blame for the fans' disappointment that night. As I was leaving the stage between the two shows, I suffered a stroke.

I wish I had been more aware of my responsibilities as an observing artist. It would have been quite a coup for me to be able to describe to you exactly what happened to my body as I stepped with my usual stork-like grace. But I can't for the life of me remember the process, the actual changes that my body went through. I suppose it would read like those two-page centerfold stories in the *National Enquirer*: "I Died and Came Back to Life," by Jesus Christ or something.

The best I can do for you is a before and after. The before was the first show. Me on stage with my band, working hard, enjoying myself and the crowd. Immediately before, I was standing in the center of the stage introducing and pointing to the members of the band over the closing coda of "The Bottle." Everybody was smiling, huge to the point of laughter, lights coming up, crowd screaming, me raising both of my arms to embrace the applause.

And then . . . hot, real hot, but not sweating. Something happened—the stroke—on the way down those few steps at the front of the stage, before you took a right turn and headed toward the dressing room. An instant or so before is me starting down those steps, head down, some kind of cap on, not a baseball cap, my face in shadows, still smiling and happy because the band sounded good. Everybody was playing well and we sounded *energy* loud but not *volume* loud. The energy and adrenaline had not pushed tempos up and over the point where my smile was remembered rather than genuine. And I was already assembling and arranging the order of tunes we would do in the second show. This was a useless process, to be sure, because I would not decide more than the first two or three songs with certainty.

The after begins on the stairs with someone holding my arm and guiding me sightless past murmuring fans who had swallowed their cheers and perhaps even forgotten them, as I had.

I was totally blind. And I remember what I could not see. Maybe I mean I remember not being able to see.

No, this was not a reach for any closer relationship with Stevie. The blindness that I experienced struck me like lightning but without the electrical burns or the flash of light.

I was there—but-not-there, and treated that way by the time my guide and I reached the dressing room and I was led to a chair. I collapsed into it and sat up as though posture was important. I heard myself being spoken about. Actually, around and about, because I was referred to in the third person as if I wasn't there.

The voice I most remember after, in the dressing room, was Vernard Dixon, the road manager the band members called Swee' Pea, because he like to wear a Swee' Pea–type sailors hat. The dressing room filled and emptied a couple of times, with band members and the curious drifting about until someone closed the door to the hallway. I didn't know where I was sitting in the room, but from time to time people briefly took the chairs around me, next to me. No one talked to me.

Band members were collecting their gear. Discussing how they were going to get back to the hotel. I felt as though I was sitting in a corner facing the wall.

Vernard opened the door to leave, to collect the money—minus the tickets that were refunded—from the producer. When he opened the door, my ex-wife Brenda came in. It was good to hear her voice. She sounded kind and solicitous, her voice as soft as ever. I was no longer alone.

I was comforted by her being there. She was organizing my things, packing my bag, asking questions, collecting the key to my hotel room from Vernard. I had not gone by the hotel before the show. I was suddenly aware that no one had been talking to me because no one really had known what to say.

I was tempted to try a reassuring smile but I still felt like I was facing a wall, and I really didn't have any idea what was happening to me, why I was blind, why I didn't otherwise feel bad—just sort of stunned. Nothing like this had ever happened to me, and the more important question, I imagine, was how long my condition was going to last. But as I said, I was stunned, feeling extremely naked and exposed. Because I was at a loss for words and because the most important questions had not occurred to me.

Brenda said she was going to get her car and pull up to the door nearest the dressing room in about ten minutes. Vernard came back in talking to someone else about the money. He told me that the gate receipts were not straight yet, so it was going to take a few more minutes before he could collect everyone and pay them. I reminded him again, uselessly, to write everything down and to get a receipt. And to apologize for me.

I was kind of vague about what the apology should consist of because I didn't know what the hell was wrong.

Band members who hadn't left yet were drifting back in, still speaking about me as though I was somewhere else.

Like, "How is he?"

I ignored questions not put directly to me.

Vernard led me out the door and into Brenda's car. She and I had been formally divorced in 1987. Oddly enough, I received the documents, which had been filed by her brother, at Blues Alley. But she and I had been separated long before that, and she and Gia moved back to Don Miguel Drive—her mother's place—at the end of 1984.

Of all the locations in Los Angeles I enjoyed myself most of all there, on Don Miguel Drive. What's more, of all the people I met and got to know in Southern California, my favorite was Mrs. Elvira Sykes, Brenda's mother. There was no complicated reason. She was simply one of the most sympathetic, pleasant, and direct women I'd ever met. And perhaps I met her at a time when those qualities were so thoroughly lacking from my life. Maybe it had to do with my impression of Los Angeles. But I didn't think that made it wrong. Impressions in Los Angeles were not to be equated with wrong.

As a rule, I found first impressions to be without merit. Maybe that's because of who I am, and the way scattered rumors and a sprinkling of my attempts at art had created a persona that did not inspire initial honesty of an unguarded introduction, free of pretentions. But that's not so in L.A., or at least was not so in the L.A. of the 1970s and 1980s. There I found that a first impression was valid because it was all there was to most people until they found the role they should play to maximize their association with someone after, "How do you do?" There was nothing until this stranger decided whether you could be used and for what.

If the reputation I had amassed was acknowledged at all, it was only in passing, a blink and a slight shift in their focus like the faint echo of a ring made by pressing the *plus* key on a cash register. Everybody in L.A. was an actress, an actor, a singer whose megastardom was assured by the demo tape they'd just recorded, the screen test they were up for, the commercial they were auditioning for. Only established players, large or small stars, could afford to have a personality or genuine interest in anybody else.

Mrs. Elvira Sykes was the second member I met of a previous generation of Brenda's family. I met her grandmother first, her father's mother, from Shreveport, Louisiana. I met her on the weekend while I was playing at the Roxy and Kareem first brought Brenda over and introduced us. If her grandmother had still been at Brenda's apartment on Cahuenga Boulevard, I might have asked to go there from Club Lingerie. I believe Mama Sykes might have helped me. Instead, the Spirits helped me.

The second show had been cancelled. Not good. I calculated the lost income in my head accompanied by clip-clopping; it sounded like someone on horseback was trapped inside my skull and couldn't find an exit. Shod hooves clip-clopping in cadence around the statue of Ulysses S. Grant. And the blind guy sitting there on a bench.

I only remember one question that Brenda asked during that short ride to the Franklin Hotel. She asked me where I had gotten the sweat suit I was wearing. That's how I remembered the Porsche. Gia's godfather, Dr. Steve Rosenthal, had provided the means for me to get to Lingerie on time. His brand new Porsche was still parked on Sunset, across the street from the club.

I was only awake for a few minutes in my hotel room before I collapsed face down on the bed and was out like a light. Before my exit, I gave the keys to the car to Brenda. She retrieved the car and returned it.

I often credit the Spirits with things I cannot righteously credit any other way. On the morning after the Lingerie show, the Spirits returned my sight. That probably sounds and reads as scattered as anything I've written here. Why? Because people might ask, "If these Spirits returned your sight, why did they take it in the first place?" That seems like another road to "the Lord works in mysterious ways . . ." But I'm not trying to go there. (Although I'm sure he does.) I believe I know what blew me out on those stairs. No sweat. Wearing a sweat suit onstage that I had put on for an entirely different purpose that had nothing to do with working and building up the necessary sweat. I had spent the ninety minutes leading up to my stroke inside a hot place, working hard enough to be drenched on a normal night. I allowed myself to become dehydrated and I now equate my stroke coming off stage to some kind of heatstroke episode, a short circuit that could have inflicted more lasting evidence of its influence than it did.

It took my sight. My sight was restored. But it left its signature, a long-range reminder of its potential and my mortality. It marked me in a place where I could not forget the circumstances that created it. On the right side of my face, it marked the cheek with a wrinkling, folding effect that takes hold of my expression at times like someone prematurely yanking down a venetian blind at an awkward angle. It also warned me because it occasionally slurred my speech, and as it adjusted aspects of me it left me unaware.

I heard about it before I heard it.

I don't particularly know why I sat blind, feeling as though I had disrupted a kindergarten class and been sentenced to face the wall. Responding more or less mechanically with my voice sounding like it carried a new echo that attached itself randomly to words. But it was a Sunday night sliding toward midnight, and there was nowhere to go that sounded better than the hotel.

309

43

It was New York City, 1999, and I was finally "being permitted" into the apartment I had shared with my mother at the time of her death. The first time I was allowed to enter, months after her funeral, I got lost at the threshold of my mother's deserted, dust-choked apartment.

I ignored the young brown-skinned security guard assigned to me by the manager of the complex. We walked down the hallway to the living room where he sat with a magazine as I returned and settled stiffly on her unmade bed in the bedroom nearest the front door. I got up without any defined place to start a review of our belongings in this place filled with her absence.

I felt like a burglar rummaging through her dresser drawers, full of her underclothes, stockings and pantyhose, thin spring blouses and sweaters, and a top drawer assortment of small unnamed lotions, hair clips and pens, hair nets and rollers, a small plastic bag with extra eyeglasses of varied prescriptions. This carry-all of glass and plastic came to represent the fierce indignity of death, which leaves even a dedicated fixture of the Sunday services on Park Avenue and Eighty-sixth Street without defense against any stranger's avaricious exploration.

Before I could reason against it, I felt ugly drops of salt and rage twisting their way down my cheeks, away from my red eyes. I wondered, without the strength to generate anger, whether the young brother in our living room had heard me crying as I wiped my face with a Kleenex. On legs locked at the hips without knees, I was a metal man with no more flexibility from forehead to foot than the tin man frozen rust-rigid in a pose speaking of unfulfilled intentions.

In the empty attic that was my mother's son's head, I saw that her direct moments of criticism protected me from more flaws than the obvious "selfish" one that she once handed me so plainly that I was aggravated by her clarity. I had always enjoyed and even taken a vicarious pride in her understated handling of all-comers through our lives together. And I was not spared entirely. I was reminded of how her jabs carried more hurt than the telegraphed roundhouse rights from celebrated bigwigs of the entertainment world. Their cotton candy excursions into colloquialisms showed more evidence of the harm my sorties against their character and integrity had done than they could respond to in kind. Her observations, delivered without elevated volume or aura of discovery, brought a lasting sharpness that left no visible bruise on me but smuggled a bone-deep ache past my skin with a package of detonations that would fracture my facade of unaffected nonchalance. And delivered without malice.

The pain of the truth was not "permanent" when it spoke to a fault we did not or could not correct. When I chose "did not," I arrogantly proclaimed that it was because the Spirits supplied me with what I needed and pointed out a debilitating generosity that belied or balanced "selfish." When I chose "could not," I admitted that I didn't know how and told myself I was raised by Lily Scott. But so was my mother.

I am a refugee from the college of clowns who was too impatient to wait for graduation day, which would have included a speech by a previous inmate who was released with honors at the top of his class. Had I waited, I would have heard his warning. So I just *thought* I was funny and that funny would fix everything, change every flat tire, arguably without even stopping; no time on the side of the road. There were no clown escape hatches that occurred to me now, paralyzed and immobile in my mother's room.

I was repulsed by my lifelong insistence on fucking isolation. Some of it has been justified by a real fear of the consequences awaiting those who befriended me and drew close, tried to settle within an umbrella's ceiling of cover. When I was younger, everything in life was an experiment and a new thrill. On a rainy day, you could find the high-end joy of another body, another soul, squeezing shoulder to shoulder, giggling, sharing warmth deliberately, two midgets who gallop on marionette legs, now jammed in a space that posed a challenge for one. I loved that kind of silliness, but life has taught me that I have to avoid that kind of close.

There was no one I could be close to now.

Real grief had overwhelmed my body's working parts. All of these little parts of my mother and her day-to-day stability were rising up from where they were left for the night months ago. They had been expecting *her* and I am not her. But they know me because I had been around fretting when they came

312

for her before, the ones with the IVs and the stretchers. It was obviously my fault that she wasn't here to resume whatever they were doing that was left to be continued. When I walked around without purpose and then stopped to cry, they became annoyed and started to move on their own. When I saw them move, I called for the guard and told him it was time to go.

I am honestly not sure how capable I am of love. And I'm not sure why. The older I get, the more I tend to question the elements of emotion and intimacy as genetic parallels with height and hair color. I truly believe that I love my mother and grandmother, but beyond them I have lived in a circle of small values that have a startlingly limited reach. And a stunted amount of emotion is attached to it. This is not an evaluation that builds a wall around my family, closing out other people. It reflects the fact that I am closer to people I know, but no closer to cousins and aunts and uncles than to good friends.

I have been blessed with three children. They have been blessed with beautiful mothers and touched with brushes of eccentricity donated by a father who could have done more for them and with them, but could not have loved them more. Because he did not have enough practice.

I am sure I was loved by the Scotts. I am sure I was loved by Lily Scott and Bobbie Scott. And probably by my precise and proper uncle, William Scott. And to a lesser extent by Sammy and Gloria Scott, my spinster aunts, who slipped into their spinsterhood from the north and south poles of that status. The key to the Scotts was understanding and what you didn't understand you had to trust.

313

Love was not an active verb in my family or in my life. There were few demonstrations, few hugs and embraces, and few declarations among us about love. I was a full-grown adult who had been married, a father, and divorced before I consciously put "I love you" into conversations with my mother, before I made sure I got a hug from her and gave her a big hug each time we met. I can't remember ever hearing "I love you" pass between the generations of Scotts that preceded me. Or recall with any clarity hearing those words from them to me or being inspired to say those words to them. Yet I can't imagine there being more warmth and laughter shared with genuine empathy and respect and consideration and . . . but not affection.

Our codes and slang terms that slip easily in and out of vogue go from addition to meaningful exchanges of emptiness and impotence rather quickly as people and music and movies and what-means-what to us and each other goes in and out of style in the blink of an eye. Right now everybody is using the ill-suited "be there for you" or "be there for me." That expression was perfect for the Scotts, because if there was one thing you could count on, it was the fact that we would be there for each other. A hundred times more likely to "be there," wherever "there" was, than to say "I love you" and share a genuine hug. And I say that as someone who wished for a hug and a word of encouragement on a thousand nights when tired and beat up by the world. I would have traded a hundred be-there's for one heartfelt hug.

And it may be that I never get another chance to say this to those children, as well as I know I have never taught them by example so that they can turn to each other for this when they need it. I hope there is no doubt that I loved them and their mothers as best I could. And if that was inevitably inadequate, I hope it was supplemented by their mothers, who were all better off without me.

Publisher's Note

Publishing a book posthumously inevitably creates a number of challenges, and *The Last Holiday* has been no exception. The words that make up the final, printed version of Gil Scott-Heron's memoir were written over many years, starting in the 1990s and all the way up to 2010, and during this period the book has undergone some significant transformations. Even calling it a memoir may be misleading, because it is certainly not a memoir in the conventional sense of the word.

The first pages that I read were given to me by Gil when he was staying at the Chelsea Hotel in New York in the late 1990s. They included his account of the night that John Lennon was murdered (entitled "Deadline") and chapters on growing up in Jackson, Tennessee, and on Stevie Wonder (entitled "Makes Me Wonder"). These original chapters were recounted in the third person, by a narrator called The Artist, as Gil felt that this allowed him to write more freely and objectively about the events he needed to describe.

In 2004, at my prompting, Gil began rewriting the book as a first-person narrative, after recognising that the device of using an Everyman narrator for a memoir created more

317

problems than it solved. Although, as he wrote in a letter on 29 September 2005, "I am adjusting to the first person as these things will show, but I find it totally unnerving and self-serving at times because I have to describe shit from the 'Watergate' point of view: what I knew and when I knew it." The "Interlude" chapter in this book is the only remnant of the original draft that has made it into the final version.

One of the reasons Gil had been drawn to the third-person narrator was because his primary motivation in writing *The Last Holiday* was to tell the story of the Hotter than July tour. He felt that Stevie Wonder had never received the recognition that he deserved for the key role he played in bringing about the legislation that made Martin Luther King, Jr.'s birthday a national holiday (this eventually happened in 1986). Gil believed that *The Last Holiday* could be an objective account by a first-hand witness to this historic tour. He wanted to ensure that people could not forget what had really happened. And it is for this reason that there is so little in *The Last Holiday* that recounts what took place after the rally in Washington in January 1981. What happened to him after 1981 did not seem relevant to the book that he wanted to write.

However, it was clear to Gil that in order to tell Stevie Wonder's story, he would have to tell his own story, and that "in writing about yourself, you write about your parents and their parents automatically because you are all of those people." It was only by opening up his own past that he felt he could properly explain why he had ended up on the tour with Stevie Wonder.

Gil's death in May 2011 has made it impossible to ask him

questions that we would dearly love to know the answers to. The manuscript he left had been sent to me in a very piecemeal fashion, over a number of years and written on various archaic typewriters and computers. From countless conversations we had and from certain notes he left, it was clear that his original vision for the book was not as a straight chronological narrative. But as time went by, Gil leaned towards a simpler approach and dispensed with the more complex structure. He also decided to write about some very personal events from the later part of his life, including the death of his mother, the stroke he suffered in 1990 and his estranged relationships with his three children. These were never part of the original plan and they add real poignancy to the concluding chapters of the book.

We are greatly indebted to Tim Mohr, whose editing skills and commitment to the project have resulted in *The Last Holiday* reading as smoothly as it does. Gil was a very appreciative man and I know how grateful he would have been for all the hard work that Tim, Dan Franklin, Amy Hundley at Grove/Atlantic and Rafi Romaya, Norah Perkins and Nick Davies at Canongate have put into *The Last Holiday*. And I like to think that he would have loved Oscar Wilson's stunning jacket artwork.

As Gil so memorably sang,

"Peace Go With You, Brother"

Jamie Byng, CEO, Canongate Books

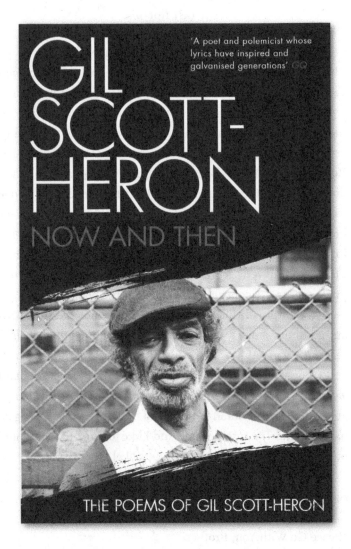

GIL SCOTT-HERON

NOW AND THEN

'A poet and polemicist whose lyrics have inspired and galvanised generations' *GQ*

THE POEMS OF GIL SCOTT-HERON

'Accessible, intelligent, rhythmic writing'
The List

CANON‖GATE

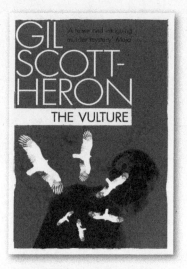

'These are impressive and ambitious works that vigorously mix street savvy and intellectual flair'
GQ

CANON‖GATE